SHELTON STATE COMM
COLLEGE
JUNIOR COLLEGE DIVISION
LIBRARY

W9-BRL-090

DISCARDED

B
821
.L33
1965

Lamont, Corliss, 1902-

The philosophy of humanism

DATE DUE			
OCL 8 '88	.		
FEB 0 9 1989			
DEC 0 8 1999			

THE PHILOSOPHY OF HUMANISM

Other Books by Corliss Lamont

FREEDOM IS AS FREEDOM DOES
A HUMANIST FUNERAL SERVICE
THE ILLUSION OF IMMORTALITY
THE INDEPENDENT MIND

(as editor)
MAN ANSWERS DEATH: AN ANTHOLOGY OF POETRY

THE PHILOSOPHY OF HUMANISM

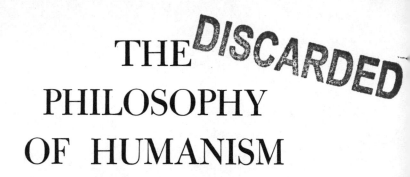

CORLISS LAMONT

Fifth Edition, Revised and Enlarged

Foreword by
EDWIN H. WILSON

FREDERICK UNGAR PUBLISHING CO.
NEW YORK

Tenth Printing, 1979

Copyright © 1949, 1957, 1965
by Corliss Lamont

Printed in the United States of America

ISBN 0-8044-6378-6
Library of Congress Catalog Card No. 65-16612

To My Mother

FLORENCE CORLISS LAMONT

*discerning companion
in philosophy*

Foreword

When Francis Bacon wrote his *Novum Organum,* he attempted to formulate a new synthesis of human knowledge. He pointed the way out of the darkness of the Mediterranean into the broader waters of the Atlantic. He urged men to depart from scholasticism and "pursue science in order that the human estate may be enhanced." The direction was away from supernaturalism to naturalism, from concern with the next world to the life that now is, from revelation and magic to science and reason.

As the power of the Spanish and Italian churchmen in Vatican Council II has shown, the influence of the Middle Ages lingers. We are still only at the beginning of the new synthesis. But around the earth, thought and belief are astir and converge on an explicit global philosophy. It is present with us, operative in the mainstream of culture. Whatever they profess, statesmen and others in vital decision-making or creative positions act on its implicit premises. It is accurate to call this new synthesis evolutionary or naturalistic Humanism. On the one hand it builds on the scientific spirit and method, accepting the natural and verifiable findings of science as a far more stable foundation for faith and conduct than supernatural and unverifiable revelation ever could. On the other hand, the new synthesis accepts the ethical ideal of concern for *all men;* it embraces the democratic faith in the worth of the individual and seeks the welfare of all humanity.

This modern Humanism needs to be made explicit, to be spelled out in a philosophy whose ethics extend beyond national boundaries. No one has yet enunciated the principles of this emerging philosophy as comprehensively as has Dr. Corliss Lamont in *The Philosophy of Humanism*. In designating the trends and personalities that have contributed to the development of this Humanism, Dr. Lamont is conservative, claiming only those persons and events which can, on the record, clearly be seen to have accepted and helped develop the general spirit and tenets of Humanism as he outlines it.

It is a curious fact that no other American author has published a comparable over-all history and systematic statement of the principles of Humanism. Yet there are many Humanists among university teachers and professional philosophers in the United States. Most Humanist writings have dealt either with prophecies of change to come, or with specific applications of Humanism to particular human problems. Perhaps the hour has not yet struck for recognition by humanity of its own true beliefs. Pre-scientific and outmoded professions of belief, undergirded by vast endowments, linger to receive lip service while men act on an emerging philosophy whose beginnings are all around us as contributing trends.

"Religious Humanists" who have arrived at the philosophy through the critical study of the materials of religion and the effort to meet the needs of their people in terms of today's orientation are of increasing influence in both the liberal and traditional churches. Neo-orthodoxy was launched as a last-ditch attempt to turn men back from preoccupation with human well-being in this world to their supposed eternal salvation. But now the erosions of modern thought are causing a retreat from Neo-orthodoxy and causing a renewal of the social gospel. In the wake of peace and civil rights efforts, churches and their doctrines are to a degree becoming instruments of social action.

Humanistic psychologists such as Erich Fromm and A. H. Maslow offer the churches a way to save face. Religious experience, state the humanistic psychologists, is possible within a naturalized and humanized setting. Eventually the churches

that have so desperately fought Humanism may try to say
that it is what they meant all the time.

The Philosophy of Humanism has always rewarded re-read-
ing. That is especially true of this fifth edition, which has
undergone extensive editing with updating and amplifying on
the basis of changing experience. British Humanists have
praised the clarity of style of this book. The author, both by
diligent study and by active organizational participation, has
been in a favorable position to keep fully abreast of developments. He has been a member of the Boards of the American
Humanist Association and the International Humanist and
Ethical Union. He has lectured widely on Humanism. Hence
he has confronted the practical problems of organizing that
which is almost unorganizable. The strength of Humanism is
still in its richly diverse diffusion in society, as was recognized
by the World Council of Churches over a decade ago when
it called scientific Humanism "one of the leading rivals of the
Christian hope." The Humanism to which they referred was
and is operative in the assumptions of creative workers in
many activities such as science, education, social work, liberal
religion, art and government. Dr. Lamont gives us the philosophy of something which is still largely unorganized and yet is
very large in influence.

In the meanwhile, without closing doors to new developments, Corliss Lamont is on solid ground in tracing the reality
of an ethical and scientific Humanism as a philosophy. And
he shows that Humanism involves far more than the negation
of supernaturalism. It requires an affirmative philosophy such
as is presented in this volume, translated into a life devoted
to one's own improvement and the service of all mankind.

The still inadequately explored dimension of Humanism is
that in which the Humanist goes beyond reason into areas of
experience where emotion and imagination—under the discipline of reason and science, of course—will yield a quickened
sense of the beauty, richness and worth of life. Men cling
to the idea of God so tenaciously precisely because they feel

that it ties the loose ends of fact and experience together and gives life meaning. *The Philosophy of Humanism* demonstrates that belief in a supernatural God, or any God, is not necessary to furnish that unity and significance for the human quest. Artists, poets, dramatists, musicians, and especially psychologists can help us in the discovery of new meanings in this added dimension. All theological problems are perhaps but a pre-scientific version of psychological problems.

As the new synthesis develops integrally with the achievement of a shared world at peace, it will come into its own. Men must first be liberated from many fears: the fears inherited with the dark sanctions of the priests—hell and its lake of fire; the fear of nuclear holocaust; the loss of identity in the sheer bigness of a confused humanity. Later, perhaps, ecstasy and jubilation will return to human living in a setting more honest, more dependable, more enduring than that offered in the revelation imagined by theologians who lacked the discipline of scientific method and the faith of man in man.

EDWIN H. WILSON
Executive Director
American Humanist Association, 1949-1961
Former Editor, The Humanist

Preface to the Fifth Edition

This book is a philosopher's testament. In it I have tried to describe in clear and simple terms the fully rounded philosophy of life known as naturalistic Humanism. In its fundamentals Humanism goes back at least as far as Athens of the fifth century B.C. and the great Age of Pericles. With Materialism and Naturalism, Dualism and Idealism, it stands out as one of the major systematic philosophies in the history of civilization. And it expresses a significant viewpoint which no intellectually alert person of the twentieth century can afford to overlook.

In my treatment of this viewpoint I have aimed at conciseness and have written what is essentially an introduction to the Humanist philosophy. Accordingly, I have discussed only briefly or have omitted entirely the details of some philosophic problems that in a longer work would merit extended consideration. For example, though I am well aware of the profound influence of social and economic factors upon philosophy, I have sketched in but little of that background.

This study, first published in 1949 under the title *Humanism as a Philosophy,* constitutes an expansion and revision of a lecture course that I gave on "The Philosophy of Naturalistic Humanism," at Columbia University from 1946 to 1959. Students in this course made many helpful criticisms of my book over the years. I have also profited from comments expressed in reviews, letters, and conversations. All of these opinions I have borne in mind while revising the book from start to finish for this fifth edition.

One of the most interesting criticisms I received was contained in a letter about this volume from George Santayana. Mr. Santayana wrote that he was glad to know I was as much of a materialist and naturalist as he, and then added: " 'Humanism' has this moral defect in my opinion, that it seems to make all mankind an authority and a compulsory object of affection for every individual. I see no reason for that. The limits of the society that we find congenial and desirable is determined by our own condition, not by the extent of it in the world. This is doubtless the point in which I depart most from your view and from modern feeling generally. Democracy is very well when it is natural, not forced. But the natural virtue of each age, place and person is what a good democracy would secure—not uniformity." [1]

I am not sure how far Mr. Santayana and I actually disagreed concerning the points that he mentioned. Certainly I had no intention of making all mankind "a compulsory object of affection" for anyone; I too would have democracy come as a natural and not a *forced* development. I would also decry the establishment of uniformity. But these opinions are not inconsistent with urging that a general pattern of international peace and of democratic procedures would further the welfare of mankind.

Where Santayana and I really differed, as two talks with him at Rome in the summer of 1950 clearly brought out, is that he was no social reformer and no crusader, even for his own philosophy. He cared little whether his conception of the truth or someone else's prevailed in the world. Now I care a great deal. I do want to see the fundamental Humanist and naturalist features of Santayana's work win out over supernaturalism. Without being dogmatic or intolerant about it, I wish to see the philosophy of Humanism steadily increase in influence. In the spacious mansions of philosophy there is room, I believe, for both my own crusading type of temperament and the retiring, above-the-battle kind represented by

George Santayana, so brilliant and productive in his relative isolation during the last twenty-five years of his life.*

In the writing and various revisions of this book, as in most other aspects of my life, my indebtedness to fellow philosophers, editorial assistants, and others approaches infinity. Greatly as I have profited from the wisdom and counsel of these many individuals, I have throughout this study given my own version of the much-debated concept of Humanism.

A major reason for the republication of this book after four editions and the passage of sixteen years is that the Humanist movement is steadily growing, so that there is an increasing need of over-all summaries of naturalistic Humanism. I hope that this fresh presentation may help to serve as an antidote to some of the irrational tendencies of the present era.

The Humanist synthesis that I offer is by its very nature an unfinished and undogmatic philosophy which is certain to be improved upon by future generations. And I expect and welcome disagreement with my formulations by both Humanists and non-Humanists.

CORLISS LAMONT

New York City
January 1965

---

* For a further discussion of Santayana, see pp. 46-47.

CONTENTS

THE PHILOSOPHY OF HUMANISM

BACKGROUND AND AFFILIATIONS
OF THE HUMANIST PHILOSOPHY

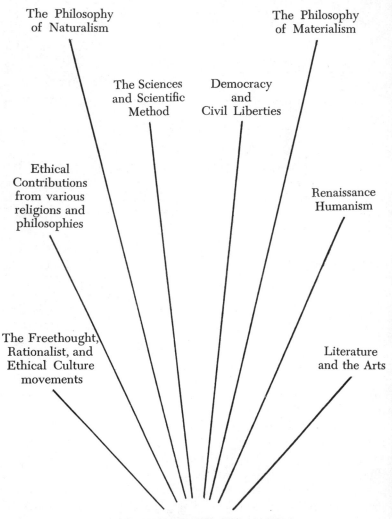

The Philosophy of Naturalism

The Philosophy of Materialism

The Sciences and Scientific Method

Democracy and Civil Liberties

Ethical Contributions from various religions and philosophies

Renaissance Humanism

The Freethought, Rationalist, and Ethical Culture movements

Literature and the Arts

CONTEMPORARY HUMANISM

CHAPTER I

The Meaning of Humanism

1. THE IMPORTANCE OF PHILOSOPHY

Since the earliest days of philosophic reflection in ancient times in both East and West thinkers of depth and acumen have advanced the simple proposition that the chief end of human life is to work for the happiness of man upon this earth and within the confines of the Nature that is his home. This philosophy of enjoying, developing, and making available to everyone the abundant material, cultural, and spiritual goods of this natural world is profound in its implications, yet easy to understand and congenial to common sense. This man-centered theory of life has remained relatively unheeded during long periods of history. While it has gone under a variety of names, it is a philosophy that I believe is most accurately designated as *Humanism.*

Humanism as a philosophy has ever competed with other philosophic viewpoints for the allegiance of men. But however far-reaching its disagreements with rival philosophies of the past and present, Humanism at least agrees with them on the importance of philosophy as such. That importance stems from the perennial need of human beings to find significance in their lives, to integrate their personalities around some clear, consistent and compelling view of existence, and to seek definite and reliable methods in the solution of their problems. Philosophy brings clarity and meaning into the careers of individuals, nations, and civilizations.

As Aristotle once remarked, everyone adheres to a philosophy whether he is aware of it or not. Every adult conducts his life according to some general pattern of behavior that is more or less conscious, more or less consistent, more or less adequate, to cope with the everyday affairs and inevitable crises of the human scene. This guiding pattern in the life of every person *is* his philosophy, even though it be implicit in his actions rather than explicit in his mind; "his inarticulate major premise," as Justice Oliver Wendell Holmes put it. Such is the strength of tradition that men have always tended to accept the particular philosophy or religion prevailing in the group into which they were born. In any case, human beings, primitive or civilized, educated or uneducated, plodding or brilliant, simply cannot escape from philosophy. Philosophy is everybody's business.

As a developed study and discipline, philosophy has for its purpose the analysis and clarification of human aims and actions, problems and ideals. It brings into the light of intelligence the half-conscious, half-expressed gropings of men and of peoples. It teaches us to say what we mean and to mean what we say. It is the tenacious attempt of reasoning men to think through the most fundamental issues of life, to reach reasoned conclusions on first and last things, to suggest worthwhile goals that can command the loyalty of individuals and groups. Philosophy as criticism boldly analyzes and brings before the supreme court of the mind prevailing human values, ideas, and institutions. Though it often succeeds in reconciling apparently conflicting viewpoints, "the mission of philosophy," as Professor Morris Cohen has said, "is to bring a sword as well as peace." This means that philosophers have the obligation of opening up the closed questions of the past, of exposing fanaticism and folly, of raising provocative issues where none were seen before.

Philosophy as synthesis attempts to work out a correct and integrated view of the universe, of human nature, of society, and of the chief values man should seek. This is an immense and unique task. It was Plato's ambitious claim that "the philosopher is the spectator of all time and all existence." This statement is true, though I hasten to add that the philosopher should not be merely a spectator. Plato's observation makes plain that the philosophic enterprise covers, in its own particular way, practically the whole gamut of human thought and activity. In order to attain a reasoned interpretation of Nature and man, the philosopher must inquire into the major branches of the natural sciences, such as chemistry, astronomy, and biology, and likewise of the social sciences, such as history, economics, and politics. Moreover, he must study carefully the realms of religion and art and literature, and cast a discerning eye over the day-to-day preoccupations and common-sense attitudes of the average person.

The philosopher need not (and hardly can) know all that these different fields have to offer; his function is to draw from them the data and principles that are particularly relevant to his problems, his broad generalizations, and his audacious syntheses. He constantly weaves back and forth between fact and theory, scientific law and far-flung cosmic speculation, always trying to be objective in his conclusions and faithful to the method of reason. The philosopher, to take over a thought from Matthew Arnold, is he who makes the determined and continued effort to see life steadily and see it whole. Or, in the words of Professor F. C. S. Schiller of Oxford, he is the man who learns "how to fit together into a significant picture the bits of a great world jig-saw puzzle."

The history of thought records many different philosophic systems that have had in their day a great appeal to the minds of men. We can see now that some of these systems were primarily artistic creations on the part of thinkers who let themselves be carried away by their imagination or who obviously overemphasized some limited aspect of existence. System-building philosophers only too often have mistaken their daring and original inspirations for a reliable representation of reality, or have sought to reconcile the irreconcilable, or have treated their particular philosophies, grounded in a certain age and culture, as the complete and final word on the nature of things.

For these reasons there has been some justifiable reaction against philosophic "systems." And contemporary philosophers have tended to confine themselves to certain circumscribed problems and areas rather than striking out boldly toward a comprehensive world-view or *Weltanschauung*. Yet they cannot really escape from the responsibility of endeavoring to provide a systematic answer concerning the main issues in philosophy, however unfinished and tentative their conclusions may be. Over-specialization within the field of philosophy is a convenient way of avoiding major controversial questions.

Though the vast extent of human knowledge in this twentieth century renders present philosophical pursuits a good deal more complicated than in the time of Plato and Aristotle, nonetheless the very growth of knowledge in the modern era gives us a considerable advantage. Likewise current-day philosophers are able to acquire valuable background and perspective from an analysis of the strength and weaknesses of numerous past philosophies. In the Occident the philosophic tradition goes back some 2,500 years to the ancient Greeks; in the Orient it is of about equal length if we take the teachings of Confucius in China and Buddha in India as our starting points. During these twenty-five centuries a vital core of philosophic wisdom has been gradually accumulating.

Despite constant talk that philosophy as a separate field of investigation has become outmoded and unnecessary, I cannot imagine a time when it will cease to play a significant role in human affairs. True enough, certain branches of knowledge once within the province of philosophy, such as psychology, government, and sociology, have developed into sciences on their own account. But philosophy blazed the way for these disciplines. And whatever subfields break away from it in the future, philosophy will always retain the important function of providing a critique of fundamental concepts and values and of offering to men an intellectually valid, over-all view of life and death, the individual and society, mind and matter, the universe and destiny.

That very compartmentalizing of knowledge that has so stimulated the progress of modern science makes philosophy perhaps more essential now than ever before. Philosophers are our experts in integration; they form a general staff for coping with the increasing fragmentation of our culture. They are liaison officers among the many different and often isolated branches of knowledge; between the civilizations of the past and the present; between the great, living systems of belief that move the various nations of our day. Philosophers are always reminding people of the interrelatedness of things, always bringing together what has been artificially torn apart and disunited. In short, in this age of growing specialization it is more than ever the business of the philosopher to specialize in generalization.

It is obvious from what I have said about the functions of philosophy that it is very much concerned with fundamental moral, social, and political issues. The great tradition in philosophy, stemming from Plato and his most notable book, *The Republic,* has always paid marked attention to the definition of the good and the road to its attainment by individuals and groups. The problem of the good has become increasingly complex in modern times, with a resulting obligation on the part of philosophers to think of the good society in terms of populous nations and indeed the entire world.

A number of the traditional philosophic positions concerning the nature of the universe and of man constitute in their very essence disguised apòlogias for or ideological escapes from existing conditions. Thus the discerning intellect will discover that certain abstruse philosophic issues, which at first glance may seem far removed from everyday life, have deep and definite roots in economic and social tensions. Philosophy is not above the battle, but directly or indirectly is affected by and reacts upon the fortunes of manifold individuals and social groups engaged in earning a living, reproducing the species, establishing governments, fighting wars, making peace, and pursuing happiness.

There can be no doubt that if a philosophy of life is to fulfill its proper role, it must be a philosophy of living, a philosophy to live by, a philosophy of action. Philosophy at its best is not simply an interpretation or explanation of things. It is also a dynamic enterprise that aims to stimulate men in the direction of those ends and values that are supremely worthwhile and desirable; to bring mankind closer to those standards of truth and methods of truth-seeking that are most reliable. All this implies the working out of effective methods for the application of tried and tested philosophic wisdom. Hence philosophy has the task, not only of attaining the truth, but also of showing how that truth can become operative in the affairs of men, of helping to bridge the age-long gap between thinkers and doers, between theory and practice. Philosophy could well recommend as a universal motto Henri Bergson's striking epigram: "*Act* as men of thought; *think* as men of action."

The old phrase "taking things philosophically" has come to have a connotation of acquiescence and defeatism that Humanists cannot possibly accept. As Professor Ralph Barton Perry of Harvard remarked, philosophers who emphasize "the cult of resignation . . . have made philosophy the opium of the intelligentsia."

Philosophy's constant involvement in the issues that mean most to men and in the defense of truth is dramatically brought out in the career of Socrates. Just as in the Western tradition the great martyr-death in religion was that of Jesus, so in philosophy it was that of Socrates. And just as the New Testament tells in simple and beautiful language the unforgettable story of Jesus, so the *Dialogues* of Plato permanently enshrine the memory of Socrates. The powers that were in ancient Athens accused Socrates of corrupting the minds of youth by raising too many thought-provoking questions and giving those questions unorthodox answers. Rather than remain silent or compromise, Socrates defied the authorities and drank the hemlock. "The unexamined life is not worth living," said Socrates in his final remarks to the judges, as recounted in the *Apology*. "I would rather die," he continued, "having spoken after my manner, than speak in your manner and live. . . . The difficulty, my friends, is not to avoid death, but to avoid unrighteousness. . . . No evil can happen to a good man, either in life or after death." [2]

Then and there, in the year 399 B.C., Socrates once and for all established a moral imperative for philosophers: that no matter what the personal consequences, it is necessary for them to exercise their freedom of speech and stand firm for what they consider the truth and the right. Indeed, no man has a philosophy worthy of the name or has achieved full stature as a human being unless he is willing to lay down his life for his ultimate principles.

In addition to Socrates, there have been other outstanding heroes in the philosophic pantheon, such as Giordano Bruno, the Italian Pantheist, burned at the stake by the Catholic Inquisition in 1600, together with his books, after he refused to recant; and Benedict Spinoza, a Dutch Jew of the seventeenth century, ostracized and excommunicated at an early age by the Amsterdam Synagogue and hounded throughout life because of his opinions in philosophy.

But since philosophers are, after all, only human and are subject to most of the same pressures as other men, they do not always demonstrate intellectual and moral courage of the highest order. It is not surprising that some of them should be intellectually timorous, out of touch with the everyday world, and fearful of becoming embroiled in those deep-reaching disputes that are the heart of the philosophic quest. One familiar way of evading fundamental issues is to throw around them an intricate net of unintelligible verbiage, to redefine ordinary words in such an extraordinary manner that utter confusion is the result. Another favorite method is to assume an attitude of noble impartiality toward those recurring controversies that mean most to the common man, or to turn aside every question of consequence by asking another question in return. Yet it is precisely the business of philosophers to do their best to give honest answers to honest inquiries.

One of the chief troubles with philosophy has been that most of the works on the subject have been written *by* professional philosophers *for* professional philosophers or have been addressed to an intellectual elite. There are of course technical problems in philosophy, as in other spheres of knowledge, that only specialists can understand and fruitfully pursue, but there is no reason under the sun why the basic ideas in this field should not be presented in a simple, concise, and understandable fashion. Philosophy has always been both in need of and susceptible to such humanization. Again, Socrates, by making philosophy an absorbing and exciting thing to the young men of Athens, set an excellent example that philosophers have rarely taken seriously enough.

Socrates lived and taught in Greece during a time of far-reaching social turmoil and disintegration. This leads me to say that important as philosophy always is, it assumes even greater significance during periods of crisis. If philosophy is worth anything, it should be able to bring to men and nations some measure of poise, steadfastness, and wisdom in exactly such a tumultuous epoch of world history as that of the twentieth century. A people without a clear and recognized philosophy is likely to falter in a serious crisis because it is confused about the central issues or has no supreme loyalty for which it is willing to make supreme sacrifices.

America and all mankind continue to live through critical days. Philosophy should have much to say on why the human race, despite all its much-vaunted progress, fought two devastating world wars within the space of thirty years, and still faces the awful possibility of the Great Nuclear War. Indubitably philosophers possess the right and duty to pass some severe moral judgments on modern man. And their broad perspectives may well lead us to regard with a good deal of skepticism the widespread prophecies about civilization collapsing or coming to an end; or to realize that if our civilization does perish, another and perhaps better one may succeed it.

The fact is that the entire world is in want of a sound and dynamic philosophy adequate to the spirit and needs of this twentieth century; a generalized view of human life and all existence that will give the peoples of every continent and country a total and integrated perspective; a universal goal, method, and hope that will lift mortal men above their personal limitations and provincial interests to a vision of the magnificent possibilities of humanity as a whole. In my judgment the philosophy best calculated to liberate the creative energies of mankind and to serve as a common bond between the different peoples of the earth is that way of life most precisely described as Humanism.

2. HUMANISM DEFINED

Humanism has had a long and notable career, with roots reaching far back into the past and deep into the life of civilizations supreme in their day. It has had eminent representatives in all the great nations of the world. As the American historian Professor Edward P. Cheyney says, Humanism has meant many things: "It may be the reasonable balance of life that the early Humanists discovered in the Greeks; it may be merely the study of the humanities or polite letters; it may be the freedom from religiosity and the vivid interest in all sides of life of a Queen Elizabeth or a Benjamin Franklin; it may be the responsiveness to all human passions of a Shakespeare or a Goethe; or it may be a philosophy of which man is the center and sanction. It is in the last sense, elusive as it is, that Humanism has had perhaps its greatest significance since the sixteenth century." [3]

It is with this last sense of Humanism that this book is mainly concerned. And I shall endeavor to the best of my ability to remove any elusiveness or ambiguity from this meaning of the word. The philosophy of Humanism represents a specific and forthright view of the universe, the nature of man, and the treatment of human problems. The term *Humanist* first came into use in the early sixteenth century to designate the writers and scholars of the European Renaissance. Contemporary Humanism includes the most enduring values of Renaissance Humanism, but in philosophic scope and significance goes far beyond it.

To define twentieth-century humanism briefly, I would say that it is a philosophy of joyous service for the greater good of all humanity in this natural world and advocating the methods of reason, science, and democracy. While this statement has many profound implications, it is not difficult to grasp. Humanism in general is not a way of thinking merely for professional philosophers, but is also a credo for average men and women seeking to lead happy and useful lives. It does not try to appeal to intellectuals by laying claim to great originality, or to the multitude by promising the easy fulfillment of human desires either upon this earth or in some supernatural dream world. But Humanism does make room for the various aspects of human nature. Though it looks upon reason as the final arbiter of what is true and good and beautiful, it insists that reason should fully recognize the emotional side of man. Indeed, one of Humanism's main functions is to set free the emotions from cramping and irrational restrictions.

Humanism is a many-faceted philosophy, congenial to this modern age, yet fully aware of the lessons of history and the richness of the philosophic tradition. Its task is to organize into a consistent and intelligible whole the chief elements of philosophic truth and to make that synthesis a powerful force and reality in the minds and actions of living men. What, then, are the basic principles of Humanism that define its position and distinguish it from other philosophic viewpoints? There are, as I see it, ten central propositions in the Humanist philosophy:

First, Humanism believes in a naturalistic metaphysics or

attitude toward the universe that considers all forms of the supernatural as myth; and that regards Nature as the totality of being and as a constantly changing system of matter and energy which exists independently of any mind or consciousness.

Second, Humanism, drawing especially upon the laws and facts of science, believes that man is an evolutionary product of the Nature of which he is part; that his mind is indivisibly conjoined with the functioning of his brain; and that as an inseparable unity of body and personality he can have no conscious survival after death.

Third, Humanism, having its ultimate faith in man, believes that human beings possess the power or potentiality of solving their own problems, through reliance primarily upon reason and scientific method applied with courage and vision.

Fourth, Humanism, in opposition to all theories of universal determinism, fatalism, or predestination, believes that human beings, while conditioned by the past, possess genuine freedom of creative choice and action, and are, within certain objective limits, the masters of their own destiny.

Fifth, Humanism believes in an ethics or morality that grounds all human values in this-earthly experiences and relationships and that holds as its highest goal the this-worldly happiness, freedom, and progress—economic, cultural, and ethical—of all mankind, irrespective of nation, race, or religion.

Sixth, Humanism believes that the individual attains the good life by harmoniously combining personal satisfactions and continuous self-development with significant work and other activities that contribute to the welfare of the community.

Seventh, Humanism believes in the widest possible development of art and the awareness of beauty, including the appreciation of Nature's loveliness and splendor, so that the aesthetic experience may become a pervasive reality in the life of men.

Eighth, Humanism believes in a far-reaching social program

that stands for the establishment throughout the world of democracy, peace, and a high standard of living on the foundations of a flourishing economic order, both national and international.

Ninth, Humanism believes in the complete social implementation of reason and scientific method; and thereby in the use of democratic procedures, including full freedom of expression and civil liberties, throughout all areas of economic, political, and cultural life.

Tenth, Humanism, in accordance with scientific method, believes in the unending questioning of basic assumptions and convictions, including its own. Humanism is not a new dogma, but is a developing philosophy ever open to experimental testing, newly discovered facts, and more rigorous reasoning.

I think that these ten points embody Humanism in its most acceptable modern form. This philosophy can be more explicitly characterized as scientific Humanism, secular Humanism, naturalistic Humanism, or democratic Humanism, depending on the emphasis that one wishes to give. Whatever it be called, Humanism is the viewpoint that men have but one life to lead and should make the most of it in terms of creative work and happiness; that human happiness is its own justification and requires no sanction or support from supernatural sources; that in any case the supernatural, usually conceived of in the form of heavenly gods or immortal heavens, does not exist; and that human beings, using their own intelligence and cooperating liberally with one another, can build an enduring citadel of peace and beauty upon this earth.

It is true that no people has yet come near to establishing the ideal society. Yet Humanism asserts that man's own reason and efforts are man's best and, indeed, only hope; and that man's refusal to recognize this point is one of the chief causes of his failures throughout history. The Christian West has been confused and corrupted for almost 2,000 years by the idea so succinctly expressed by St. Augustine, "Cursed is everyone who places his hope in man."

In an era of continuing crisis and disintegration like that of the twentieth century, men face the temptation of fleeing to some compensatory realm of make-believe or supernatural solace. Humanism stands uncompromisingly against this tendency, which both expresses and encourages defeatism. The Humanist philosophy persistently strives to remind men that their only home is in this mundane world. There is no use in our searching elsewhere for happiness and fulfillment, for there is no place else to go. We human beings must find our destiny and our promised land in the here and now, or not at all. And Humanism is interested in a future life, not in the sense of some fabulous paradise in the skies, but as the on-going enjoyment of earthly existence by generation after generation through eternities of time.

On the ethical and social side Humanism sets up service to one's fellowmen as the ultimate moral ideal. It holds that the individual can find his own highest good in working for the good of all, which of course includes himself and his family. In this sophisticated and disillusioned era Humanism emphatically rejects, as psychologically naïve and scientifically unsound, the widespread notion that human beings are moved merely by self-interest. It repudiates the constant rationalization of brute egoism into pretentious schemes on behalf of individuals or groups bent on self-aggrandizement. It refuses to accept the reduction of human motivation to economic terms, to sexual terms, to pleasure-seeking terms, or to *any* one limited set of human desires. It insists on the reality of genuine altruism as one of the moving forces in the affairs of men.

Since we live during a time of nationalism run wild, of terrible world wars, of hate and misunderstanding between peoples and governments, I want to underscore at the start Humanism's goal of the welfare of *all* mankind. In its primary connotation Humanism means simply human-being-ism, that is, devotion to the interests of human beings, wherever they live and whatever their status. Though certain groups in cer-

tain countries have in the past put themselves beyond the
pale of human decency, and though this could happen again,
Humanism cannot tolerate discrimination against any people
or nation as such. And it reaffirms the spirit of cosmopolitanism,
of international friendship, and of the essential brotherhood
of man. Humanists feel *compassionate concern* for their fellowmen throughout the globe.

An English bishop recently asserted that "50 per cent of
the intelligent people of the modern world are Humanists." [4]
Most of the individuals to whom he refers probably do not
call themselves Humanists and may never have taken the
trouble to find out to what precise school of philosophy they
belong. It is important, however, that all those who actually
are Humanists should come to recognize in the word *Humanism* the symbol of their central purpose in life, their community
of interests and their sense of fellowship. As Walter Lippmann
has written in his Humanist book, *A Preface to Morals*, "If
civilization is to be coherent and confident it must be *known*
in that civilization what its ideals are." [5] This implies that
those ideals shall be given a habitation and a name in some
philosophy.

Now much that is essentially Humanist in twentieth-century
civilization is not openly acknowledged to be so. In the United
States, where there is so much confusion of spirit and intellect,
lip service to outworn religious concepts or their mere cere-
monial use has steadily increased among those who profess
some form of supernatural faith. No nation in the world is
more secular and this-worldly in its predominant interests than
America. These secular trends have extended to the Sabbath.
Automobiles, the massive Sunday newspapers, golf and baseball, radio, television, and motion pictures have all made
tremendous inroads on the day of worship.

In order to keep their following, the churches themselves
have turned more and more to philanthropic activities and
the Social Gospel, that is, away from concern with the future
joys and punishments of the next world to a concern with

the present needs of their parishioners and humanity in this world. Modern secularization has penetrated deep into the great organized religious bodies. In Protestant circles the Young Men's Christian Association and the Young Women's Christian Association have sought to attract youth into religious paths by providing facilities for social life, lodging, sports, and vocational training. Even the Catholic Church, which has retained with little compromise its traditional theology, has bowed to secular pressures by instituting organizations with a lay purpose and program, such as the Knights of Columbus and the National Catholic Welfare Conference.

America's belief in democracy and progress, its buoyant optimism and idealism, its reliance on science and invention, all fit into the Humanist pattern. Our increasing dependence on the machine and on scientific techniques tends to do away with old-time appeals to the supernatural. The stronghold of supernatural religion has always been in the country rather than in the city. But today the spread of urban culture generally and of scientific methods in agriculture has radically altered the outlook of the rural population. Modern farmers turn more and more to tractors, irrigation, flood control, and the rotation of crops to solve their problems, in place of last-minute prayers to supernatural forces.

There is a great deal in the American tradition that is fundamentally Humanist in character. In fact, our Declaration of Independence gave resounding affirmation to the social aims of Humanism when it proclaimed that "all men" have the inalienable right to "life, liberty and the pursuit of happiness." This generalization was clearly meant to apply to human beings everywhere and not just to the inhabitants of the thirteen colonies. Accordingly, the famous document that launched the United States on its career as an independent nation makes a close approach to the cardinal Humanist doctrine that holds out the welfare of humanity at large as the final goal.

The author of the Declaration himself, Thomas Jefferson,

described by Charles and Mary Beard as "the natural leader of a humanistic democracy," alluded to the Declaration in these words: "May it be to the world, what I believe it will be (to some parts sooner, to others later, but finally to all), the signal of arousing men to burst the chains under which monkish ignorance and superstition had persuaded them to bind themselves, and to assume the blessings and security of self-government." [6]

Abraham Lincoln expanded on these Humanist sentiments in his Independence Hall speech of 1861 in which he defined the "great principle" that had held the United States together for so long: "It was not the mere matter of separation of the colonies from the motherland, but that sentiment in the Declaration of Independence which gave liberty not alone to the people of this country, but hope to all the world, for all future time. It was that which gave promise that in due time the weights would be lifted from the shoulders of all men, and that all should have an equal chance." [7]

The Preamble to the American Constitution gives a significant summary of Humanist purposes limited to a national scale. Thus: "We, the people of the United States, in order to form a more perfect Union, establish justice, insure domestic tranquility, provide for the common defence, promote the general welfare and secure the blessings of liberty to ourselves and our posterity, do ordain and establish this Constitution for the United States of America." The specific concern here for future generations is unsual and is definitely an advanced Humanist idea. It is worthy of note, too, that both the Preamble and the Constitution itself omit all reference to Deity. The Bill of Rights further clears the way for secular interests by guaranteeing separation between the state and religion.

While the American people today do not yet recognize clearly the direction in which they are moving, their highest aims and much in their everyday pattern of existence implicitly embody the viewpoint of Humanism. As for the large social-economic programs of the contemporary world centering around such terms as capitalism, free enterprise, collectivism, socialism, and communism, Humanism should be able to illumine them to a considerable degree. But no matter what happens to these programs in the light of human events and the march of history, no matter which ones succeed or do not succeed, the philosophy of Humanism will always remain pertinent.

If this philosophy approximates the truth in its underlying generalizations, then it is a philosophy which, with some changes in phraseology, was appropriate to ancient times and which in the main will hold good for the shape of things to come. Economic and political systems will come and go, nations and empires and civilizations rise and fall, but Humanism, as a philosophic system in which mankind's interests upon this earth are the first word and the last word, is unlikely to become obsolete. Naturally, however, any particular expression of Humanism will eventually be superseded.

The humanistic spirit, then, while finding wider and more conscious formulation in the modern era and in the more developed nations, has been inherent and struggling for expression in the race of man since first he appeared upon this planet. So Humanism sums up not only the current tendencies of mankind to construct a more truly human world, but also the best in men's aspirations throughout the age-long history of human thought and endeavor.

3. DIFFERENT KINDS OF HUMANISTS

As I pointed out earlier, Humanism as a word has several meanings and it is essential to distinguish among them. If we are considering the history of culture, the term usually refers to the European Renaissance or awakening, which started in Italy during the fourteenth century and later spread to the rest of the continent and to England.

Renaissance Humanism was first and foremost a revolt

against the other-worldliness of mediaeval Christianity, a turning away from preoccupation with personal immortality to making the best of life in this world. Renaissance writers like Rabelais and Erasmus gave eloquent voice to this new joy in living and to the sheer exuberance of existence. For the Renaissance the ideal human being was no longer the ascetic monk, but a new type—the universal man—the many-sided personality, delighting in every kind of this-earthly achievement. The great Italian artists, Leonardo da Vinci and Michelangelo, typified this ideal.

The Renaissance also constituted a revolt against the authority of the Catholic Church and against the religious limitations on knowledge. And there developed among the most influential figures of this period an increasing reliance on reason instead of faith. But so far as the advancement of knowledge was concerned, the Humanist intellectual awakening consisted largely in a rediscovery of and a return to the Greek and Latin classics. This was a progressive step at the end of the Middle Ages, and obviously a knowledge of the ancient classics is always worthwhile. During this period, however, concentration on the culture of Greece and Rome finally became an obstacle to the extension of knowledge in the broadest sense and particularly to the development of modern science. The fact is that many of the Renaissance Humanists displayed a profound and active disdain for natural science.

One of the most acute Renaissance thinkers, the Italian Pietro Pomponazzi, cast doubt on the idea of immortality and contended that a high-minded ethics did not require belief in a future life. In his treatise *On the Immortality of the Soul,* Pomponazzi took an Aristotelian position and argued that natural reason must hold that there is no personal survival. Only faith, revelation, and scripture, he said, can demonstrate that immortality exists. In this manner Pomponazzi gave expression to the convenient theory of "the double truth," whereby man's intelligence reaches one conclusion while religion reveals the opposite. Despite this effort of Pomponazzi to avoid offending the authorities, the Inquisition at Venice burned his book on immortality.

Brilliant and far-ranging as were the thinkers and writers of the Renaissance, neither Pomponazzi nor better-known Humanist figures like Erasmus and Montaigne, Francis Bacon, and Thomas More, worked out an inclusive metaphysics or theory of the universe that rejected Christian supernaturalism.

The features of permanent value in Renaissance Humanism that can be taken over by present-day Humanism are its insistence on getting away from religious control of knowledge; its immense intellectual vitality; its ideal of the well-rounded personality; and above all, its stress on man's enjoying to the full his life in this world. The philosophy of Humanism, then, as I am presenting it, reveals a continuity with the vital Humanist tradition of the Renaissance, as exemplified in its great artists and authors, and carries on their spirit in contemporary form.

Humanism is such an old and attractive word and so weighted with favorable meanings that it has been currently adopted by various groups and persons whose use of it is most questionable. Thus the Academic Humanism founded in the early nineteen-thirties by Irving Babbitt, a Harvard professor, and Paul Elmer More, an author and editor, emphasized a literary and educational program with supernaturalistic and reactionary tendencies. In philosophy it adhered to a false Dualism of man versus Nature. And it revived some of the bad features of Renaissance Humanism by setting up a return to the ancient classics as the foundation stone of education and by opposing the Humanities to science. Finally, it turned the obvious need of human self-control in the sphere of ethics into a prissy and puritanical morality of decorum. This Academic Humanism had only a brief vogue and has all but disappeared from the American scene.

Then there is Catholic or Integral Humanism stemming from the impressive mediaeval synthesis of Thomas Aquinas. The foremost exponent of this theocentric Christian philosophy is the French thinker, Jacques Maritain. Though we can agree with Maritain upon certain broad ethical and social aims, his general position is far removed from that of man-centered Humanism.

Still another version of Humanism was the subjective variety put forward early in this century in England by Professor Schiller. His Humanism, borrowing from the more questionable elements in the Pragmatism of William James, centered around a theory of knowledge in which the personal, subjective human factor was paramount and in which objective truth tended to melt away in the haze of moral and religious wish-fulfillment. Schiller also made unacceptable compromises with supernaturalism. At the same time he was one of the few modern philosophers of note who used the word *Humanism* to denote a whole system of philosophy and who saw the great possibilities of this term.

The Humanist philosophy which is the subject matter of this book can be distinguished primarily from these other types by referring to it as *naturalistic* Humanism. The adjective *naturalistic* shows that Humanism, in its most accurate philosophical sense, implies a world-view in which Nature is everything, in which there is no supernatural and in which man is an integral part of Nature and not separated from it by any sharp cleavage or discontinuity. This philosophy, of course, recognizes that vast stretches of reality yet remain beyond the range of human knowledge, but it takes for granted that all future discoveries of truth will reveal an extension of *the natural* and not an altogether different realm of being, commonly referred to as *the supernatural.*

I shall now mention a number of representative individuals who, regardless of the terminology they use, belong in general to the category of naturalistic Humanism. First of all we have the three greatest American philosophers since William James, namely Morris R. Cohen, John Dewey, and George Santayana. Other professional philosophers who are in essence Humanists include Professors Van Meter Ames of the University of Cin-

cinnati; Barrows Dunham, formerly of Temple University; Abraham Edel of the College of the City of New York; Sidney Hook of New York University; Horace M. Kallen of the New School for Social Research; Max C. Otto, Professor Emeritus, of the University of Wisconsin; Roy Wood Sellars, Professor Emeritus, of the University of Michigan; Gardner Williams of the University of Toledo; and Joseph L. Blau, Charles Frankel, Ernest Nagel, John H. Randall, Jr., and Herbert W. Schneider, Emeritus, all of Columbia University. The late Professor Irwin Edman of Columbia, an especially persuasive teacher and writer, was likewise a Humanist.

Prominent scientists on the roster of naturalistic Humanism are Luther Burbank, celebrated botanist; Brock Chisholm, physician and formerly Director General of the U. N. World Health Organization; Pierre and Marie Curie, the discoverers of radium; Albert Einstein of relativity fame; Sigmund Freud, founder of psychoanalysis; Erich Fromm, one of America's leading psychoanalysts; Sir Julian Huxley, English biologist and former Director General of UNESCO; Professor James H. Leuba, psychologist and expert on religious mysticism; Linus Pauling, Professor of Chemistry and winner of the Nobel Peace Prize in 1963; Vilhjalmur Stefansson, anthropologist and Arctic explorer; and James Peter Warbasse, surgeon and leader in the cooperative movement.

Also coming within the Humanist classification are well-known authors such as Harry Elmer Barnes, Van Wyck Brooks, E. M. Forster, Harold J. Laski, Walter Lippmann, Archibald MacLeish, Thomas Mann, Somerset Maugham, Henry L. Mencken, Gilbert Murray, Jean-Paul Sartre, and Sherman D. Wakefield; the eminent American painter, John Sloan; the French statesman, Eduard Herriot; Jawaharlal Nehru, independent India's first Prime Minister; and Sun Yat-sen, great Chinese revolutionary leader of the nineteen-twenties.

One of the most important groups believing in naturalistic Humanism calls itself *religious* Humanists. These derive their main strength from the ranks of Unitarian clergymen, such as John H. Dietrich, formerly minister of the First Unitarian Church in Minneapolis; Charles Francis Potter, long head of the now defunct First Humanist Society of New York City; Curtis W. Reese, former Dean of the Abraham Lincoln Centre in Chicago; and David Rhys Williams, retired pastor of the First Unitarian Church in Rochester. These men, with ten additional clergymen, twelve educators, and other progressive intellectuals, issued in 1933 the vigorous *Humanist Manifesto*, comprehensively summing up their philosophic viewpoint in fifteen brief propositions.*

In 1961 the U.S. Supreme Court took official cognizance of religious Humanism in the case of Roy R. Torcaso, a Humanist who was refused his commission as a Notary Public under a Maryland law requiring all public officers in the State to profess belief in God. In delivering the unanimous opinion of the Court that this statute was unconstitutional under the First Amendment, Justice Hugo L. Black observed: "Among religions in this country which do not teach what would generally be considered a belief in the existence of God are Buddhism, Taoism, Ethical Culture, Secular Humanism and others."

Very close to religious Humanism in their philosophy and often cooperating with the Humanists are the Ethical Culture Societies. They consider themselves religious fellowships. Several adherents of Ethical Culture were signatories of the *Humanist Manifesto*. The oldest and strongest of the Ethical groups is the Society for Ethical Culture of New York, founded in 1876 by Dr. Felix Adler, a teacher of philosophy at Columbia. The Society is "dedicated to the ever increasing knowledge and practice and love of the right." It is federated in the American Ethical Union with twenty-seven other Ethical Societies and Fellowship Groups throughout the United States. The Union's object is: "To assert the supreme importance of

---

* For the complete text and list of signers of the *Humanist Manifesto*, see the Appendix, pp. 285-89.

the ethical factor in all relations of life—personal, social, national and international—apart from any theological or metaphysical considerations." True to this fundamental formulation, the Ethical Culturists have put their emphasis on the this-earthly welfare of mankind and have followed the motto of "Deed, not creed."

Prominent figures in the American Ethical Union today and officially designated as Leaders are Algernon D. Black, Horace L. Friess, Henry B. Herman, James F. Hornback, David S. Muzzey, and Jerome Nathanson. In 1964 V. T. Thayer, one of the senior Leaders, received the Humanist Pioneer Award annually bestowed by the American Humanist Association. While the Ethical movement originated in America, it has been quite influential in England, where its outstanding leaders were Stanton Coit and Frederick J. Gould and where it has included some of Britain's most distinguished philosophers, scientists, and authors. It has also spread to the European continent and to Japan.

Making a somewhat different approach to naturalistic Humanism are the miscellaneous varieties of contemporary Freethinkers and Rationalists in America and other countries. The Freethinkers of the West have a long tradition going back to France of the eighteenth century when Freethought societies helped lay the intellectual foundations for the Revolution of 1789. Always anticlerical and opposed to religious revelation and authority, the Freethinkers for a considerable period bore the brunt of the battle against ecclesiastical repression of thought. The Freethinkers in the United States are a small but militant band who, although split into several different organizations, carry on useful educational activity through their journals and meetings. In recent decades the Freethought movement has repeatedly affirmed its solidarity with modern Humanism.

The Rationalists as an organized group have been strongest in England. Their moving principle may be defined as "the mental attitude which unreservedly accepts the supremacy of reason and aims at establishing a system of philosophy and ethics verifiable by experience and independent of all arbitrary assumptions or authority." The English thinker J. A. Hobson struck a prevailing note of present-day Rationalism when in his book, *Rationalism and Humanism,* he called upon British Rationalists to move on to Humanism as "the next step," an affirmative one, following what had been a predominantly negative and iconoclastic attack on traditional religious concepts. In 1957 the British Rationalists changed the name of their monthly journal to *The Humanist.* On the other side of the world the Freethought Society of the Philippines became in 1964 the Humanist Association of the Philippines.

Even more significant for the Humanist movement is the fact that in 1963 two of its leading organizations in England, the Ethical Union and the Rationalist Press Association, while maintaining their own identities, founded the British Humanist Association and agreed to cooperate within it. Launched at a large dinner in the House of Commons, the BHA has Sir Julian Huxley as its President, Professor A. J. Ayer of Oxford University as Vice-President, and H. J. Blackham, Editor of *The Plain View,* as Director. In due course the two initiating groups will probably merge altogether into the new organization.

Finally, we find in the category of naturalistic Humanists the followers of Karl Marx, who call themselves variously Marxists, Communists, or Socialists. On economic, political, and social issues the Marxist Humanists are of course much to the left of the other types of Humanists I have described. Ordinarily they use the formidable phrase *Dialectical Materialism* to designate their philosophy, though they often talk in a general way about the *Humanist* civilization of Soviet Russia and of the socialist world. The Marxist materialists disagree sharply on certain philosophic issues with me and with other Humanists, particularly in their ambiguous attitude toward democracy and their acceptance of determinism. They are, however, unquestionably humanistic in their major tenets of rejecting the supernatural and all religious authority, of setting up the welfare of mankind in this life as the supreme goal, and of relying on science and its techniques.

My résumé of the main groups that support naturalistic Humanism may make the subject seem rather complex. But the very fact that a number of different philosophic and religious groups, whatever their public designation, are all converging on the same general Humanist position gives to this philosophy an added significance and shows how widespread it has become in the modern world. The importance of the Humanist movement cannot be fairly estimated merely in terms of those who formally describe themselves as Humanists. However, the organization in which all those in the United States today who are fundamentally Humanists can unite for mutual cooperation is the American Humanist Association (AHA), founded in 1941.

The purpose of the AHA is to educate the American people on the meaning of Humanism and to persuade as many of them as possible to adopt this way of life. The AHA, with headquarters at Humanist House, Yellow Springs, Ohio, has more than sixty chapters in cities throughout the country. One of the most important chapters is the Humanist Student Union of North America, established in 1964. The AHA's publishing program includes a first-rate pamphlet series and a lively bimonthly, *The Humanist*.

The President of the American Humanist Association is Mrs. Vashti McCollum, who in 1948 won a precedent-making decision in the United States Supreme Court against religious instruction in public schools. The Executive Director is Tolbert H. McCarroll, an able attorney and former President of the Portland (Oregon) Ethical Society. A young man in his thirties, he took over this office in the AHA in 1963, replacing the Reverend Edwin H. Wilson, veteran Humanist who had successfully filled the same position for fourteen years.

In 1952 the AHA participated with a number of Humanist and Ethical Culture groups in an International Congress at

Amsterdam. This Congress established the International Humanist and Ethical Union (IHEU), with its central office at Utrecht. The IHEU, whose roots extend as far afield as India and Japan, has seven national groups that are full members and nineteen others affiliated with it. As a rule it meets every five years. In August 1962 it held its third Congress in Oslo.

My discussion of Humanism ought to have made clear already that the choice of words, in the realm of philosophy as elsewhere, is a most important matter. Philosophers cannot afford to overlook the social and psychological realities of language. *Naturalism* well expresses the world-view in which Nature and natural law are all that is; but as a word it is somewhat cold and abstract and does not in itself imply any great concern with human affairs. Moreover, in the popular mind naturalists are professional nature-lovers such as John Burroughs and Donald Culross Peattie. *Naturalism* also has its own special meaning in art and literature. *Materialism* denotes the same general attitude toward the universe as Naturalism and includes an estimable code of moral values. But it has been misunderstood, particularly in the English-speaking countries, as being a crass and low-minded ethical philosophy that stresses material goods and physical pleasures to the neglect of the higher spiritual values. Moreover, as applied to Communist culture and philosophy, *Materialism* is, in America at least, not an objective descriptive term, but one of reproach and opprobrium.

Humanism, on the other hand, embodying in itself the best from the naturalist and materialist traditions, is a warm, positive, understandable term which on the face of it indicates a paramount interest in man and a corresponding lack of preoccupation with the occult and the supernatural. Out of it flows naturally the implication that the supreme ethical objective is to work for a happier existence on behalf of all humanity here and now. The wide scope and unifying possibilities of *Humanism* are self-evident in that it is derived from a root that pertains to all men and not, as with the root words of so many philosophies and religions, from the name of a single man. Admittedly, *Humanism* is ambiguous in the sense that it has been and is understood in diverse ways, but that is a drawback which holds true of many excellent words—*democracy*, for instance, or *good*. The fact is that in interpreting *Humanism* as I do in this book, I am being loyal to historical usage and to the integrity of words. And there is no doubt in my mind that this term constitutes—in philosophy—an accurate, appealing, and internationally valid symbol for the beliefs and hopes of a large segment of humanity.

Humanism is a constructive philosophy that goes far beyond the negating of errors in thought to the whole-hearted affirmation of the joys, beauties, and values of human living. This is a viewpoint that can be grasped without difficulty by the people of every culture and country. Indeed, Humanism already *is* the functioning philosophy of millions upon millions of human beings throughout the globe who are daily striving to build a better life upon this earth for themselves, their children, and their fellowmen. To a mankind not yet altogether aware of its own good and goal, Humanism offers an inclusive program of philosophical and ethical truth that can play a leading role in the future of the race.

CHAPTER II

The Humanist Tradition

1. PHILOSOPHIC FORERUNNERS

Broadly speaking, whenever a thinker in any field treats the this-worldly welfare of man as paramount, he treads on Humanist ground. For Humanism the central concern is always the happiness of man in this existence, not in some fanciful never-never land beyond the grave; a happiness worthwhile as an end in itself and not subordinate to or dependent on a Supreme Deity, an invisible King, ruling over the earth and the infinite cosmos.

From the Humanist viewpoint, supernatural religion and that major portion of philosophy which has functioned as its handmaiden have made man central in a perverse and exaggerated way, reading purely human traits into the universe at large. Thus most of the religions and religious philosophies hold that mind and personality, love and purpose, are attributes of reality in its very essence. They illegitimately extend to existence as a whole the acknowledged importance of human values upon this planet; they teach a cosmology of conceit and a superstitious anthropomorphism that militates against men's true good in their one and only life. These religions and philosophies, furthermore, by constantly resorting to supernatural explanations, take the easy way out and offer facile solutions to problems susceptible to the painstaking methods of science.* Against all of these persistent fallacies Humanism has always constituted a vigorous dissenting voice.

---

* Immanuel Kant, himself a supporter of religious Dualism, warned in his *Inaugural Dissertation* that "the hasty appeal to the supernatural is a couch upon which the intellect slothfully reclines."

The first notable Humanist of whom there is reliable record was Protagoras, a Greek teacher and philosopher of the fifth century B.C., to whom Plato devoted an entire dialogue. Protagoras formulated the famous dictum "Man is the measure of all things, of things that are that they are, and of things that are not that they are not." This statement is too vague and subjective to be taken over without qualification by modern Humanism, but was at the time a daring and unorthodox thought. Protagoras was also an outspoken agnostic. According to Diogenes Laertius, he asserted: "As to the gods, I have no means of knowing either that they exist or do not exist. For many are the obstacles that impede knowledge, both the obscurity of the question and the shortness of human life." [8] For these and similar iconoclastic sentiments the Athenians accused Protagoras of impiety, banished him, and "burnt his works in the market place, after sending around a herald to collect them from all who had copies in their possession."

A number of other Greek philosophers in the fifth century B.C. showed a Humanist bent in that they, too, concentrated on the analysis of man rather than on the analysis of physical Nature, as the earlier generation of Greek thinkers had done. Most of them, like Protagoras, were Sophists, that is, wandering "teachers of wisdom" who discussed practically all the major issues that have ever arisen in philosophy. Plato criticized and satirized the Sophists in a way that was somewhat unfair, making them the foil of a fellow-Sophist, the wise and lovable Socrates, intellectual and moral hero of the *Dialogues*. Socrates brilliantly expounded typically Humanist maxims such as "Know thyself" and "The good individual in the good society." While believing in a God himself and having hopes of immortality, he tried to work out an ethical system that would function independently of religious doctrine. Throughout the chief Socratic dialogues of Plato—such as the *Apology*, the *Crito*, the *Phaedo*, the *Symposium*, and the all-embracing *Republic* itself—there is an abundance of mellow ethical philosophy, relevant for Humanism, that can be sifted out from the frequently supernaturalist and antidemocratic currents of thought in these works.

Especially in the field of ethics Humanism finds it profitable to be eclectic and to select from the most disparate philosophies and religions whatever ideas or insights seem of value. In the present chapter, however, I wish to stress the outstanding philosophies that in their world-view as well as their ethics take a Humanist position. Such, in the history of thought, are all the leading Naturalisms and Materialisms. These systems are alike opposed to the religious-tending Dualisms, like those of Plato and René Descartes, which hold that there are two ultimate substances, mind and matter; and to the religious-tending Idealisms, like those of G. W. F. Hegel and Josiah Royce, which claim that mind or idea is the basic stuff of existence.

Naturalism considers that man, the earth, and the unending universe of space and time are all parts of one great Nature. The whole of existence is equivalent to Nature and outside of Nature nothing exists. This metaphysics has no place for the supernatural, no room for superphysical beings or a supermaterial God, whether Christian or non-Christian in character, from whom men can obtain favors through prayer or guidance through revelation. But the adherents of Naturalism recognize and indeed rejoice in man's affinity with the mighty Nature that brought him forth and do not, like the more naïve type of atheist, go about shaking their fists at the universe.

From the beginning, Naturalism has supported and helped to develop the scientific outlook and man's reliance on reason. Accordingly it views man as entirely a creature of this earth and as an indissoluble unity of personality—including mind —on the one hand, and body or physical structure, on the other hand. This naturalistic psychology is the antithesis of the dualistic psychology that denaturalizes and supernaturalizes man by placing him, or at least his mind and soul, outside of and above Nature. The naturalistic interpretation makes any form of personal survival after death out of the question and so carries with it the implication of an ethics limited to this-worldly actions and aims.

The first great naturalist in the history of philosophy, though by no means a consistent one, was Aristotle, most universal of Greek philosophers, who lived in the fourth century B.C. Aristotle, student of Plato at the renowned Academy in Athens and tutor of Alexander the Great, was a biologist and psychologist as well as a philosopher. He not only provided powerful sinews for the life of reason by clarifying and codifying the laws of logic, but was also the founder of science as a discipline and an organized, interrelated body of fact. His broad and penetrating genius explored, and then extended, practically the whole range of knowledge as it existed in his day. Though Aristotle's underlying purpose was to explain rather than to reform the world, he arrived at many conclusions that are usable by those who would remake society. Perhaps most important in this connection was his emphasis on the fact of process in Nature and civilization, although his analysis of motion and change remained far from scientific and although the idea of biological evolution apparently did not occur to him.

Then, too, he established on a firm foundation that naturalistic psychology, still frequently called the "Aristotelian" psychology, which looks upon man as a living combination of soul and body. This view rules out the possibility of a personal after-existence; nevertheless Aristotle talked of the "active intellect" as immortal, without meaning that he thought there was a worthwhile future life for the full human personality with its memory and sense of self-identity. He likewise used the word *God* in an abstract manner very different from its customary significance. Aristotle's God was not a personal one consciously caring for the world and mankind, but the Prime Mover, an Unmoved Magnet, the eternal source of motion in the universe, stirring everything to activity through the force of attraction.

Thus Aristotle marred the purity of his Naturalism by in-

dulging in a confusing redefinition of supernaturalist concepts
—a tendency that has ever been the bane of philosophy—and
made it easier for the Catholic Church many centuries later to
incorporate his thought with seeming logic into its theology.
There were other serious faults in the philosophy of Aristotle,
such as his justification of slavery and belief in the natural in-
feriority of women. Both the virtues and defects of his system
had an undue influence because of the tremendous prestige of
the man himself, referred to until the modern era as "the
Master . . . of those that know," in Dante's admiring words.
Mankind should always be on guard against becoming subservient to the geniuses of the past.

The tradition of philosophic Naturalism that Aristotle established, while entering to some extent into various materialistic
world-views, did not really come into its own again until more
than two thousand years later when Benedict Spinoza appeared upon the scene in Holland of the seventeenth century.
Spinoza is considered by many as the most eminent of all
modern philosophers. His greatest book was the *Ethics,* which
treats not merely of ethical problems, but compresses into its
fewer than 300 pages a complete philosophy of life. Cast into
the general pattern of geometry, with numbered propositions,
demonstrations, corollaries, and Q.E.D.'s following one another in strictly logical sequence, this brilliant volume of Spinoza's is generally acknowledged as one of the supreme mas-
terpieces of the philosophic intellect.

Spinoza's stress on mathematical method and form shows to
what an extent he had absorbed and approved the new
science. His philosophical Naturalism and naturalistic psychology embodied the epoch-making scientific developments of the
two past centuries starting with the Copernican revolution.
However, like Aristotle in ancient Greece, Spinoza compro-
mised with religious terminology by bringing into his philosophy something he called *immortality* and something he called
God.

Again, as with Aristotle, his definition of these terms was

far removed from ordinary usage. By immortality Spinoza meant, not the duration of the personality beyond the grave, but the attainment of a certain high quality of thought and action in the present existence; and the fact that a man's life, when it is over, becomes part of the unchanging and eternal past. By God he meant, not a supermaterial being possessing the attributes of purpose, justice, consciousness, and love, but simply the totality of Nature.

Spinoza has constantly been accused of being an atheist, and I believe rightly so in relation to the Judeo-Christian tradition. At the same time, because he so accented "the intellectual love of God" (or Nature), he is often referred to as "the God-intoxicated man." The truth is that Spinoza did not believe in either God or immortality as usually defined; but subject as he was to persecution by both Church and State on account of his unorthodox ideas, it may be that he stayed out of jail and preserved his life through his highly intellectualized redefinitions of God and immortality.

Spinoza had good grounds for being nervous, since Bruno had been executed as a heretic at the beginning of the seventeenth century and Galileo had been forced to recant by the Inquisition during Spinoza's own lifetime. Furthermore, two of Spinoza's best friends in Holland were the victims of a brutal political murder by a mob and his own security was continually threatened. His chef-d'oeuvre, the *Ethics*, actually did not appear until after his death for the reason that Spinoza kept postponing its publication for fear of the consequences. In a letter to a friend Spinoza said that because his enemies had lodged "a complaint against me with the prince and magistrates" and because "the theologians were everywhere lying in wait for me, I determined to put off my attempted publication until such time as I should see what turn affairs would take." [9]

After Spinoza, Naturalism, everywhere a minority and unpopular viewpoint for all but a fraction of history, lapsed again to a large degree until the second half of the nineteenth century. It then came back into the mainstream of Western thought with renewed vigor, receiving a fresh and lasting impulse from Charles Darwin's *The Origin of Species,* published in 1859. What Darwin and his fellow biologists did, through marshaling incontestable evidence of the evolution of man from lower forms of life, was to demonstrate that no wide and impassable gulf exists between Homo sapiens and the rest of Nature. This undermined some of the most powerful arguments of religious supernaturalism and of the traditional philosophies associated with it, giving most convincing support to the major naturalist thesis that man and all of his experience are in every respect a part of Nature.

Naturalist trends in Europe greatly increased as a result of Darwin's work. But the revival of Naturalism as an explicit philosophy in intellectual and academic circles took place chiefly in the United States, where its strongest and most influential school developed at Columbia University under the original inspiration of Professors John Dewey and Frederick J. E. Woodbridge. That school continues to flourish under the leadership of exceptional teachers and scholars such as John H. Randall, Jr., the leading Naturalist in present-day America; Ernest Nagel, a specialist in the philosophy of science; and Justus Buchler, Chairman of the Columbia Philosophy Department.

John Dewey, who saw so clearly the full implications for philosophy of the Darwinian revolution in biology, was born in the very year in which *The Origin of Species* appeared. It is Dewey's hardheaded empirical viewpoint, as set forth in books like *Experience and Nature* and *Reconstruction in Philosophy,* that constitutes the most scientific and up-to-date version of Naturalism. While Dewey makes room for a very much refined "religion," he completely discards all supernatural forces and entities and regards mind as an instrument of survival and adaptation developed in the long process of evolution. In much of his work Dewey followed the lead of William James, Harvard's versatile physiologist, psychologist, philosopher, and teacher, but he eliminated the subjective elements that marred the latter's pragmatism. -

In my opinion Dewey is the twentieth-century philosopher who so far has best understood modern science and scientific method and who most cogently developed their meaning for philosophy and culture. Throughout he places reliance on experimental intelligence as the most dependable way to solve the problems that face the individual and society. Now intelligence, reason, thought, when most effective, are all nothing more nor less than scientific method in operation; and Dewey's most persistent plea is that men should apply that method to every sector of their lives and that the most profound need of our day is to extend scientific thinking from the natural sciences to the broad field of social, economic, and political affairs. His full-fledged Naturalism is, then, a massive philosophic system which is not only itself based on science, but which also considers the advancement of science in every sphere as the best hope of the human race.

Since the First World War, Naturalism has come increasingly to the fore in American philosophy and promises to continue its gains in the future. For three centuries antinaturalist and anti-Humanist philosophies were dominant on the American continent. These consisted either of Protestant and Catholic theologies or, in the nineteenth century, of transcendental and idealistic metaphysics originating primarily in Germany, and inspired particularly by Hegel and Kant. The influence of Idealism became especially marked in the universities. Paradoxically, however, while "our professed philosophies have endlessly refuted Naturalism . . . our practiced philosophies have steadily confirmed it." [10] And the recent advance of Naturalism has without question furthered the Humanist goal of bringing American theory consciously into line with the secular and scientific temper of America in action.

Closely related to Naturalism in its basic world-view and similarly a strong bulwark for Humanism is the philosophy of Materialism, holding that the foundation stone of all being is matter in motion. Like Naturalism, Materialism relies first and foremost on scientific method, believes in the ultimate atomic structure of things, and finds in Nature an order and a process that can be expressed in scientific laws of cause and effect. But Materialism has stressed matter as such more than Nature and tended until recently to oversimplify and overmechanize, reducing in theory the whole complex behavior of living creatures and human beings to the operation of the same laws that apply to inanimate existence. The correct view, however, would seem to be that while the laws of physics and chemistry are necessarily germane to many aspects of living forms, they are not sufficient in themselves to explain organic structure and functioning. Human thinking and feeling, for instance, although functions of the body and dependent upon it, operate at a level qualitatively far removed from atomic energy in its simpler forms.

Materialism has usually gone hand in hand with an outspoken antireligious position and has been less prone to compromise with religious terminology. It has also been associated, particularly in modern times, with radical political movements. Naturalism's less militant attitude in general is perhaps the chief reason why it is sometimes called a "polite" Materialism.

Materialism has exercised as long and far-reaching an influence on human thought as Naturalism. The earlier Greek philosophers of the sixth century B.C., men like Thales, Anaximander, and Heraclitus, tended in the direction of a naïve Materialism. They made brilliant guesses to the effect that everything is part of one substance or stuff such as water, air, or fire. The first complete and consistent materialist, however, was Democritus, the so-called laughing philosopher, who flourished about the year 400 B.C. and developed systematically the idea that the whole universe is composed in the last analysis of tiny material particles—atoms of different size, shape, and configuration whirling swiftly through the void and interacting according to a definite causal sequence. Thus Democritus was the father of the atomic theory, finally proved true by science some 2300 years later.

An old anecdote about Democritus well illustrates the difference between the scientific and the supernaturalist approach. A respected citizen of Democritus's town, we are told, was out walking one day, with no covering on his bald head, when a tortoise inexplicably fell upon him out of the sky and killed him. Since an eagle, the bird of the god Zeus, had been seen hovering above at the time of the accident, the neighbors began to spread the rumor that the death of their fellow citizen was a miraculous happening of divine portent. But "Democritus gave the event a thoroughly naturalistic explanation, resolutely dismissing talk of the supernatural or of fate. Eagles like the meat of tortoises, but sometimes find it difficult to get from the shell. They have, therefore, learned to drop the creatures from a great height on shining rocks, which shatter the shell and make available the meat. The eagle had simply mistaken the man's bald head for the splendor of a rock." [11]

More than a century later Epicurus took over the theory of Democritus, adding the important point that in the swirl of the atoms chance deviations take place that break the chain of complete determinism and make room for human freedom of choice. Epicurus had strong ethical grounds for preferring a materialistic system, since he wanted to see men live in the light of reason and without fear. Accordingly, he tried to eliminate apprehensions about the supernatural by teaching that there were no deities who intervened in human affairs and that mortal men had no existence after death. This negation of religious doctrines was a prerequisite, in the judgment of Epicurus, for attaining individual happiness on earth. Such happiness he defined in terms of the more refined pleasures, guided by wisdom and adjusted to the hard realities of life. The Epicureans placed affection or friendship among the highest goods of experience. Epicurus himself retired to his garden to live quietly, abstemiously, and nobly, achieving a kind of philosophic saintliness. Yet Epicureanism has come to mean generally the pursuit of sensual enjoyment; the philosophy par excellence of wine, women, and song. And Epicurus remains perhaps the outstanding example of a great philosopher who has been perpetually misunderstood.

When we come to the period of Rome's supremacy in the ancient world, we find that the greatest of Roman philosophers, Lucretius, was a disciple of Epicurus and based his masterly work, *On the Nature of Things,* upon his system. This classic of both literature and philosophy, the finest philosophic poem ever produced as well as the most eloquent exposition of Materialism, rendered into Latin verse a detailed account of the Epicurean view of life. Lucretius had a profound appreciation for the beauty and sublimity of Nature, and his magnificent descriptions of the natural world in its various aspects of loveliness and grandeur have hardly been equalled in philosophic writing since his day.

Despite their frank and open crusade against religious superstition, both Lucretius and Epicurus made one concession to convention and tradition. That was their admission that far away in the intermediate spaces of the heavens there existed blessed beings or gods who led a life of uninterrupted enjoyment and contemplation, totally undisturbed by any duties pertaining to the management of the cosmos or the fate of men. Since these do-nothing gods had no concern with human affairs, men need have no concern with them and could go their way as free and unperturbed as if such beings were purely fanciful. Lucretius and Epicurus regarded their gesture toward the old mythology as harmless and evidently indulged in it mainly to escape being branded as outright atheists, ever a dangerous accusation in most cultures and countries.

Like Naturalism, Materialism as a system found little favor or expression during the long period between the civilizations of antiquity and the modern era. Following the efforts of Francis Bacon, himself no materialist, on behalf of a revival of science to substitute the Empire of Man over Nature for that of Man over Man, his former secretary, Thomas Hobbes, gave Materialism a methodical and thoroughgoing formulation in the seventeenth century. Hobbes's interpretation of Materialism was unusual in that he made it the basis for political conservatism and suggested that God was *corporeal*. This latter idea, paradoxical as it may seem, stems from the logical position, likewise held by some of the early Church Fathers, that there can be no such thing as an incorporeal substance and that God, if he exists, must have a body. Hobbes was also an iconoclast in undertaking criticism of the Bible on documentary grounds. It is no wonder that the Church of England looked upon him as a doubtful ally, some of the more intolerant bishops wishing to have him burned as a heretic. And it is more than possible that Hobbes, who in his best-known book, *The Leviathan,* attacked even Aristotle for compromising with religion because of "fearing the fate of Socrates," at times wrote about God and other religious topics with his tongue in his cheek.

The most significant resurgence of Materialism, however, took place in France during the second half of the eighteenth century as part of the great Enlightenment that stirred to its depths the Western World. The French Encyclopedists, such as La Mettrie and Helvetius, Holbach and Diderot, were able to utilize the materialist philosophy as a powerful weapon against religious superstition and the reactionary Catholic Church. In his *System of Nature* Baron d'Holbach summed up the materialist attitude toward religious supernaturalism: "If we go back to the beginning of things, we shall always find that ignorance and fear created the gods; that imagination, rapture, and deception embellished or distorted them; that weakness worships them; that credulity nourishes them; that custom spares them; and that tyranny favors them in order to profit from the blindness of men." [12] And the uncompromising Diderot exclaimed: "Men will never be free until the last king is strangled in the entrails of the last priest!" [13]

These French materialists, however, maintained the mechanistic fallacies I have already mentioned and in addition extended them to their social theory.

During the nineteenth century leadership in the materialist
movement passed to Germany and to such men as Jacob
Moleschott and Ernst Haeckel, Ludwig Buchner and Ludwig
Feuerbach, Karl Marx and Frederick Engels. Haeckel was
the first important German biologist who wholeheartedly
accepted the Darwinian doctrine of organic evolution. He
used that theory as the cornerstone of his popular philosophic
work, *The Riddle of the Universe,* wherein he showed conclusively that the mind as well as the body of man had evolved
from animal species.

The brilliant Feuerbach, a much underrated figure in most
histories of philosophy, broke with orthodoxy early in his
career and lost his teaching post after it was discovered that
he was the author of an anonymous treatise attacking the
idea of personal immortality. In his most significant book,
The Essence of Christianity, Feuerbach demonstrated that the
mythologies of traditional religion have their source in unfulfilled human feelings, longings, and needs. Men deify their
inward nature by projecting it outward as the idea of God;
"God is the highest subjectivity of man abstracted from himself." [14] The essential predicates of Divinity, such as personality
and love, are simply the human qualities men value most
highly. Although Feuerbach is ordinarily classified as a materialist, he himself at one time considered Humanism as the
most appropriate name for his philosophy.

Feuerbach had a profound influence on the philosophic
development of Marx and Engels. It was he, as Engels states,
who "in many respects forms an intermediate link between
Hegelian philosophy and our own conception." [15] The Dialectical Materialism of Marx and Engels corrected the mechanistic
errors of the earlier materialist tradition and gave full recognition to the dynamic, ever-changing character of existence
and to the infinite interrelatedness of phenomena in both

Nature and society. While Dialectical Materialism considers that human thought is a function of the bodily organism, it believes that the mind is no mere passive reflector of the outside world, but that it possesses a fundamental initiative and creativity, a power of working upon and remolding the environment through the force of new ideas.

At the same time the Marxist materialists have carried on and developed the intransigent antireligious doctrines of the materialists who preceded them. Today there can be little question that Dialectical Materialism, while having its own shortcomings, is the most influential variety of Materialism, both because of its consistency and inclusiveness and also because it is the official philosophy of Communist governments and parties throughout the world.

There are other philosophies of the past which, while not specifically within either the naturalist or materialist category, give strong support to the Humanist position. For example, Auguste Comte, French thinker of the middle nineteenth century, made a stimulating if somewhat erratic approach to a consistent Humanism. Taking the facts and methods of science as his starting point, Comte worked out a far-reaching system, which he called *Positivism*. He used the word *positive*, not as the opposite of *negative*, but as meaning scientifically certain or assured.

During his late forties Comte reacted against his earlier intellectualism following a deep emotional crisis associated with his passionate, though Platonic, love for a beautiful and intelligent woman, Clotilde de Vaux, and her untimely death at thirty-one after he had known her for only a year. Comte mourned at her tomb once a week and invoked her memory in prayer three times a day. He referred to her as his angel of inspiration and as a second Beatrice. Finally, he formally ensconced her in his system as a virtual saint and as the personification of the Ideal Female symbolizing the Great Being (humanity).

All this accompanied Comte's unfortunate transformation of

Positivism into a complex Religion of Humanity, replete with rituals, sacraments, priests, and temples. For the worship of God he substituted the worship of Man and for the calendar of Christian saints a select list of the heroes of human progress. Positivism, patterning its liturgy closely after that of the Roman Catholic Church, assumed some of the objectionable features of a religious cult, and was soon dubbed "Catholicism minus Christianity." It was, moreover, a cult overpersonalized in the image of its egotistic founder, who in effect became the high priest of the new religion and whose statue was prominently displayed in all the Positivist temples.

Comte had a considerable vogue throughout the Western World, but his thought took deeper root in Latin America than in the United States. His followers have been particularly active in Brazil, where in 1881 they established a Positivist Church. Its headquarters in Rio de Janeiro still functions on a regular basis. Comte's lasting influence on Brazil is seen in the fact that inscribed on the national flag is his maxim, "Order and Progress." This is the only national emblem in the world that perpetuates the words of a philosopher.

In England the versatile John Stuart Mill developed and included in his philosophy of Utilitarianism the more scientific aspects of Comte's work, shunning its religious and mystical elements. Mill's writings also served as an invaluable stimulus to the democratic ideals that mean so much to Humanism. His essay *On Liberty* ranks with Milton's *Areopagitica* as one of the classic statements on freedom of thought and the rights of the individual. "If all mankind minus one were of one opinion," declared Mill, "and only one person were of the contrary opinion, mankind would be no more justified in silencing that one person, than he, if he had the power, would be justified in silencing mankind. . . . All silencing of discussion is an assumption of infallibility." [16]

Positivism also inspired Herbert Spencer, systematic and system-building British philosopher who outlined a general theory of evolution several years before Darwin issued *The*

Origin of Species and who continued, after that notable event, to apply the evolutionary hypothesis to every sector of human history and thought. Spencer promoted his interpretation of evolution with such zeal that he overreached and discredited himself. For he advocated a hard-boiled theory, supposedly based on the Darwinian principle of the survival of the fittest, that in society the economically successful, the biologically fit, and the morally good are roughly equivalent. In regard to supernaturalism, Spencer was an agnostic, that is, one who believes there is not sufficient evidence either to prove or disprove the existence of God and immortality. The originator of the useful word *agnostic* was Thomas H. Huxley, noted English biologist and popularizer of the Darwinian theory. Since agnostics are doubtful about the supernatural, they tend to be Humanists in practice.

Although it is difficult to classify Bertrand Russell, the leading English philosopher of the twentieth century and a member of the House of Lords, he properly belongs, I think, in the tradition of naturalistic Humanism. This is attested by the fact that he is president of the leading British Rationalist organization and a member of the Advisory Council of the British Humanist Association. Lord Russell's system is not free of contradictions and has never shaken off entirely the taint of subjectivistic theories of knowledge. Yet there is no trace of supernaturalism in his conclusions; and he stands thoroughly committed to the methods of democracy and science. Russell's most original contribution to philosophy lies in his demonstration of the essential identity of logic and pure mathematics. Early in his career he became a militant social reformer. On account of his pacifist views during the First World War, Cambridge University dismissed him, and the British Government imprisoned him for six months.

In 1940 political and ecclestiastical pressures resulted in Russell's losing his appointment as professor of philosophy at the College of the City of New York. A censorious faction led by Episcopal Bishop William T. Manning had demanded that Russell be ousted on the grounds that his books were "lecherous, salacious, libidinous, lustful, venereous, erotomaniac, aphrodisiac, atheistic, irreverent, narrow-minded, untruthful and bereft of moral fibre." [17] Although CCNY itself stood firm for academic freedom in the Russell case, the higher city authorities overruled the College.

After the Second World War and despite his advanced years, Russell took active leadership in the British and worldwide movements for the ending of nuclear bomb testing, for total disarmament in nuclear weapons, and for the abolition of international war. Participating at the age of ninety in a big peace demonstration in London in 1962, he was arrested and sent to jail for a week.

Another distinguished thinker not easy to label is George Santayana, who has likewise made signal contributions to Humanism. Born in Spain, he came to maturity in the United States and taught philosophy for many years at Harvard University.* He spent the latter part of his life in Rome, where he resided in comparative solitude until his death in 1952. It is my considered judgment that Santayana's prose style is more beautiful than that of any other philosopher since Plato; and his work, which includes poetry, the novel, and autobiography, can be read as much for its literary charm as for its intellectual stimulus. His philosophic approach is always sophisticated and urbane, treating supernatural religion, for instance, as poetic myth to be enjoyed and understood rather than as dark superstition to be fought and eradicated. Santayana's essential tenderness toward the religious tradition has led one wit aptly to say: "Santayana believes that there is no God, and that Mary is His mother."

Santayana's volumes abound with aphorisms that plainly have a Humanist intent, as when he tells us that "men became superstitious not because they had too much imagination, but because they were not aware that they had any"; [18] that "the

---

* See also pp. xii-xiii.

fact of having been born is a bad augury for immortality"; [19] and that "the love of God is said to be the root of Christian charity, but is in reality only its symbol." [20]

As contrasted, however, with the sound approach of his earlier period and his greatest work, *The Life of Reason*, Santayana in his later years somewhat weakened his philosophy by adopting an esoteric doctrine of essences, which, much like the old Platonic ideas, are supposed to subsist in an eternal realm apart from the regular course of Nature. It is this feature of Santayana's thought that led John Dewey to criticize it as "broken-backed Naturalism." Santayana sometimes talked of himself as a naturalist, sometimes as a Humanist, but preferred to think of his system as a species of Materialism. On political and economic issues he was distinctly conservative.

Dr. Albert Schweitzer, world famous for his humanitarianism and opposition to nuclear weapons, has sometimes called himself a Humanist; and his central philosophic principle, "Reverence for Life," has a fine ring. But when we analyze what he means by this phrase, we discover that for him "life" includes physical objects and the whole material universe, so that he turns out to be in a vague way an animist or a panpsychist. Furthermore, so far as biological species are concerned, Dr. Schweitzer's infinite benevolence extends to the mosquitoes and microbes that may bring death to a man. This is going a bit far for a Humanism primarily concerned with the welfare of humanity; and it also imposes psychological guilt on man for killing the worms and germs that threaten his life. Naturalistic Humanism, however, agrees fully with Dr. Schweitzer in favoring kindness to animals as a principle of human conduct.

Though contemporary Humanism cannot accept *in toto* any of the Naturalisms, Materialisms, or allied philosophies discussed above, it must draw primarily, insofar as it depends on past thought, upon these great systems that I have outlined. Today all philosophy of the first rank must to some extent be eclectic and acknowledge its heavy debt to earlier thinkers. To maintain otherwise is to strike an intellectual pose. Humanism is not interested in novelty as such. Its question is not whether an idea is old or new, familiar or daring, but whether it is true and whether it is relevant to the Humanist outlook.

Even systems such as those of Dualism and Idealism, with which Humanists so profoundly disagree, have much to teach us. Almost every philosophy contains some important elements that are sound. And in general it is far more fruitful to try to understand why certain philosophers went astray than to neglect or scorn them. Brilliant errors, tenaciously pursued unto their remotest implications, can be most illuminating and suggestive in the search for truth. That search follows no royal road, straight and smooth, but meets many obstacles, makes many false starts, goes off on many attractive but misleading bypaths. It is a search, too, which is never-ending, yet which each generation can push forward to new discoveries and triumphs.

2. RELIGIOUS ROOTS OF HUMANISM

Unquestionably the great religious leaders like Buddha and Confucius and Jesus have made a substantial contribution, on the ethical side, to the Humanist tradition. The original teachings of both Buddha and Confucius are to some degree shrouded in obscurity, but it seems most unlikely that either of them believed in supernaturalism in the sense of the existence of a personal God and personal immortality. And it is dubious indeed whether either of these wise and humble men would have approved of the complex priest-ridden religions, interlarded with all sorts of naïve superstitions, that eventually became organized around their names. Buddha, especially, would no doubt have been surprised and horrified to find himself elevated to the status of a Divinity, devoutly worshipped by hundreds of millions of people throughout the East and his image graven in innumerable stone, metal, and wooden statues.

Buddha's sayings, such as those embodied in the Eight-fold Path of Virtue, dealt primarily with a code of conduct for this world. He was not interested in ordinary religious rituals, sacrifices, and other observances. He believed that men could overcome the miseries of life by giving up their narrow personal aims and tormenting desires. It was a high doctrine of altruism and self-renunciation, with a somewhat negative and individualistic emphasis on one's avoidance of pain and sorrow rather than an affirmative stress on building happiness within the good society and through social cooperation.

Confucius was much more concerned with political and social life than Buddha and presented the ideal of the noble man in the noble state. He laid his heaviest stress on an ethical system which looked to men's happiness here and now and, like the ethics of Plato and Aristotle, exalted the importance of knowledge and of human interrelationships. Concerning survival beyond the grave, Confucius would only say: "While you do not know life, what can you know about death?" He was equally uncertain concerning God and the gods.

Lin Yutang, the contemporary Chinese author, is convinced that Confucius was a true Humanist; and he describes Chinese Humanism, faithful to the spirit of Confucius, in this way: "For the Chinese the end of life lies not in life after death, for the idea that we live in order to die, as taught by Christianity, is incomprehensible; nor in Nirvana, for that is too metaphysical; nor in the satisfaction of accomplishment, for that is too vainglorious; nor yet in progress for progress's sake, for that is meaningless. The true end, the Chinese have decided in a singularly clear manner, lies in the enjoyment of a simple life, especially the family life, and in harmonious social relationships. . . . There is no doubt that the Chinese are in love with life, in love with this earth, and will not forsake it for an invisible heaven. They are in love with life, which is so sad and yet so beautiful, and in which moments of happiness are so precious because they are so transient." [21]

Turning to the West, we find that the Old Testament Hebrews, despite their vigorous supernaturalism, had little faith in a worthwhile immortality for the human personality and were primarily interested in the future of the tribe or nation *in this world*. It was their earnest expectation that God would finally deliver Israel, the chosen people, into a heaven or New Jerusalem situated on this terrestrial globe. Throughout the Old Testament there runs a strong sense of the values attainable in earthly living. And a book like Proverbs contains a wealth of moral insight and worldly wisdom that stands up independent of sanctions or revelations from on high. Moreover, Old Testament prophets such as Amos and Isaiah, Jeremiah and Ezekiel, denounced in no uncertain language the selfishness, corruption, and oppression of their day. They fought on behalf of the people against their exploiters.

Two books of the Old Testament are themselves among the greatest Humanist documents in all literature. I refer to The Song of Solomon, with its superb and poetic love passages, and Ecclesiastes, with its central theme of enjoying life while one is able, even though all human happiness and achievement are transient and in the end perhaps mere vanity. Greek influence in Ecclesiastes is unmistakable and its message bears a distinctly Epicurean flavor. Since the book was probably written about 200 B.C. or later, its author or authors may well have been affected directly or indirectly by the school of Epicurus.

Passing to the New Testament, we see plainly that its theology, taken literally, is totally alien to the Humanist viewpoint. Yet when we objectively analyze New Testament Christianity, with its emphasis on the resurrection and eternal life of the individual, we are able to understand that this religion has displayed in its worship what is essentially a veneration of man's own highest qualities. These it attributed to God the Father and to Jesus the Son, whose deification fulfilled the need for a more human God. And when this Christ became a bit too distant, the Church wisely brought in the Virgin Mary and other saints to reintroduce the human touch.

New Testament ethics is based on the assumption that the most meaningful and worthwhile part of man's life lies in the realm of immortality. The New Testament as a document is so full of ambiguities as to correct human conduct that the devil is always quoting it for his own devious purposes. Nonetheless, the gospels have much to offer any generous and humane ethical philosophy. Running through them is a radically democratic spirit, a deep equalitarian feeling, that has been the inspiration of numberless workers for a happier mankind in this mundane sphere. Jesus raised his voice again and again on behalf of broad Humanist ideals such as social equality, the development of altruism, the brotherhood of man, and peace on earth. According to the gospel story, he was much aware of the material needs of men and himself fed the hungry and healed the sick. Some of his specific sayings can be given a this-worldly interpretation consonant with Humanism. I am thinking of such familiar statements as: "Ye shall know the truth, and the truth shall make you free"; and "I am come that they might have life, and that they might have it more abundantly."

Humanism, then, holds that certain of the teachings of Jesus possess an ethical import that will always be an inspiration for the human race; and that the Jesus portrayed by the gospels represents one of the supreme personalities of all time. He was a most effective fighter against the hidebound Pharisees of his day, the greatest free speech victim in the history of religion * and a radiant martyr for the cause of humanity. This interpretation of Jesus as a great good man

---

* See Clifford J. Durr's suggestive essay, "Jesus: A Free Speech Victim," in *Three Biblical Lessons in Civil Liberties,* American Humanist Association, 1963, pp. 5-12.

instead of a god has found ample support within Christianity itself. Early in the fourth century A.D. Arius, a Christian presbyter, initiated the famous Arian controversy by stressing the human attributes of Jesus and claiming that he was of a different substance from God the Father. In 325 the Council of Nicaea outlawed this Arian view as heresy and drew up the official Nicene Creed affirming that God was a Trinity of Father, Son, and Holy Spirit. But the more simple and sensible Arian doctrine never died out in Christian circles and for centuries had its secret adherents.

Arianism broke forth into the open again as a major issue during the first century of the Protestant Reformation when Michael Servetus, a Spaniard, took up the battle and declared: "Your Trinity is a product of subtlety and madness. The Gospel knows nothing of it. . . . God is one and indivisible." [22] Both Catholic and Protestant authorities banned and burned Servetus' book *On the Errors of the Trinity*. Servetus escaped from the agents of the Catholic Inquisition only to be recaptured by the police of John Calvin, Protestant "Pope" and dictator of Geneva. Calvin, whose own intolerance was scarcely less than that of the Inquisition itself, brought Servetus quickly to trial for his heresies and had him burned at the stake in 1553. Far from halting the ideas of Michael Servetus, the flame that reduced his body to ashes helped mightily to fan into vigorous life the modern Unitarian movement throughout Europe.

This Unitarian movement, insisting on the oneness of God and the essential humanity of Jesus Christ, became a powerful influence in Poland at the end of the sixteenth century under the leadership of Faustus Socinus, spread to England in the seventeenth century, and took root across the Atlantic in America in the eighteenth. For a long time the Unitarians did not favor setting up a separate denomination. It was only in 1825 that they broke away from the Congregationalists and officially established their own Unitarian organization in Europe and the United States. From the beginning the stronghold of the American Unitarians was in New England, where William Ellery Channing, Theodore Parker, and Ralph Waldo Emerson were their acknowledged leaders. While the world-view of the Unitarians was certainly non-Humanist, they were on the whole liberals in theology and also backed most of the important social reforms of the nineteenth century. They gave emphasis, too, to the right of individual religious freedom and welcomed into the Unitarian fellowship even those who questioned the existence of a personal God.

Approximately a hundred years after the founding of Unitarianism the more advanced members of this sect, most of them from the Middle West, started the movement known as religious Humanism. Dr. Curtis W. Reese, a Unitarian pastor, precipitated the discussions that led to religious Humanism by a challenging sermon at Des Moines in 1917 and an address at the Harvard Divinity School in 1920. Philosophers, teachers, writers, and clergymen quickly entered into the debate; and the result was the definite emergence of Humanism in religion, eventually culminating in the *Humanist Manifesto* of 1933. This key document was initiated by three Unitarian ministers: L. M. Birkhead, Raymond B. Bragg, and Edwin H. Wilson; and by two university teachers, Dr. A. Eustace Haydon, a professor of religion, and Dr. Roy Wood Sellars, a professor of philosophy. Dr. Sellars drew up the *Manifesto's* first draft, which served as the essential frame and basis for the final formulations.

In a sermon delivered in 1925 the Reverend John H. Dietrich showed how Unitarianism had naturally laid the basis for Humanism. "Unitarianism," he asserted, "offered opportunity for the enunciation of Humanism by virtue of its underlying spirit of spiritual freedom, by its insistence upon intellectual integrity rather than intellectual uniformity, by its offer of religious fellowship to every one of moral purpose without regard to his theological beliefs. But this is not the important thing. The real reason why Unitarianism was the natural soil for the growth of Humanism is the fact that Unitarianism was

a revolt against orthodox Christianity in the interest of the
worth and dignity of human nature and the interest of human
life." [23] A large proportion of the Unitarian churches in the
United States are acknowledgedly Humanist.

The Universalist Church, an American and Canadian denomination somewhat smaller than the Unitarian, also had
an influential Humanist wing. The Universalists became active
in the latter part of the eighteenth century and represented
a revolt of the heart against certain Christian dogmas such as
that of eternal punishment for sinners. The Universalists take
their name from their belief in universal salvation, the doctrine
that God "will finally restore the whole family of mankind to
holiness and happiness." The outstanding Humanist among
Universalist clergymen is the Reverend Kenneth L. Patton,
pastor of the Charles Street Meeting House in Boston. Mr.
Patton's poems, and his Responsive Readings, such as those in
Man Is the Meaning, rank high as sensitive and eloquent expressions of the Humanist spirit.

During the past few decades it became evident that the
Unitarians and the Universalists were growing closer together
in their general religious attitudes. In 1950 top officials of both
organizations began negotiations for a merger. And in 1961
the two movements formally united in a single liberal church
under the name of the Unitarian Universalist Association. This
Association, of which the Reverend Dana M. Greeley is President, has about 155,000 members divided among 1,000
churches and fellowships.

In the complex history of the Christian religion there have
been still other developments that have encouraged a Humanist attitude. Thus, insofar as the Protestant revolt led
to a stress on good works and moral achievement rather than
on ritual performance and priestly magic for the attainment
of supernatural salvation, it led in a Humanist direction. So
also did those tendencies within the Protestant Church which
looked to a religion based upon reason instead of revelation.

We can take as the prime example here the religion of Deism, which found wide acceptance in Western Europe and America during the eighteenth century.

The viewpoint of Deism was essentially that God created the universe at the beginning of things and then, retiring to the comfortable status of Deity Emeritus, left the great world-machine to work out its own self-evolution according to natural law. This form of religious rationalism placed miracles and prophecy in the class of mere superstition; and further undermined revealed religion by stimulating objective and scholarly criticism of the Scriptures. Deism retained the belief in a future life with appropriate rewards and punishments. The deist position in general strengthened the secular, Humanist trends of the modern era, since it implied that men should depend on their own efforts and intelligence and not feel that they could fall back on a Divine Being who would do the job for them or rescue them in an emergency.

Deism reached its peak in the eighteenth century when many of the most eminent intellects on either side of the Atlantic came to support this religion. They included Sir Isaac Newton in England, the irrepressible Voltaire in France, G. E. Lessing in Germany, and Benjamin Franklin, Thomas Jefferson, and Thomas Paine in America. Jefferson, who suffered every sort of calumny and slander for his liberalism in religion, wrote: "Fix reason firmly in her seat, and call to her tribunal every fact, every opinion. Question with boldness even the existence of a god; because if there be one, he must more approve of the homage of reason than that of blindfolded fear." [24] Paine's widely circulated book *The Age of Reason* did much to popularize the deist view. A number of the lesser lights of the American Revolution were also Deists. There is no doubt, either, that George Washington, a rather indifferent member of the Episcopal Church, and John Adams, second President of the United States and sympathetic to Unitarianism, were strongly influenced by Deism, both through their colleagues and as a result of the general intellectual atmosphere.*

Deism in the United States, however, was soon on the wane. Professor Harold A. Larrabee reveals why: "So sharp and so general was the American reaction to the French Revolution and its aftermath, turning public sentiment away in horror from all forms of unbelief toward a re-energized Protestantism, that it virtually closed the national mind for the greater part of the nineteenth century to all philosophies except religious versions of realism and idealism. So violent was the counter-attack on Deism that it left no tenable middle ground between evangelical fervor and odious infidelity." [25]

Throughout the course of Christianity, and more particularly subsequent to the Reformation, certain individuals and groups have concentrated on humanitarianism and the Social Gospel rather than on the hope of immortality and the abstract disputes of theology. Typical of this attitude have been the Quakers, or Society of Friends, first organized in Britain by George Fox in the latter part of the seventeenth century. The Quakers, like the Unitarians, repudiated the doctrine of the Trinity and religious formalism, advocating *individual* divine guidance through the "inner light." They were philanthropic in spirit and early took an advanced position on many social issues, being pioneers for the abolition of slavery, the protection of oppressed races such as the American Indian, and the improvement of prison conditions. From the start they were uncompromising opponents of militarism and war. They were the first Christian denomination to give women equal rights with men in church organization. And to demonstrate in their daily conduct their sympathy with the poor and their disap-

---

* It was President Adams, not President Washington, who in 1797 confirmed and signed the Treaty between the United States and Tripoli in which appears the significant statement: ". . . the Government of the United States of America is not in any sense founded on the Christian Religion."

proval of luxury, the Quakers dressed simply, spoke simply and lived simply.

Most famous of all Quakers was William Penn, who in 1681 founded the colony of Pennsylvania as a refuge from religious persecution. He had been a militant advocate of Quaker beliefs in England at a time when it was extremely unpopular and indeed illegal to support the Friends publicly. Penn repeatedly suffered imprisonment, including nearly nine months in the Tower of London, rather than compromise on his views. Today the main stronghold of the Quakers is in the United States, where the liberal or Hicksite wing of this sect has made the closest approach to Humanism.

Another religious movement primarily concerned with social reform was that of Christian Socialism, which got under way in the British Isles in the middle of the nineteenth century. At first much influenced by Thomas Carlyle, Christian Socialism found its most effective leaders in Frederick Denison Maurice, a forward-looking Anglican, and Charles Kingsley, chiefly remembered today for his novels *Westward Ho!* and *Hypatia*. Writing under the assumed name of Parson Lot, Kingsley told his readers in 1848: "We have used the Bible as if it were a mere special constable's handbook—an opium-dose for keeping beasts of burden patient while they were being overloaded—a mere book to keep the poor in order. . . .* We have told you that the Bible preached to you patience while we have not told you that it promised you freedom. We have told you that the Bible preached the rights of property and the duties of labor, when (God knows!) for once that it does that, it preaches ten times over the *duties of property* and the *rights of labor*." [26]

Christian Socialism, taking its chief inspiration from a

---

* Compare Karl Marx's statement, first published in 1844 in his essay *Introduction to a Critique of Hegel's Philosophy of Law:* "Religion is the sigh of the hard-pressed creature, the heart of a heartless world, as it is the soul of soulless circumstances. It is the opium of the people."

radical interpretation of the Bible, soon expanded into numerous other countries. In the United States it has had capable reresentatives such as Walter Rauschenbusch, a Baptist; Harry F. Ward, a Methodist and former head of the American Civil Liberties Union; and John C. Bennett, a Congregationalist and President of Union Theological Seminary.

At the present time it is safe to say that each of the main denominations of Protestantism, as well as the Catholic and Greek Orthodox Churches, contains a considerable number of persons whose greatest interest, regardless of the theology that they formally profess, is in the alleviation of human suffering and the extension of human happiness upon this earth. We can make the same generalization about non-Christian religions such as Buddhism, Confucianism, Judaism, Mohammedanism, and so on. Philosophic Humanists, while continuing to disagree with supernaturalism in whatever guise it appears, welcome as allies on specific economic, social, and ethical issues all supernaturalists who sincerely agree with them on such questions.

The philosophy of Humanism is well aware that the various supernatural religions, as systems of thought and as institutionalized in the churches, have on the whole acted as a conservative force to preserve the existing order in social and economic affairs. Yet in certain countries at certain times supernatural religion has played a progressive role. And individual members of different sects have again and again shown magnificent courage and idealism in the service of humanity. In the history of the West innumerable martyrs for freedom of conscience and religion have made a major contribution to the long uphill struggle for democratic rights and civil liberties.

Above all, traditional religion has offered men an organizing principle of existence, however unsound that principle has been, and a compelling interest, beyond petty personal desires, for which to work. At its best it has given them the opportunity of losing themselves in something greater than any individual and of finding themselves in consecration to an ideal. Any present philosophy worthy of the name must fulfill this historic function of religion.

Even its most enthusiastic supporters, however, must admit that so far religion has signally failed to bring about unity among mankind. No realistic observer today believes that any extant religion has such powers of conversion that it can succeed in achieving religious accord among the different nations and people of the globe. Some Western theologians still claim that the world can establish peace and international harmony only under the banner of Christianity. Actually there is little chance of reconciliation even among the numerous Protestant sects, let alone between them and the Catholic Church, between the Catholic Church and the Eastern Orthodox Church, or between Christianity as a whole and the other great faiths. Nor is there much hope of lasting concord among those non-Christian faiths.

The traditional religions make such absolute and unyielding claims for the truth of their respective revelations that substantial agreement among them in regard to theology seems out of the question. What President Jefferson wrote almost 150 years ago is still relevant: "On the dogmas of religion as distinguished from moral principles, all mankind, from the beginning of the world to this day, have been quarrelling, fighting, burning and torturing one another, for abstractions unintelligible to themselves and to all others, and absolutely beyond the comprehension of the human mind." [27]

The Christian faith bears the additional handicap of being identified throughout the continents of Africa and Asia with Western imperialism and the hated, discarded colonial system. The black, brown, and yellow peoples in the fast evolving "underdeveloped" countries think of Christianity as the religion of the white man who has for centuries been their greatest oppressor and who in our era has been guilty of the most shocking racism in Germany, South Africa, and the United States.

Humanism does not suffer from any of these handicaps that beset the traditional religions. Precisely where religion throughout history has demonstrated the most serious weaknesses, the philosophy of Humanism promises to show particular strength. It is a philosophy that has striking potentialities for unification both within nations and among nations. This is why Sir Julian Huxley, when he was head of UNESCO, suggested that the general philosophy of that United Nations agency should be "a scientific world Humanism, global in extent and evolutionary in background." [28]

3. THE CULTURAL BACKGROUND

Apart from philosophy and religion, a great deal in the cultural life of the West has been characterized by a distinctly Humanist spirit. This was eminently true of the supreme flowering of Greek genius, centering in Athens, that took place during the Golden or Periclean Age of the fifth century B.C. The dominant loyalty of this age was devotion to the welfare and glory of the city-state. This was a limited type of Humanism, to be sure, but was genuine Humanism in the sense of setting up human accomplishment in this world as the chief end of man.

Allegiance to the city is a constant theme throughout Greek philosophy and literature. The city-state is the political unit which Plato and Aristotle have in mind throughout their work. The brilliant Greek dramatists, Aeschylus, Euripides, Sophocles, and Aristophanes, continually discuss in their plays the city patriotism of the Greeks. The full nature of this deep feeling for the city is perhaps best expressed in the famous Funeral Oration of Pericles, greatest of Greek statesmen, as handed down to posterity by the pen of the historian, Thucydides. This speech was made in 431 B.C. in tribute to the Athenians who fell during the first year of the Peloponnesian

War. Pericles as head of the Athenian State sums up the virtues of his city in both peace and war.

"Our constitution," he declares, "is named a democracy, because it is in the hands not of a few but of the many. Our laws secure equal justice for all in their private disputes, and our public opinion welcomes and honors talent in every branch of achievement, not for any sectional reason, but on grounds of excellence alone. . . . We are lovers of beauty without extravagance, and lovers of wisdom without unmanliness. Wealth to us is not mere material for vainglory but an opportunity for achievement. . . . In a word I claim that our city as a whole is an education to Greece, and that her members yield to none, man by man, for independence of spirit, many-sidedness of attainment, and complete self-reliance in limbs and brain. . . . Great indeed are the symbols and witnesses of our supremacy, at which posterity, as all mankind today, will be astonished." [29]

No single document that has survived the ravages of time sums up more succinctly and accurately the highest Athenian ideals of his period than does Pericles' address. It is significant that in his oration Pericles neither mentions the name of a single god nor alludes to a future existence for the Athenian dead. He makes clear that the luster they have achieved is a this-worldly, humanistic one. They sacrificed themselves "to the commonwealth and received, each for his own memory, praise that will never die, and with it the grandest of all sepulchres, not that in which their mortal bones are laid, but a home in the minds of men, where their glory remains fresh to stir to speech or action as the occasion comes by. For the whole earth is the sepulchre of famous men; and their story is not graven only on stone over their native earth, but lives on far away, without visible symbol, woven into the stuff of other men's lives." [30]

Actually, though certain cults of ancient Greece promised a worthwhile personal immortality to men, Greek religion in general, with its gloomy Hades, was similar to that of the ancient Hebrews in conceiving of the afterlife as a sad and forbidding place to which rational beings could hardly look forward. The Olympian religion of the Athenians was pagan, poetic, and polytheistic, and laid much stress on the proper rites and sacrifices required by the numerous and lively gods and goddesses of the ancient pantheon. "Nevertheless the devotion and worship given to these gods was paid to them as symbols of the glory and the power of the city-state, rather than as deities." [31] Undoubtedly the better educated and more sophisticated among the Greeks, like Pericles himself, did not take the existence of the Olympian gods seriously and well knew that they were mere personifications of natural forces and human powers, artistic allegories pleasing to the imagination.

All the same it was not healthy in Athenian civilization to deny directly the existence of the traditional gods. The conservatives were convinced that many social values were bound up with the old beliefs and that their negation constituted a dangerous challenge to the very principle of authority in government. Socrates was executed and Protagoras exiled because they so vigorously questioned the *status quo* in ideas. Anaxagoras, another noted Greek philosopher of the fifth century B.C. and a personal friend of Pericles, was found guilty of impiety and condemned to death after he had fled from Athens. In his investigations of the heavenly bodies Anaxagoras advanced a number of hypotheses confirmed some two thousand years later by modern science, but he unfortunately ran afoul of an Athenian law forbidding the study of astronomy. The major crime for which he was convicted was his assertion that the sun was "a mass of red-hot metal . . . larger than the Peloponnesus," instead of a deity as tradition taught. It is painful to record that Athenian civilization, the most democratic of the ancient world, prevented free inquiry that seemed to conflict with religion and persecuted some of its profoundest minds.

The Humanist viewpoint permeated much of Greek culture during the Periclean Age. As Gilbert Murray has said: "The idea of service to the community was more deeply rooted in the Greeks than in us. And as soon as they began to reflect about literature at all—which they did very early—the main question they asked about each writer was almost always upon these lines: 'Does he help to make better men? Does he make life a better thing?' " [32]

In his play *Antigone* Sophocles writes:

> Many are the wonders of the world
> And none so wonderful as Man.

He goes on to describe the extraordinary capacities of men, such as their "wind-swift thought," and their amazing inventions "beyond all dream." And he concludes, in a vein altogether relevant to our atomic era, that the important thing is not man's power as such, but whether it is used for good or for evil. Closest, however, of the great Greek writers to being a complete Humanist was the scintillating Euripides, the Voltaire of the ancient world. Euripides, skeptical and agnostic, satirized Athenian society and religion throughout his dramas, though he covered his tracks and saved his skin by inserting pious lines now and then.

Religious skepticism combined with official obeisance to the gods was also a feature of Roman culture. In the first century B.C. the Roman orator Cicero showed an absolute disbelief in all the accepted practices of divination, but thought they should be fostered "on account of popular opinion and of their great public utility." Julius Caesar avowed his unbelief in immortality and was contemptuous of the supernaturalist rituals and sacrifices that he carried out for the sake of political expediency. Ovid and Horace, both outstanding writers of this period, had no faith in personal survival after death. Nor did Pliny the Elder. The supreme lyric poet of Rome, Catullus, whose love poems are among the most moving in all literature, was a sort of ancient Omar Khayyám in his

general attitude of irrepressible pleasure-seeking in this vale
of delight. Though the poet Terence was no Humanist, he
gave expression to a famous Humanist sentiment: "I am a
man, and nothing that concerns a man do I deem a matter of
indifference to me." [33]

Subsequent to the emergence of Greek Humanism, the next
notable Humanist period did not come until the European
Renaissance beginning in the fourteenth century A.D. I discussed earlier the significance of the Renaissance for the Humanist movement.* The essential point to remember is that
the Renaissance Humanists insisted, in contradistinction to
the prevailing Christian tradition, that men possess intrinsic
ethical and intellectual worth instead of being morally depraved and mentally impotent; and that human individuals,
no matter what may be in store for them beyond the grave,
should look upon this-earthly enjoyment as a natural and
wholesome part of the good life. It was Erasmus himself,
author, scholar, and generally acknowledged as the most representative Humanist of all, who ended his characteristic book,
The Praise of Folly, with the lines:

> Drink deep, live long, be jolly,
> Ye illustrious votaries of folly.

At times Renaissance Humanism's revulsion against the repressive otherworldliness that had held human nature in
bondage for so many centuries turned into almost pure paganism.

On the continent the Humanist spirit of life—ardent and
overflowing in beauty, pleasure, and action—received its most
magnificent rendering in the work of the supreme masters of
Renaissance art. The Italian painters Raphael, Leonardo,
Michelangelo, Titian, and Tintoretto, though they utilized
Christian mythology to a large degree, at one and the same
time depicted in sublimest color and form the glories of ex-

---

* See pp. 19-21.

istence in the here and now. Farther north the Rabelaisian Rubens crammed into his sprawling canvases all the gusto of life in Flanders; while the restrained yet vital Rembrandt, with his balanced light and shade, gave a sense of the infinite power and possibilities of the human personality. In Elizabethan England it was the poets who most completely and convincingly expressed the Humanist attitude. And there William Shakespeare, in the endless profusion of his dramatic genius, achieved heights never transcended by anyone writing in the English language.

Shakespeare himself indicated little interest in or support of religious supernaturalism. As Santayana points out in his penetrating essay "The Absence of Religion in Shakespeare," England's greatest poet, while making a few allusions to the Christian faith in order to round out his characters, "chose to leave his heroes and himself in the presence of life and of death with no other philosophy than that which the profane world can suggest and understand," [34] namely a species of Humanism. Shakespeare's mind was on men and women living out their diverse lives in diverse types of society; he dwelt upon the human foreground without much attention to the cosmic background. And in *Hamlet* Shakespeare gives one of the most memorable of Humanist perorations:

"What a piece of work is a man! how noble in reason! how infinite in faculty! in form and moving, how express and admirable! in action how like an angel! in apprehension how like a god! the beauty of the world, the paragon of animals!"

Another profound Humanist upsurge took place as part of the eighteenth-century French Enlightenment which I have already mentioned in connection with the philosophy of Materialism.* Besides the materialist philosophers of that time, the most influential intellect was that of the bold, witty, all-encompassing Voltaire. He typified perfectly Humanism's reliance on reason and science, its faith in the educability of

---

* See p. 41.

man, and its determination to do away with the evils that
afflict the human race. This burning interest in the welfare
of humanity was long known as *humanitarianism*, though this
word has now come to have the rather limited meaning of
preventing the more immediate and obvious kinds of physical
suffering through philanthropic and reform measures.

Voltaire was in the forefront of the fight against the Catholic
Church and in fact author of the stirring anticlerical battle cry,
"Ecrasez l'infame!" ("Crush the infamous thing!"). But he
was not so radical in philosophy as his materialist colleagues
and is on record as stating that "If there were no God, it
would be necessary to invent him." As we have seen, in
religion Voltaire supported Deism and helped to spread its
reputation as an "anticlerical theism." Because of his unceasing
and effective attacks on orthodoxy, he was exiled during much
of his life from his native France.

Voltaire and his fellow French Encyclopedists eloquently
voiced the ideals of international peace and cosmopolitanism,
of human freedom and democracy, that are so integral to the
Humanist outlook. Voltaire's conception of the basic spirit behind free speech and civil liberties has been well paraphrased
in the familiar words often directly attributed to him: "I
wholly disapprove of what you say, but will defend to the
death your right to say it." Voltaire and his co-workers had
an invincible belief in the possibility, and indeed probability,
of unceasing social progress. In truth, the modern idea of
progress came to maturity during this Age of Reason in France.

That idea, so commonplace in our own times, was quite
original in those. As Professor Randall tells us: "It is difficult
for us to realize how recent a thing is this faith in human
progress. The ancient world seems to have had no conception
of it; Greeks and Romans looked back rather to a Golden
Age from which man had degenerated. The Middle Ages, of
course, could brook no such thought. The Renaissance, which
actually accomplished so much, could not imagine that man
could ever rise again to the level of glorious antiquity; its

thoughts were all on the past. Only with the growth of science in the seventeenth century could men dare to cherish such an overweening ambition." [35]

Still another contributor to the French Encyclopedia who should not be overlooked was the fiery Jean Jacques Rousseau. In the Age of Reason he offered a sloppy religion of feeling, so that Voltaire wrote that he resembled a philosopher "as a monkey resembles a man." Yet even this anti-intellectual Rousseau was humanistic in the sense of passionately advocating a better life for humanity and a more democratic organization of society. "Man is born free and everywhere he is in irons!" he cried. Rousseau was also one of the first modern writers who gave conscious expression to that appreciation of Nature as a thing of beauty which ought to be a part of any fully rounded philosophy. And while he reveled in romantic exaggerations, he always serves as a vivid reminder that Humanism must make room for human emotion, especially feelings of social sympathy, as well as for reason.

In England of the eighteenth century there were a few literary tendencies of a Humanist flavor, with Alexander Pope composing, in his *Essay on Man,* the celebrated couplet:

> Know then thyself, presume not God to scan;
> The proper study of mankind is man.

At the beginning of the nineteenth century William Blake, no Humanist and a pronounced mystic in both his art and poetry, nonetheless produced a stanza, in his "Milton," that has been an inspiration for generations of British Humanists:

> I will not cease from mental fight,
> Nor shall my sword sleep in my hand,
> Till we have built Jerusalem
> In England's green and pleasant land.

It was only a little later that the youthful genius of Percy Bysshe Shelley startled the literary and academic world of England. Expelled from Oxford University in 1811 at the age of eighteen for his essay "The Necessity of Atheism," Shelley shortly afterward extended and refined its theme in the spirited though immature "Queen Mab," a long poem denouncing supernaturalism and the evils of Christianity. The British authorities refused to grant Shelley the usual copyright for this work, on the ground that no author deserved copyright protection for a book advocating clearly pernicious opinions. In "Queen Mab," there are already suggestions of Shelley's more mature belief in the immanent World Spirit of Pantheism.

Of far greater poetic and intellectual merit is Shelley's drama *Prometheus Unbound*, in which he recounts how Prometheus, representing the human mind and will, gives over his powers to the god Jupiter, who thereupon enchains Prometheus and enslaves the race of man. But Jupiter is finally overthrown, with the result that both Prometheus and man become free. The symbolic meaning of this poem is that the anthropomorphic God of theology is a brain-spun creation of the human imagination and that man remains in thralldom to this nonexistent being until he takes his destiny into his own hands, winning salvation by bringing about an earthly millennium in place of the Christian heaven.

In the closing stanza of *Prometheus Unbound* Shelley, in a final summing up of the spirit of Prometheus himself, wrought one of the most moving passages of militant Humanism in all poetry:

> To suffer woes which Hope thinks infinite;
> To forgive wrongs darker than death or night;
>   To defy Power, which seems omnipotent;
> To love, and bear; to hope till Hope creates
> From its own wreck the thing it contemplates;
>   Neither to change, nor falter, nor repent;
> This, like thy glory, Titan, is to be
> Good, great and joyous, beautiful and free;
> This is alone Life, Joy, Empire, and Victory.

In Germany it was Goethe, whose long career lasted well into the nineteenth century, who gave unrivalled expression to the Humanist love of earthy, wholehearted, many-sided life. His poetic drama *Faust*, sometimes called The Divine Comedy of modern Humanism, constitues a reaffirmation of the liberating spirit of the original Renaissance. Like Shelley, Goethe retained a vague pantheistic belief.

During this same period German music took a marked turn toward Humanist themes. Beethoven is noteworthy here with his *Third Symphony* (the *Eroica*), celebrating the memory of a great man; his *Fifth Symphony*, portraying the triumph of mankind over fate; and his *Ninth Symphony*, assertive of the brotherhood of man and attaining its climax in a stirring setting to music of the poet Schiller's "Ode to Joy." There is no doubt that Beethoven himself was a real democrat at a time when it was not easy to be one. Wagner, while by no means consistent in his thought, told in *The Ring of the Niebelung* the story of disintegrating godhood and humanity supplanting it. In *The Twilight of the Gods*, the final opera of the tetralogy, this theme reaches its culmination as Valhalla crashes down in flames. Wagner's saga of the legendary Norse gods can also be interpreted as showing the dangers and evils of uncontrolled power being concentrated in the hands of a few.

In the later nineteenth century in England the Humanist literary tradition was carried on by such authors as George Eliot (Marian Evans), Edward Fitzgerald, William Morris, and Algernon Charles Swinburne. Eliot, who is best known for her novels, translated two Humanist classics from the German, *The Essence of Christianity* by Ludwig Feuerbach and *The Life of Jesus* by David F. Strauss. In her poem, "The Choir Invisible," she gives praise to the immortality of influence in place of personal survival beyond the tomb. Thus she speaks

> Of those immortal dead who live again
> In minds made better by their presence: live
> In pulses stirred to generosity,
> In deeds of daring rectitude, in scorn

> For miserable aims that end with self,
> In thoughts sublime that pierce the night like stars,
> And with their mild persistence urge man's search
> To vaster issues. . . .

Fitzgerald, a contemporary of George Eliot, translated into English quatrains the philosophic reflections of Omar Khayyám, son of a Persian tentmaker and brilliant scientist and free-thinker of the eleventh century. The result was a poetic master-piece that has become a world classic, *The Rubáiyát of Omar Khayyám*, which Fitzgerald had to print himself since at first no publisher dared touch it. *The Rubáiyát* scoffs at the idea of an after-existence and acclaims the virtues of delighting in life while we may:

> Oh, threats of Hell and Hopes of Paradise!
> One thing at least is certain—*This* Life flies;
>   One things is certain and the rest is lies;
> The Flower that once has blown for ever dies.

This nostalgically philosophical poem is the modern Bible of hedonists who devote themselves primarily to personal pleasure, free from supernaturalist restraints.

In his *News from Nowhere* William Morris, reacting against the evils and ugliness of the Industrial Revolution, sketched a Humanist Utopia in terms of a simple and secularized village economy in which crowded cities and grimy factories are both eliminated and where regular work merges with applied art and the creation of beauty. Swinburne, the finest English lyric poet of the Victorian Age, did his mature work after the publication of Darwin's *The Origin of Species* and absorbed into his thought the naturalistic implications of the revolutionary new biology. In his poem "The Garden of Proserpine," Swinburne gives thanks that individual lives come to an end with "the sleep eternal in an eternal night." His tenuous, redefined "God" is nothing more than the spiritual aspirations of humanity glimpsed as a whole. And his humanistic spirit asserts itself in the concluding line of his passionate "Hymn of Man": "Glory to Man in the highest! for Man is the master of things."

George Meredith, another leading Victorian author, revealed a Humanist bent in his poetry, while the agnostically inclined Matthew Arnold vigorously attacked religious superstition and upheld the idea that Jesus was not God but a great teacher and oracle of "sweet reasonableness." One of the supreme English novelists, Thomas Hardy, some of whose best work appeared in the twentieth century, leaned toward a pessimistic Humanism and believed that humanity is doomed to permanent frustration and tragedy. He also was a determinist and looked upon man as the puppet of fate, with the cosmos as "a viewless, voiceless Turner of the Wheel." Hardy's philosophy brings out the fact that it is possible to relinquish entirely Christian supernaturalism and at the same time retain an attitude of defeatism toward human hopes of happiness and progress on this earth. Likewise disposed to a sombre and disillusioned Humanism was A. E. Housman, author of *A Shropshire Lad* and other verse.

A twentieth-century writer who stood for the reasoned optimism that usually accompanies the Humanist viewpoint was H. G. Wells. While Wells became rather pessimistic in the last few years of his life, partly under the impact of the Second World War, he strenuously championed during most of his career all of the main Humanist ethical and social goals. In his program for the emancipation of mankind he accented the need for a radically reformed educational system, for the spread of scientific thinking and for a world economy and world state on a cooperative basis. Another famous English literary figure, John Galsworthy, was of a Humanist turn of mind and asserted: "Humanism is the creed of those who believe that in the circle of enwrapping mystery, men's fates are in their own hands—a faith that for modern man is becoming the only possible faith." [36] The novelist Arnold Bennett was also clearly Humanist in his philosophy.

Turning to the continent once more, we find that French literature after the middle of the nineteenth century was dominantly rationalistic and humanistic in its trend. Here the distinguished names of Gustave Flaubert, Émile Zola, Alphonse Daudet, Jean Marie Guyau, and Guy de Maupassant stand out preeminently. Ernest Renan's illuminating book, *The Life of Jesus*, translated into many languages, gave a Humanist interpretation of Christ as "an incomparable man" and created an international sensation. Anatole France, who died in 1924, was perhaps the most thoroughgoing French Humanist of the period. A spiritual son of Voltaire, his trenchant novels satirizing the old superstitions provoked the ire of entrenched and institutionalized bigotry throughout Europe.

In Scandinavia of the nineteenth century the Norwegian dramatist Henrik Ibsen wrote in a pronounced Humanist vein in such plays as *The Enemy of the People* and *The Emperor and the Galilean*. And in the twentieth century a Norwegian sculptor, Gustav Vigeland, struck a powerful Humanist note in his monumental series of nude figures in an Oslo park symbolizing the life and aspirations of man.

In Tsarist Russia, Ivan Turgenev and Maxim Gorky showed distinct Humanist leanings in their novels. Prince Peter Kropotkin, widely admired philosophical anarchist and agnostic, also gravitated toward Humanism in his writings. In Spain the leading Humanist was the famous Freethinker and teacher, Francisco Ferrer, who was convicted on false evidence as a revolutionary by the Spanish monarchy and executed in 1909.

In the world of art the French, again, were leaders in the direction of Humanism. The painter Eugène Delacroix participated actively in the secular and democratic tendencies of the age. He welcomed the Revolution of 1830 and shortly thereafter exhibited his most famous picture, "Liberty Leading the People to the Barricades," now in the Louvre. The sculptor Auguste Rodin created some of the most stirring of modern statuary, giving impassioned, if somewhat theatrical, expression to the radiant actualities of life on earth. The composer Claude Debussy rejected the supernaturalist creeds and insisted upon a purely secular funeral. His exquisite symphonic poems, such as *The Sea, Clouds,* and *The Afternoon of a Faun,* reflected varying moods of Nature and introduced a delicate and subtle originality into the portrayal of natural beauty in musical composition.

As for twentieth-century painting, the great muralists of Mexico—José Clemente Orozco, Diego Rivera, and David Alfaro Siqueiros—concentrated on Humanist themes in their work. The magnificent murals of these three artists not only adorn the walls of many public buildings in Mexico, but are also to be found in various educational and other institutions throughout the United States.

In the United States the most effective single voice in the second half of the nineteenth century in opposition to supernaturalist myths was that of Robert G. Ingersoll. One of the most alert thinkers and persuasive orators in the history of America, he was a pillar of the Republican Party. In his campaign against religious intolerance and credulity, he lectured far and wide throughout the country for three decades. Ingersoll's Humanist credo was:

> *Justice is the only worship.*
> *Love is the only priest.*
> *Ignorance is the only slavery.*
> *Happiness is the only good.*
> *The time to be happy is now,*
> *The place to be happy is here,*
> *The way to be happy is to make others so.*
> *Wisdom is the science of happiness.*[37]

In academic circles Andrew D. White's scholarly study, *A History of the Warfare of Science with Theology in Christendom,* proved of signal service to the documentation of Humanism by showing that the theologians had fought practically every forward step in scientific investigation since the founding of Christianity, much to the detriment of religion as

well as of science. In the realm of social thought Edward
Bellamy produced the most influential of American visions of
Utopia in his amazingly popular novel, *Looking Backward*.
Bellamy vividly portrayed an ideal socialist commonwealth
for the United States, with public ownership of the main
means of production and distribution recognized as in the
true interests of all classes. Also a severe critic of the prevailing
economic system was Lester F. Ward, founder of American
sociology. Ward worked out an original and rational cosmic
philosophy that clearly places him in the ranks of Humanism.
He energetically and effectively attacked supernaturalism as
an obstacle to science and progress, at one time editing an
antireligious journal called *Iconoclast*.

As for outstanding literary figures in America with a consistent Humanist outlook, there have been far fewer of them
than in Europe. Henry David Thoreau, though retaining his
belief in a Creator, rebelled against some of the cardinal
supernaturalist dogmas, questioning that it is the chief end
of man "to glorify God and enjoy Him for ever." He com-
plained that men rarely express "a simple and irrepressible
satisfaction with the gift of life"; and commented on the idea
of immortality with the observation, "One world at a time."
Thoreau was also a militant fighter against slavery and for
democracy. His most valuable contribution to the Humanist
philosophy came in his detailed descriptive writing on the
beauties of external Nature, especially in *Walden or Life in
the Woods,* the classic prose work in this field.

Contemporary with Thoreau was Walt Whitman, whose
intimate and large-visioned appreciation of Nature had a
singular quality. Humanists, however, remember Whitman
particularly for his eloquent and sustained panegyric to the
democratic ideal and consider him perhaps the most representative poet of democracy. He was humanistic, too, in his
glorification of the infinite enjoyments possible in human experience; and was, to use one of his own expressions, a "ca-

resser of life wherever flowing." For him merely to be alive and healthy amounted to a kind of ecstasy: "Henceforth I ask not good fortune, I myself am good fortune." Although by no no means free of supernaturalist illusions, Whitman sang of the robust pleasures of the whole man, body and soul, and heartily disbelieved in all asceticisms.

Another nineteenth-century American writer with Humanist leanings was Mark Twain, who evinced a solid skepticism toward supernatural beliefs in *What Is Man?* and other books. Twain lived on into the twentieth century and died in 1910. His most savage attack on orthodox Christianity is contained in *Letters from the Earth,* a posthumous volume suppressed by his daughter, Clara Clemens, for many years and not published until 1962.

In a most thoughtful paper * Maxine Greene, Associate Professor of Education at Brooklyn College, suggests that the leading characters portrayed in the mainstream of American literature affirm and control their own energies, define their own standards and use their own minds in an essentially Humanist fashion without reliance on God or the supernatural. She illustrates this thesis by analyzing the novels of Nathaniel Hawthorne, Herman Melville, Mark Twain, John Steinbeck, Ernest Hemingway, and others. And she sums up her central point in this comment. "We go to sea repeatedly from Melville's time on—and the image of men at sea—like the image of men in the wilderness—seems to me to be almost an archetypal image of human beings on their own, human beings making their own way, guiding themselves by the stars they can see—rather than by faith or prayer or invisible forces."

We find an excellent example of Miss Greene's theme in Hemingway's novelette, *The Old Man and the Sea,* in which

* "Man Without God in American Fiction," an essay read December 14, 1962, at a meeting of the New York Chapter of the American Humanist Association.

an old, weather-beaten Cuban fisherman pits his skill and endurance against the strength of a huge marlin. He finally catches the great silver-black fish after more than two days of terrific struggle. But when he lashes his prize to the hull of his small boat to tow it to a Havana beach, the ferocious sharks quickly close in, biting and tearing away the flesh of the fish. The old man tries to fight them off with harpoons and knives, and even clubs them with the tiller; but as he nears the shore, he realizes that only the bony skeleton of the beautiful marlin is left. Yet the fisherman will not admit failure and says with Promethean defiance: "Man is not made for defeat. Man can be destroyed, but not defeated."

Further representative of the Humanist viewpoint in the United States were the realistic novelists Jack London, Theodore Dreiser, and Sinclair Lewis. In 1927 Lewis published his novel *Elmer Gantry*, a scathing satire of a Baptist-Methodist minister. In writing the book he relied upon a long-time Humanist clergyman, L. M. Birkhead, as his adviser on matters ecclesiastical. In a carefully documented study, "Authors and Humanism," Warren Allen Smith, a Humanist teacher, quotes Lewis as stating: "Yes, I think that naturalistic Humanism—with dislike for verbalistic philosophy—is my category." [38]

American poets of the twentieth century with a Humanist outlook are Conrad Aiken, Witter Bynner, Arthur Davison Ficke,* Archibald MacLeish, Edwin Markham, Edgar Lee Masters, and Carl Sandburg. In 1915 Masters gave to the world his *Spoon River Anthology*, a collection of apocryphal epitaphs in an Illinois graveyard that has become an American classic. MacLeish's *J. B.*, a dramatization of the Book of Job, was successfully produced on Broadway and abounds with Humanist implications. Markham puts into simple and unsophisticated language some of the key concepts of Humanism in his poems "Brotherhood" and "Earth Is Enough." Thus the latter starts:

---

* See pp. 180-81.

> We men of Earth have here the stuff
> Of Paradise—we have enough!
> We need no other stones to build
> The Temple of the Unfulfilled—
> No other ivory for the doors—
> No other marble for the floors—
> No other cedar for the beam
> And dome of man's immortal dream.

In *The People, Yes,* Sandburg gives voice to the long-range optimism characteristic of Humanists:

> And man the stumbler and finder, goes on,
>   man the dreamer of deep dreams,
>   man the shaper and maker,
>   man the answerer. . . .
>
> Man is a long time coming.
> Man will yet win.[39]

In my survey of the Humanist tradition I have not attempted to give an account of the rise of modern science or the major role that philosophers have played in its increasing progress and prestige. Scientific developments, however, have been of enormous effect in weakening attitudes of otherworldliness and in furthering the Humanist philosophy. In the first place, scientific discoveries and the scientific temper have done much to revise, in the direction of Humanism, traditional ideas and methods in religion and philosophy, though usually it has not been the scientists themselves who have worked out the deeper implications of the new findings in astronomy, physics, chemistry, biology, psychology, and other fields.

In the second place, applied science in its development of the machine and modern technology has opened up possibilities of earthly abundance and human advancement that were hardly dreamt of before. In the economic sphere the new machine techniques led directly to the far-reaching Industrial

Revolution of the late eighteenth and early nineteenth centuries. The accompanying growth of the factory system and the working class, together with the enormous increase in the production of goods, has resulted in an almost universal demand for a higher standard of living for the masses of the people. This altogether Humanist objective the Swiss historian Jacob Burckhardt called "the dominating feeling of our age."

I have obviously not tried to cover all those manifold events of a political and social character that have had significance for the flowering of the Humanist spirit. Most relevant here are the great political revolutions of modern times: the American Revolution of 1776, the French Revolution of 1789, the various Communist revolutions beginning with Russia in 1917, and the far-flung anticolonial, nationalist revolutions that have brought independence to most of the peoples of Africa and Asia. These tremendous mass upheavals have transformed much of the world and have had an immense impact throughout the globe. They have opened up new pathways to mankind's eventual achievement of a truly Humanist order. Yet every step forward raises new problems, even though they be at a higher level. Each one of these major upheavals entailed an immense amount of suffering and violence, and each one fell short of its stated aims in many particulars. But each of them wrought enormous gains for the peoples immediately concerned.

As we study the historic roots of Humanism, it becomes increasingly clear that the social and political penalties following upon the open espousal of a Humanist philosophy have in general been very great and have prevented many enlightened persons in every era from speaking out with entire frankness. This is one reason for the constant and confusing redefinition of religious terms like *God* and *immortality*. Retention of at least these *words* in a man's vocabulary has been necessary during certain periods to preserve his life or prevent his imprisonment. Equivocation in philosophy and religion has deep social roots in the repressive tendencies of undemocratic communities. And centuries-old habits of compromise or silence illustrate once more Karl Marx's remark that "The legacy of the dead generations weighs like an alp on the brains of the living." [40]

There is considerable validity in the saying attributed to the first Earl of Shaftesbury and later popularized by Benjamin Disraeli: "All wise men have the same religion, but wise men never tell." However, the worldly discretion of the sophisticated concerning otherworldly affairs has often been due, not so much to personal fear as to belief in the Machiavellian myth that religious superstition is a needful restraint upon the masses of the people. The theory and practice of "the double truth," * so useful at one time in blunting the impact of religious heresy, today goes by the name of "double-talk" and applies to all fields of thought.

Our survey also indicates the importance of literary men and nontechnical philosophers in the history of philosophy. Professional philosophers are necessarily intellectuals, in fact college or university teachers in nine cases out of ten; and they tend to take a somewhat intellectualistic attitude toward the human scene. Many of them have been so busy thinking that they have shut themselves off from a well-rounded existence. We need the poets and the writers to make philosophy full-blooded, to take it out of the study and into the world. We need Shakespeare, Goethe, Shelley, Swinburne, Sandburg, and the rest to remind us that life can be a wonder and a wild desire, an adventure and a thing of joy forever.

In this chapter I have treated only the highlights of the great Humanist tradition in philosophy, religion, and culture, calling attention to the fact that some of the most illustrious minds of the past have been in essence Humanist. Modern Humanism is proud of this long tradition that gives to it an

---

* See pp. 20-21.

impressive continuity reaching back to ancient Greece and Rome, and coming down through the European Renaissance, through the French Enlightenment, through the flowering of nineteenth-century Western culture to many eminent thinkers of our time. Present-day Humanism offers its philosophy to the world, not with any pretentions of having attained intellectual finality, yet with the hope and belief that it can serve as a rallying point for men of intelligence and good will in our modern era.

CHAPTER III

This Life Is All and Enough

1. THE UNITY OF BODY AND PERSONALITY

For Humanism, as for most philosophies, the most important and far-reaching problem connected with the nature and destiny of man is what sort of relationship exists between the physical body and the personality, which includes the mind in its every aspect. Is the relation between body and personality so close and fundamental that they constitute an indissoluble unity (the monistic theory); or is it so loose and unessential that the personality may be considered a separable and independent entity which in the final analysis can function without the body (the dualistic theory)? Are men, in short, fundamentally a one-ness or a two-ness? Is the human self built and nurtured and maintained only on the basis of living flesh and blood, or can it somehow—like the surviving captain of a ship that sinks—continue its existence after the dissolution of its life partnership with the bodily organism?

Involved in this issue to a considerable extent are problems of knowledge, of ethics, of education, and of individual freedom. Most directly involved of all for philosophy and religion is the question of death and of personal immortality. If the dualistic theory or psychology is true, as the traditional religions of the world hold, then a future life is probable or at least possible. If, on the other hand, the monistic theory or psychology is true, as Naturalism, Materialism, and Humanism claim, then there is no possibility that the human consciousness, with its memory and awareness of self-identity intact, can survive the shock and disintegration of death.

According to this view, the body and personality live together; they grow together; and they die together.

The issue of mortality versus immortality is crucial in the argument of Humanism against supernaturalism. For if men realize that their careers are limited to this world, that this earthly existence is all that they will ever have, then they are already more than half-way on the path toward becoming functioning Humanists, no matter what their general attitude toward the universe and no matter what they think about a Deity. In my opinion the history of philosophy and religion demonstrates that in the West, at least, the idea of immortality has on the whole played a more important part than the idea of God. William James asserts unqualifiedly that "the popular touchstone for all philosophies is the question, 'What is their bearing on a future life?' " [41] If this is true, then James is also correct in observing that for most men God has been primarily the guarantor of survival beyond the grave.*

Christianity in particular, with its central emphasis on the resurrection and eternal life, came into being first and foremost as a death-conquering religion. In modern times the priority of immortality as an article of the Christian faith has become ever more insistent, with the very existence of God being more and more frequently deduced from the alleged perseverance of the human personality after death. A brilliant student of religious psychology, Professor James B. Pratt, penetrates to the heart of the situation when he writes: "As the belief in miracles and special answers to prayer and in the interference of the supernatural within the natural has gradually disappeared, almost the only *pragmatic* value of the

---

* *Immortality* has sometimes been defined as the attainment here and now of a certain "eternal" quality of life and thought; as the lasting social influence a man may have; as the handing down of the torch of life to one's descendants, or as the indestructibility of the ultimate material elements of the human body. But the real issue is and always has been whether there is an enduring personal, conscious career after death.

supernatural left to religion is the belief in a personal future life." [42]

Fraught with the greatest significance, then, is the Humanist position affirming the truth of the monistic or naturalistic psychology, with its sweeping implications regarding the idea of immortality. I believe that the facts of science offer overwhelming evidence in support of the Humanist thesis of the inseparable coexistence of body and personality.

To begin with, biology has conclusively shown that man and all other forms of life were the result, not of a supernatural act of creation by God, but of an infinitely long process of evolution probably stretching over at least two billion years. In that gradual evolutionary advance which started with the lowly amoeba and those even simpler things marking the transition from inanimate matter to life, body was prior and basic. With its increasing complexity, there came about an accompanying development and integration of animal behavior and control, culminating in the species man and in the phenomenon called mind. Mind, in short, appeared at the present apex of the evolutionary process and not at the beginning.

The human body itself is an organism of the most prodigious intricacy, its multitudinous parts adjusted to one another to the last degree of nicety and its billions upon billions of cells normally working together in all but perfect harmony. Specifically it is the relatively greater complexity of the brain in man, and particularly of the cerebral cortex, that has bestowed on him the power of thought and thus raised him immeasurably above all other creatures of the earth.

Just as in the evolution of species, mind and personality appear when bodily organization has reached a certain stage, so it is in the history of every normal human being. Neither the embryo nor the newborn infant possesses the distinguishing features of mind, though their potentialities for eventual mental development are of course already present. The laws of heredity, with the hundreds of thousands of genes from each parent determining the inherent mental and physical characteristics of each individual, show in the first instance the intimate correlation between the physical organism and the self. The laws of sex, with their ever-powerful influence on behavior, character, and aptitude, tell the same story. It is obvious that certain profound differences between the male and female personalities depend primarily upon different bodily organization. Always the general rule is that the kind of personality one has is conditioned by the kind of body one has and by the more fundamental changes that take place in that body.

Any father or mother who carefully watches the growth of a child from birth through adolescence to maturity can make a thousand and one commonplace observations that convincingly testify to the progressive unity of body and mind. This correlation of the physical and the psychic continues through adulthood and old age to the last hour of breath. In the words of Lucretius 2,000 years ago: "We feel that the understanding is begotten along with the body and grows together with it, and along with it comes to old age. For as children totter with feeble and tender body, so a weak judgment of mind goes with it. Then when their years are ripe and their strength hardened, greater is their sense and increased their force of mind. Afterward, when now the body is shattered by the stern strength of time, and the frame has sunk with its force dulled, then the reason is maimed, the tongue raves, the mind stumbles, all things give way and fail at once." [43]

Of course Lucretius's statement requires qualification. Men can grow very old and remain quite alert and clear in their minds until the very end. However, some slowing down in the mental processes does take place in practically all persons during advanced years; and definite personality changes usually occur beyond middle age if only for the reason that the human organism then no longer possesses the same physical strength and recuperative powers as in the days of youth.

The very process of dying throws additional light on the relation between body and personality. As at the beginning of an individual's life, during gestation and infancy, the body is controlling, so it is, too, at the end of life. Just as no personality can enter this world until some body issues, as it were, a passport, so no personality can depart this life until the body gives leave by ceasing all vital functions. Men can be recalled from what is almost equivalent to a state of death, as when they are revived from drowning, suffocation, or electric shock, through various types of artificial respiration or of drastic therapy directly involving the heart. The clear implication of these different medical techniques is that personalities, or *souls* in the older phraseology, are very intimately bound up with their this-earthly bodies and that in such situations as I have indicated they come and go according to the expert manipulation of these bodies.

Psychology and its associated sciences give the most conclusive proof of all in support of the oneness of body and personality. Our conscious experience depends on the nervous system with its numberless circuits running through the brain, the spinal cord, the sense organs, and indeed all parts of the body. Our thinking processes are centered in the outer layer of the brain, the cerebral cortex, which consists of more than ten billion nerve cells or neurons. The total number of distinct and different connections, both actual and possible, in this organ is simply staggering and for practical purposes approaches infinity. Along the neural pathways of the cortex are laid down those enduring memory patterns which are essential for the operation of the mind and whose persistence is in great measure a necessity for personal immortality. It is difficult to see how they could possibly outlast the dissolution of the living brain where they originated and had their being.

Analysis of different types of mental states, including outright abnormality or insanity, strengthens these conclusions. A severe blow on the head, a fracture of the skull, deterioration of the brain tissue through disease, lack of thyroid secretion, diminution of the blood supply to the brain, alteration of its quality or rate of circulation through the use of alcohol or drugs—all of these things impair more or less seriously normal intellectual activity. Backing up this evidence of the close interrelation between the brain and thought is the scientific correlation of functions such as seeing, hearing, and speech coordination with identifiable sections of the cerebral cortex.

The common processes of sleep and fatigue well illustrate some of the points I have been making. As the body grows tired, the mind grows tired with it. Though it is possible to fight off sleep for no little time, the natural thing is for the whole man as a unit to want and take repose. During slumber a person remains unconscious, except in the sense of occasionally having dreams. Were it not for the substantial and efficacious connecting links that memory provides between the successive days of our lives, we should arise each morning with no consciousness of the past and without the awareness of continuing self-identity so essential to human selfhood. And surely it is legitimate to infer that if a person temporarily loses consciousness in sleep for a third or fourth of every twenty-four hour day, he may at death lose that consciousness permanently.

If one sleeps poorly or perhaps not at all for even a single night, the deleterious effects on the mind and especially on its ability to concentrate become quickly apparent. Bad digestion is likewise a well-known enemy of clear and unimpeded thinking; and in fact any sort of ill health may impair intellectual efficiency to some extent.* Not everything, however, that goes on in the body at large has immediately important consequences for the brain and its powers of thought. This is why people may have serious, long-drawn-out, and often fatal diseases, such as cancer or tuberculosis, without their mental

---

* The various alterations I have mentioned in the operation of the mind attributable to physical causes help to establish the monistic psychology through the method of concomitant variation in a functional relationship.

faculties being substantially impaired. Cases of this kind show that while the human organism is a closely integrated system, some parts of it in some ways are relatively independent of other parts.

It is of course undeniable that mental states like fear and anger, optimism and good humor, can and do have far-reaching results on the condition of the physical organism. Good morale can be as important to the functioning of individuals and groups as good food. A physical process such as the knitting of a broken limb is sometimes prevented or delayed by faulty nutrition resulting from anxiety. Lovesickness is a real disease in both men and women. And without accepting all the conclusions of psychoanalysis, we can safely say that the subconscious, or unconscious, exercises a profound influence on human behavior and that repressions connected with sex sometimes adversely affect an individual's health. These and many other related facts, far from indicating that the mind can become completely independent of the body, point to a connection between the two so intimate and inclusive that it is inconceivable how thought could function without its earth-sustained biological base.

One of the most easily discernible indications of the pervasive unity of personality and body is the way in which the physical exterior of a man reflects his essential being. The gait, the carriage, the voice, the eyes, the smile, the faint wrinkling of the brow, however easy or difficult to interpret correctly, do mirror the varying mental and emotional characteristics of a person. Just because of this well-known fact, conscious volition often steps in to control facial reactions.

The English poet and bishop John Donne puts our whole point beautifully in describing the animated features of a high-spirited young girl:

> Her pure and eloquent blood
> Spoke in her cheeks, and so distinctly wrought
> That one might almost say her body thought.[44]

Her body thought. Here in a phrase Donne, a good orthodox Christian of the seventeenth century, sums up a central tenet of the naturalistic psychology. *Human bodies think.* Precisely! And the extraordinary thing, if we wish to talk in superlatives, is that there should be thinking at all, not that a material organism should do that thinking.

Another most important consideration is the great extent to which the personality is moulded by the human environment. All of us are born into a family and into a society. Our parents, our teachers, our friends, our nationality, our language, our economic condition, and many other social factors influence enormously the growth of our characters and minds. Weighty and dramatic evidence here comes from a number of well-authenticated cases of children who during their early years were totally isolated from human beings or who had practically no normal contact and communication with them. Such children led an animal-like existence, could not talk, frequently could not walk and were so mentally retarded that they had almost no "mind" at all. Later some of them, after long and painstaking training, developed into normal individuals.

Our conclusion must be that even a normal human body does not automatically produce a normal human personality, but only when that body is subject to certain environmental and social influences. Not only do our individual minds depend upon the accumulated intellectual and cultural heritage of the race, but mind as we know it is in its very origin a social product. For the human mind matures and attains its distinctive powers of abstract thought only through the symbols of speech and language. Men are born with brains; *they acquire minds.*

Speech is admittedly not a biological function. In man's evolution, teeth, tongue, vocal cords, and lungs were not developed as part of a speech mechanism, but had their own special functions and survival value. Speech, then, came into existence only through men associating together and developing—from elementary movements, grunts, and cries—definite, recognizable signs which serve as a medium of communication.

Spoken and written words are not, of course, the only form that language can take. The pointings and gestures of the deaf and dumb, the dots and dashes of the Morse code, the smoke signals of Indian tribes, are all well-established modes of human expression. Whatever means are used, however, for the interchange of thought, ideas always arise as concomitants of a thoroughly material brain in action and are always communicated through some symbol that is also material in quality. The intimate connection between mind and language is well brought out by the parable of the old lady who remarked, "How do I know what I think till I hear what I say?"

Moral standards, like the categories of mind, originate and evolve in the course of human association. Hence morality, too, is a social product. The notion that a supernatural soul enters the body from on high, already endowed with a pure and beautiful conscience, runs quite counter to the findings of anthropology, psychology, and scientific ethics. We can summarize, then, by saying that, in addition to the indissoluble union between body, on the one hand, and mind and personality, on the other, there is also an indissoluble connection between the body-mind-personality, that is, the whole man, and the sustaining and conditioning environment, both human and nonhuman.

As we have seen, language and abstractions are necessary to the operation of the mind; it is the *misuse* of abstractions that is one of the prime causes of confusion regarding the body-mind problem. The terms "mind" and "personality" are concepts that we use, like "digestion" and "respiration," to designate certain activities of the human being. Unfortunately our language habits make it dangerously easy to separate such abstractions from the original functionings that gave rise to them and then to treat them as if they were somehow independent and self-subsistent.

It is so evident that digestion and respiration are functions, primarily, of the stomach and the lungs that it would at once seem absurd to imagine them as operating without these organs. But since the complete functional dependence of personality and mind on the body and brain is less generally known and accepted, it does not offhand appear so unreasonable to talk of them as if they existed minus their indispensable physical base. Actually it makes no more sense to postulate a special brain-soul in order to account for the activities of the brain than to postulate a special stomach-soul in order to explain the functioning of the stomach or a special lung-soul to explain the phenomenon of breathing. Mind is not a separate agent or substance, but is a particular type of doing, of activity, on the part of a human being. Thought always signifies thinking; reason is always reasoning.

Certain eminent twentieth-century philosophers, such as Henri Bergson, have persisted in adhering to the dualistic psychology; but their theory of a separable and independent soul involves them in a number of unresolvable dilemmas. It is, for example, impossible either to understand how an immaterial soul can act upon and control a material body or to distinguish between those human characteristics which belong to the immortal soul and to the mortal this-earthly organism. The hypothesis that the brain-body acts as a transmissive apparatus through which the soul manifests itself, as a light shines through a colored glass, also breaks down at numerous points.

The dualistic position becomes especially vulnerable when we bring into play the scientific law of parsimony, which requires that any scientific explanation be based on the fewest possible assumptions that succeed in accounting for all the facts. The dualist assumption of a supernatural soul violates this law because such an assumption is superfluous for explaining the emotional profundities and the intellectual powers of men. It is as much out of place as the old-time notion that invisible little devils or demons cause insanity and hysteria. The amazing complexity and resources of the human body as a whole, evolved from the lower forms of life through veritable aeons of time, and the infinite intricacy of the brain and its cerebral cortex are fully competent to sustain the multifarious activities and achievements of human personalities.

It is the organism's reserve power or what Professor Walter B. Cannon in his aptly titled book *The Wisdom of the Body* calls "the margin of safety" that explains those well-known cases in which the brain continues to function unimpaired even after a part has been injured or entirely removed. This helpful faculty, however, does not extend to certain indispensable portions of the brain; and their destruction inevitably brings about death. In general the active tissues of most organs in the human body greatly exceed in quantity what is necessary for normal functioning. Not a few human organs, such as the kidney, are paired; and in such instances the body often maintains comparative efficiency with only one of the paired organs working. Thus Nature has constructed us on the principle of generous superabundance, with the result that we are able to cope with all sorts of emergencies and tests of endurance. In his stimulating essay "The Energies of Men," William James, telling of the immense reserve capacities that we humans can summon up from the depths of our being, gives in graphic language convincing support to Dr. Cannon's principle.

Science not only refutes dualistic psychology, but also casts a good deal of light on why this theory is so frequently advanced. For scientific analysis does make a number of valid distinctions in describing the human organism. Breathing, after all, is not the same as digesting; nor does one eat ideas. Furthermore, there are certain natural divisions within the human brain itself. On the one hand we have the cerebral cortex, the thin, outer, upper layer of gray matter that carries on a man's conscious thinking and coordinating. On the other hand we have the thalamus, the cerebellum, and the brainstem, which together constitute the lower half of the brain. They function to a large extent as the seat of the emotions and govern automatic processes like respiration and the circulation of the blood.

This lower half of the brain developed first in evolution and is often in conflict with the upper half known as the cerebrum. This wholly *natural* dualism within the brain that I have been discussing is the basis for numerous arguments claiming a *supernatural* dualism, in which the functioning of the cortex is explained in terms of a super-physical soul. The point to keep in mind is that whatever distinctions we make within the human brain or body, they are always distinctions within the same natural body; and that whatever distinctions we draw between man and other things, animate or inanimate, they are always distinctions within the same realm of Nature.

Curiously enough, various forms of supernatural religion render striking support to the thesis of unity between body and personality implied by modern science. The religions of ancient times found it most difficult to imagine a substantial and happy hereafter for human beings who had been deprived of their natural bodies by death. So it was that the ancient Greeks had an extremely gloomy conception of the after-existence as a dark, cheerless underworld where the sickly phantoms of the departed flitted about forlorn and futile, with faint voices and nerveless limbs. It is no wonder that on one occasion the shade of Achilles, as recounted in Homer's *Odyssey*, told Ulysses: "Better to be the hireling of a stranger, and serve a man of mean estate whose living is but small, than to be ruler over all these dead and gone." [45] Plato, it will be recalled, suggested that this and similar passages be deleted from the poets, lest such ideas of the beyond make the warriors of the ideal state less enthusiastic about sacrificing their lives in war.

The ancient Egyptians thought that a desirable immortality was possible, but that it was inseparably connected with the practice of mummification and the proper preservation of the natural body. To this fact the great pyramids of Egypt, built primarily to shelter permanently the bodies of the kings and their families, bear imposing witness. I could cite many beliefs and practices akin to those of the Egyptians among a number of other peoples with a developed civilization as well as among tribes still on a primitive level. Some such tribes, for example, have followed a religious custom of killing off old people before they reach the age of decrepitude, on the supposition that only if their bodies are in fairly good condition at the time of death will their souls be able to lead a satisfactory afterlife.

The dominant views of the Old Testament Hebrews either conceived of death as the annihilation of the personality or held that the enfeebled spirits of the dead went to a sad and somber place called Sheol, quite similar to the Hades of the Greeks. In relation to this particular religious background, as described in the Bible, the resurrection idea of the New Testament Christians came as a brilliant solution. For it promised that the old this-earthly bodies would rise triumphant from the tomb, and enabled the faithful to envisage a splendid immortality in which their souls would be united with their former bodies become glorified and incorruptible. Despite a number of embarrassing questions posed by the world's stubborn refusal to come to an end, as expected by the early Christians, the resurrection dogma is still accepted by hundreds of millions of Catholics, Protestant Fundamentalists, Greek Orthodox Christians, Hebrew traditionalists, and faithful Mohammedans.

No religious doctrine has ever more dramatically reinforced the idea of a close and indissoluble union between body and personality than that of the Christian resurrection. The mainstream of Christian thought has insisted from the earliest days that it will be a resurrection of the flesh, the identical body of this world without a hair or a fingernail missing. The seriousness with which the Catholic Church believes in a literal resurrection is seen in its constant and deep-seated antagonism to the cremation of the dead, a practice which psychologically, at any rate, tends to weaken faith in the resurrection of the corpse. During the development of medicine as a science many churchmen opposed surgery and dissection on the ground that these techniques would mutilate the body and therefore interfere with a perfect resurrection.

The more modernistic and sophisticated of the Protestants, however, influenced by the rise of science and the displacement of miracle by law, found themselves compelled to give up the notion of a literal resurrection. But they filled the well-recognized need of the immortal personality for a bodily partner by inventing in its stead various spiritual, celestial, etheric, astral, and other extraordinary kinds of supernatural bodies. In so doing they assumed basically the same position—and for the same reason—taken by certain characteristically modern sects such as the Spiritualists, the Swedenborgians, and the Theosophists. Indeed, there can be no doubt that the believers in immortality, of every age and culture, bestow on the surviving personality, either explicitly or by implication, a very real body. There can be no question, either, that this constitutes a sort of backhanded recognition of the monistic principle that the human personality and the human body are fundamental and inseparable accompaniments of each other.

To summarize, my brief survey of scientific facts concerning the body-mind problem, buttressed by the reactions of simple common sense and the insistence of supernatural religion upon the need of some kind of future-life body, builds up a most compelling verdict in support of the unbreakable unity of the body and personality, including the mind and consciousness. Testifying always and everywhere to the union, one and inseparable, between body and personality, the monistic or naturalistic psychology stands today as one of the greatest achievements in the history of science. That psychology, while not yet able to describe in exact detail all the intricate workings of the body-personality, does on the whole provide a satisfactory account of the complex human organism.

The monistic relation, then, between body and personality has the standing of a proved psychological law and makes untenable any theory of a worthwhile personal survival after death. Even if there existed a wise and good God who had guided the evolution of life upon this earth, he would presumably continue to follow the natural laws that he had himself established. And he could bring about immortality for men only by violating the monistic principle that he had used in the development and construction of human beings; only by becoming a miracle worker and preternatural magician in the old style. Hence one can give credence to the idea of personal immortality only by believing in miracles; and whoever believes in miracles can literally believe in any fantasy whatsoever.

2. SOME OTHER CONSIDERATIONS

As we reflect further upon the age-long idea of immortality, reason leads us to additional doubts concerning this conception. Thus when we examine actual descriptions of the future life, we find that the activities of the death-surviving personality in any worthwhile or imaginable hereafter not only demand a bodily vehicle, but also a substantial and complex environment. It was easy enough for theologians to provide this in the old days before the evolution of modern science and the progressive onlightenment of men's mind. But in more recent times many professional portrayers of the afterexistence have felt constrained to drop out most of the concrete detail and to become increasingly vague, in order to keep their descriptions within the bounds of intellectual acceptability and spiritual dignity. In the process, however, their concepts of the future life have been largely deprived of imaginative reality and emotional efficacy. At the same time their descriptions, when strictly scrutinized by logic, are seen to imply most of what has been discarded as naïve and untenable in earlier representations.

On the other hand, modern cults like the Spiritualists, invincible in their childlike literalness, simply bring up to date the traditional kind of immortality description by locating in the hereafter all the conveniences of twentieth-century life from cheap cigarettes to expensive limousines. Raymond, Sir Oliver Lodge's dead son, speaking to his father from "the other side," outlines the fundamental pattern of the Spiritualist Beyond: "Everything that is necessary to man, everything that man in a sense makes his own, has an etheric duplicate. . . . It may be that the chair you see at home, your material chair, and the chair we see, which is your chair on our side, the etheric chair, are one and the same thing really. . . . You can mold an etheric body for a thing—a piano, a clock, a desk—by loving it and liking to have it with you." [46] It is no wonder that certain contemporary Spiritualists react strongly against this sort of thing and refuse to go into the details of the next world.

As a matter of .fact logic further demands counterparts in the hereafter for all *living* things. They are required not only to round out the environment, but also because if we grant men souls that are to exist forever, it is most difficult to draw a reasonable line barring from a like destiny the creatures of the animal world from which man is descended and to which he is kin. Thus the pageant of immortality must include, in addition to all the millions and billions of men and submen who ever lived, the entire past and present population of the animal kingdom. Surely those who appreciate the sociability and affection displayed by household pets will agree that if an infant who lives ten days or ten months goes on to life everlasting, then good old Rover, who was a beloved member of the family for ten years, should also have an honorable place in the great beyond.

Both Spiritualists and other believers' who are sufficiently stubborn in their consistency, do indeed expect to meet animals in the spirit world. If one visits the remarkable Canine Cemetery at Hartsdale, New York, one finds how the faithful, in the most touching and sentimental gravestone inscriptions, have borne witness to their confidence in the eternal survival of favorite dogs, cats, and canaries. Here, for example, is a typical inscription in the Cemetery:

My adored Zowie

I do not cringe from death so much
Since you are gone my truest friend.
Thy dear dumb soul will wait for mine
However long before the end.

Now I am fond of dogs myself. But if we confer immortality on them and other congenial forms of animal life such as seals, horses, and elephants, then on what logical basis can we deny it to snakes, jelly-fish, houseflies, and hornets? And since there is no hard and fast boundary between animal and vegetable life, how then can we rule out an after-existence for poison ivy and onions, for the beautiful flowers and the noble trees?

Our consideration of various descriptions of immortality naturally leads us to ask whether they have any true or verifiable meaning at all. I believe that they have; and that most portrayals of the future life constitute ethical judgments on this world. By carefully analyzing the ideas of immortality held by different peoples we can obtain repeated proof of how earthly circumstances are always projected into the beyond and, more especially, of how the moral standards of respective cultures are duplicated in the hereafter. Priests and preachers from the earliest times down to the present have consistently eternalized in heaven what they deemed the true, the good, and the beautiful; and eternalized in hell what they deemed the false, the evil, and the ugly.

Descriptions of immortal life have, then, almost universally symbolized the ethical patterns of mortal life. The literature of the religions, from the lengthy tomes of eminent theologians to the sermons of village ministers, abound in convincing examples of this point. Undoubtedly, however, the symbolic status and function of immortality ideas received their finest and most complete exemplification in the *Divine Comedy* of Dante. In the pages of his great epic this foremost poet of the Christian faith beautifully summed up and celebrated his own ideals and those of his age, giving a detailed representation, in supernatural terms, of every important moral good and moral evil as viewed, particularly, by the Church. Dante's work well illustrates the process by which moral ideals become intimately associated with immortality ideas in the minds of men.

Immortality concepts can also be interpreted as symbolizing, in a broad sense, the diverse motivations that have impelled men to believe in a life beyond the grave. Because of the widespread and pathetic human propensity for assuming that wishes will come true, the existence of very deep and powerful motivations toward hope in a hereafter should make us doubly cautious in accepting arguments purporting to establish personal survival. Even I, disbeliever that I am, would frankly be more than glad to awake some day to a worthwhile eternal life. Among the most important motivations toward belief in a beyond are the loss of beloved friends or relatives, dreams in which the dead appear, the psychological difficulty, if not impossibility, of imagining ourselves as non-existent, and the innate human tendency to self-preservation. This biologically instilled urge to keep on living or, negatively, to avoid dying is a major source of longings for immortality. The drive for life extends deep into the unconscious and permeates the billions of protoplasmic cells that constitute the basic units of the human body. A man's simple desire for the continuation of present life in this world is frequently expressed in terms of a desire for a future life in another world.

The harsh impact of sudden and, above all, premature death is another prime motive in the yearning for an after-existence. In India, for instance, the average expectation of life has been steadily increasing since that nation became independent in 1950, but it is still only forty-two years, an age generally considered the prime of life. Even in an advanced country like the United States infant mortality—that is, deaths under one year of age—is still about 115,000 annually. And primarily because we *are* so advanced, in terms of complicated machines like automobiles, more than 100,000 Americans a year lose their lives through accidents. Undeniably the twentieth century is an era of enormous violence in which untold multitudes have died prematurely in international wars, civil wars, revolutions, uprisings, and riots. Perhaps worst of all is to realize that the First World War (1914-1918) resulted in a death toll of approximately 10,000,000, of whom 5 per cent were civilians; and that the Second World War (1939-1945) rolled up a total five times as large—approximately 50,000,000, of whom about 50 per cent were civilians.

The New York Times of September 11, 1950, at the height of the Korean War, provides us with an excellent example of how the idea of immortality may be used as an apology for international conflict. The *Times* reports: "Sorrowing parents whose sons have been drafted or recalled for combat duty were told yesterday in St. Patrick's Cathedral that death in battle was part of God's plan for populating 'the kingdom of heaven.'" The prelate who suggested this remarkable form of consolation was Monsignor William T. Greene of the Roman Catholic Church.

Then there is the general frustration of legitimate human desires and ideals, leading immature minds to hope for their own compensation in heaven and the punishment of their oppressors in hell. If one surveys the past, it is undeniable that the overwhelming majority of mankind have had little access to the better things of life; have led narrow, frustrated, and brief careers; and have gone down to their graves with many of their higher potentialities as human personalities unfulfilled. The same holds true today for by far the larger part of the world's population.

Yet no matter how many or how natural may be the motivations toward belief in a hereafter, the agitation they create within the human breast can hardly be taken as very sound proof of immortality. If human beings aspired to be as big as all space instead of as eternal as all time, their mere longing would not be thought a dependable guarantee of its own fulfillment. Nor would a profound craving to have witnessed at first-hand the Battle of Thermopylae in 480 B.C. establish in itself the actuality of pre-existence. Yet the logic of many typical arguments for an eternal existence after death can be utilized with equal force by Buddhists and Hindus to support the idea of an eternal existence before birth.

Quite obviously a drastic change in the social and economic system in most parts of the world, ensuring to everyone a secure, abundant, and socially significant life, would greatly weaken the chief incentives to a belief in immortality. A more cooperative form of society would discourage present tendencies toward selfish individualism and expansion of the ego that foster the urge for everlasting self-perpetuation. If medical progress, combined with a general improvement in living conditions, were able to prolong the life span of most people in the world to seventy or eighty years, that potent motive toward belief in a hereafter—premature death—would tend to disappear.

I am not attempting here to mention and to answer all the abstract arguments on behalf of immortality advanced by theology and philosophy. In another book, *The Illusion of Immortality,* I have treated them fully. Suffice it to say that many of these arguments are dependent on the view that this earth is and will continue to be a vale of tears and that therefore we *must* find recompense in a realm beyond. For example, Immanuel Kant's so-called ethical argument for survival after death is of this variety; therefore the better things become for mankind in this present world, the worse they become for Kant's argument. What most of the more fundamental abstract arguments boil down to is that men are so noble, so unique, so brilliant, or altogether so important that we cannot admit they will ever perish as individuals. Yet this claim is simply another example of far-fetched wish-fulfillment.

Somerset Maugham, the English novelist, speaking of arguments for an afterlife, hits several nails on the head at once: "A very good test of the force of arguments on which you accept a belief is to ask yourself whether for reasons of equal weight you would embark on a practical operation of any importance. Would you for example buy a house on hearsay without having the title examined by a lawyer and the drains tested by a surveyor? The arguments for immortality, weak when you take them one by one, are no more cogent when you take them together. They are alluring, like a house-agent's advertisement in the daily paper, but to me at least no more convincing. For my part I cannot see how consciousness can persist when its physical basis has been destroyed, and I am too sure of the interconnection of my body and my mind to think that any survival of my consciousness apart from my body would be in any sense the survival of myself. Even if one could persuade oneself that there was any truth in the suggestion that human consciousness survives in some general consciousness, there would be small comfort in it." [47]

As for those who, like the Spiritualists and psychic researchers, advance scientific "proofs" of an afterlife, they have not in the least, in my opinion, been able to discredit that monistic psychology which makes personal immortality impossible. Experimenting on a wide scale, these groups have accumulated a large variety of extranormal phenomena and have shown conclusively that the purported spirits of the dear departed can be extremely agile in a darkened room. But these experimenters have by no means proved that the small proportion of their data which remains untainted by the fraud of mediums, or by methods something less than scientific, implies human survival after death.

The objective data actually disclosed by them are susceptible to different interpretations such as the activity of the subconscious, cryptesthesia (the existence of a hidden sixth sense) or telepathy. Telepathy across space, with the receiving and sending minds always operating as functions of definitely living bodies and brains, seems to me a fairly plausible possibility. Telepathy, however, if established, would tend to explain away many of the more mysterious revelations of mediums and might well, therefore, weaken rather than strengthen the Spiritualist case for immortality. Personally, I shall sit up and take more notice when the communications from just one Spiritualist spirit eventuate in some socially useful result such as the solution of a difficult murder case. Meanwhile I shall continue to give credence to the old adage that "dead men tell no tales" and to believe that the interesting and often intriguing phenomena collected by the psychic researchers are chiefly valuable as contributions to purely naturalistic sciences such as psychiatry and abnormal psychology.

Generally speaking, the emotional consequences of death have been so profound that discussion of the subject has rarely been carried on in an atmosphere conducive to unbiased conclusions. It is usually assumed that death as such is a very great evil and the worst enemy of man. Now certain specific ways in which death has manifested itself throughout human history, constantly striking down individuals and indeed multitudes in the prime of life and appearing in innumerable ugly forms, are correctly to be classified as evil. Yet death in and of itself, as a phenomenon of Nature, is not an evil. There is nothing mysterious about death, nothing supernatural about it, that could legitimately lead to the interpretation that it is a divine punishment inflicted upon men and other living creatures. On the contrary death is an altogether natural thing and has played a useful and necessary role in the long course of biological evolution. In fact, without this much-abused institution of death, which has given the fullest and most serious meaning to the survival of the fittest and thus has rendered possible the upward surge of organic species, it is clear that the animal known as man would never have evolved at all.

Man could not exist, either, were it not for the helping hand of death in making available the most basic means of human living. Man's fuel, food, clothing, shelter, furnishings, and reading materials all depend to a large extent upon the operation of death. Coal, oil, and peat originate in decomposed organic substances; wood for fuel, building, furniture, and the manufacture of paper comes from dead trees. The death of plant life provides man with food in the form of vegetables, grains, cereals, and fruits; with drink in the form of wine, beer, and liquor; with clothing in the form of cotton, flax, and rayon; and with rubber for tires, waterproof garments, and a thousand other things. The death of animal life brings him not only birds, fish, fowl, and meat to eat, but also fur and wool for clothing and leather for shoes. Turning to aesthetic experience, we realize that the glorious colors of the autumn landscape come from dead and dying leaves—a true resurrection of beauty.

Living and dying, birth and death, are essential and correlative aspects of the same evolutionary process. Life affirms itself *through* death, which was brought into existence *by* life and derives its entire significance *from* life. In the dynamic and creative flux of Nature the same living organisms do not go on indefinitely, but retire from the scene at a certain stage and so give way to newborn and lustier vitality.

The American novelist, Anne Parrish, expresses this truth beautifully when she writes that each one of us "must die for the sake of life, for the flow of the stream too great to be dammed in any pool, for the growth of the seed too strong to stay in one shape. . . . Because these bodies must perish, we are greater than we know. The most selfish must be generous, letting his life pour out to others. The most cowardly must be brave enough to go." [48] Death opens the way for the greatest possible number of individuals, including our own descendants, to experience the joys of living; and in this sense death is the ally of the unborn generations of the future.

Of course there are living forms like trees, far more simply organized than human beings, that endure for centuries and tens of centuries. In his novel, *After Many a Summer Dies the*

Swan, Aldous Huxley, in satirizing the desire for immortality, stresses the ability of certain species of carp to live on for hundreds of years. He pictures an English lord attaining a hideous, subhuman prolongation of life beyond two hundred years, by means of eating the intestinal flora of this fish. Apparently one price of the organic complexity that makes man's career so exciting, so splendid, and so vividly self-conscious is death for the personality at the end of a relatively brief time span.

As H. G. Wells and Julian Huxley write in their noteworthy volume *The Science of Life:* "The individual has, so to speak, made a bargain. For the individual comes out of the germplasm and does and lives and at length dies for the sake of life. It is a bit of the germ-plasm which has arisen and broken away, in order to see and feel life instead of just blindly and mechanically multiplying. Like Faust it has sold its immortality in order to live more abundantly." [49] For me, at least, the understanding of death's indispensable place in Nature and of man's unique place in the great life process is one of the best antidotes to the thought of personal extinction.

Another consideration that helps to counteract the prospect of oblivion through death is that every man carries literally all eternity in his being. I mean by this that the ultimate elements of the body, as the Law of the Conservation of Mass [*] implies, have always existed in some form or other and will go on existing forever. The infinite past comes to a focus in our intricately structured bodies; and from them there radiates the infinite future.

Biology, however, does not strictly rule out immortality for human beings, though it does insistently indicate that any kind of continued existence must be based on natural bodies. There is a fair chance that medicine will in due course discover how to preserve the average man in good health at least up to the century mark. It is also quite conceivable that at some

---

[*] Mass in this context includes both matter and energy.

very distant day science will learn how to prolong indefinitely the life of human bodies, except in cases of serious accidents or acts of violence that injure or crush the physical organism beyond all possibility of repair. Then there would be immortality in its original sense of "not-death"; for people would simply not die and the fundamental partnership of body and personality would never come to an end. Whether such a use of science would be desirable is another and a doubtful matter.

Over the years, with my Humanist premises, I have gradually come to think that death, with all its implications, is a blow of such magnitude and finality that it is always a thing of tragic dimensions—to the person who dies, or his intimate survivors, and usually to both. If the deceased was widely known in the community, his death can be a tragedy for many people—indeed for millions or tens of millions—who were not personally acquainted with him. Such was the case when President John F. Kennedy was assassinated in November, 1963. Even when death is a release from painful and incurable illness, it seems tragic that the only remedy should be complete extinction of the individual. Obviously, when death strikes someone who is young or in the prime of life, the tragedy is worse.

Yet there is tragedy, too, in the death of the old, even of those in their eighties or nineties. Some of the greatest scenes in literature concern the death of aged persons, throwing a searchlight on the living, such as that of the grandmother in Proust's *Remembrance of Things Past* and of the central character in Tolstoy's *Death of Ivan Ilyich*. I am acquainted with a number of lion-hearted individuals over ninety who are still carrying on with wonderful vitality and mental acumen. I think especially of Alexander Meiklejohn, ninety-two years old, philosopher, educator, and untiring crusader for civil liberties; ° and Bertrand Russell, likewise ninety-two, the world's most eminent Humanist and active to this day in many

---

° Professor Meiklejohn died suddenly on December 16, 1964.

good causes, particularly the struggle for international peace.

Mankind can ill afford to lose such wise and useful citizens. And their own continuing zest for life, as well as the love which their families and friends bear them, makes it sad that one day they must part from us forever. The death of anyone whom we love, no matter what his age, stabs deep into the heart and leaves a lasting pang.

The Humanist, although fully realizing the tragic aspect of death, neither agonizes over it like the existentialists; nor is preoccupied with it like the Spiritualists; nor permits it to overshadow in his philosophy the other phases of human existence and justify the conclusion that life as a whole is a tragedy. Nor does the Humanist cry out against death in the manner of Dylan Thomas in his poignant lines:

> Do not go gentle into that good night.
> Rage, rage against the dying of the light.[50]

No, Humanists look death in the face with honesty, with dignity and with calm, recognizing that the tragedy it represents is inherent in the great gift of life.

In full justice to death I must add that it is by no means so terrible a thing as many religions and philosophies have depicted. If the Humanists are right in calling immortality a brain-woven conceit, death not only does away with the possibility of an eternal paradise, but also negates the threat of hells and purgatories beyond the tomb. Death destroys unjustified fears as well as unjustified hopes. Since a man can die only once, the dead are beyond all good or ill. They are as totally unconcerned with life and existence as the unborn and unconceived. As Job said in his classic paean to the grave: "There the wicked cease from troubling; and there the weary be at rest."

Humanism, then, takes its stand with the great Greek thinker who 300 years before the birth of Christ summed up this whole matter in the pithy formula: "When we are, death is not; and when death is, we are not." So spoke Epicurus, who lived many centuries prior to the rise of modern science and when the world of Western man was yet in its infancy. For more than 2,000 years now this Western world has had its fling with all sorts of charming but extravagant myths, and romantic but fanciful philosophies. It is high time for us to cast aside the intellectual vagaries of the past, to think and act as mature men and women ready to cope with reality as it is, in its varying aspects of starkness and splendor. And in working through to a sound view of life and destiny, we can take no more important step than to discard the illusion of immortality:

> Give up the dream that Love may trick the fates
> To live again somewhere beyond the gleam
> Of dying stars, or shatter the strong gates
> Some god has builded high; give up the dream.[51]

This renunciation made by reason goes far in liberating us from the false pretensions and vain commitments of super-naturalism. Taking this path onto the plateau of truth, "we shall then be making that rare advance in wisdom which consists in abandoning our illusions the better to attain our ideals." [52] For to know clearly and finally that this is our one and only life enables men to focus their minds completely upon the consummation of human happiness here in the warmth and light of our own gracious sun.

3. THE DESTINY OF MAN

Humanism definitely places the destiny of man within the very broad limits of this natural world. It submits that men can find plenty of scope and meaning in their lives through freely enjoying the rich and varied potentialities of this luxuriant earth; through preserving, extending and adding to the values of civilization; through contributing to the progress and happiness of mankind during billions and billions of years; or through helping to evolve a new species surpassing man.

Those who cry out that human existence is meaningless and worthless without the promise of immortality are either striking a pose or expressing in extreme language the grief they have suffered from the loss of some loved one. We can say in all seriousness with Santayana "that no man of any depth of soul has made his prolonged existence the touchstone of his enthusiasms. . . . What a despicable creature must a man be, and how sunk below the level of the most barbaric virtue, if he cannot bear to live for his children, for his art, or for country!" [53] Or for his fellowmen throughout the world, I would add.

Though in the most poignant cases of "love-devouring death," as Shakespeare phrased it, nothing can really offset the tragedy, the possession of wide interests and deep loyalties beyond the immediate circle of friends and family can do much to cure the hurt. Those who are involved in some absorbing work or who give themselves to some consuming cause seem best able to rise above the narrow intensities of affection that often wreak emotional havoc in people's lives. Humanists are opposed to the expansion of personal grief over a loved one's loss into a little cult of perpetual mourning.

The death of individuals cannot defeat the ongoing life of the nation or of humanity as a whole. The affirmative philosophy of Humanism accepts the inspiration of those who have passed on and proceeds to carry forward the immense tasks of social emancipation and reconstruction. It casts aside the misleading supernaturalisms of the past and proclaims the virtues of an ethics frankly dedicated to this-earthly human happiness. Such a sane and humane ethics can be more effective, as well as more high-minded, than any based on the promise of personal immortality. It is more virtuous to act ethically without hoping for a reward in an afterlife than with such a hope in mind. It is positively indecent to claim that men will act decently only if they are guaranteed the *pour-*

boire, as Schopenhauer called it, of post-mortem existence. And it is simply untrue that the denial of immortality necessarily instils in us a philosophy of "Eat, drink, and be merry; for tomorrow we die."

If this life is our sole opportunity for self-enjoyment, it is also our sole opportunity to make our actions count on behalf of the social good, to contribute significantly to the more lasting human values, and to leave a name behind us that will be honored and beloved by the community. Whether or not, however, a man's name endures, whether or not he lives again in children and descendants, his influence flows on unceasingly in the great stream of human life. The individual will find a deeper and more sustained happiness in working for a noble purpose than in spending his fast-flying years upon personal trivialities. There will be no chance to alter the irreversible record of our lives.

As for the future, it is up to the human race to work out its own destiny upon this globe. Humanism denies that there is any overarching fate, either in the form of a Divine Providence or a malignant Satanism, that is either helping or hindering man's progress and well-being. Within certain limits prescribed by our earthly circumstances and by scientific law, individual human beings, entire nations, and mankind in general are free to choose the paths that they truly wish to follow. To a significant degree they are the moulders of their own fate and hold in their own hands the shape of things to come.

Man has already gone far since he appeared upon this planet, and during the brief episode—not more than 6,000 years—since what we call civilization came into existence. He has mastered the face of the earth, the depths of the sea and the heights of the air, subduing and turning to his own uses the mighty forces of Nature. He has charted the vast regions of interstellar space, with their billions of stars and galaxies; he has penetrated the recesses of the atom, discovering its most potent secrets. He has become a veritable Hercules by multiplying his productive power through prodigious and intricate machines. He has built great cities and civilizations upon every continent; created magnificent art and literature and other cultural forms; and invented the scientific method that leads to the attainment of the truth and to the possibility of continuing progress.

Unquestionably human beings have become the unchallenged lords of creation, so far as this earth is concerned. Biologically speaking, the animal, man, has been an enormous success. Despite the wars, plagues, and economic dislocations that have periodically afflicted humanity, the population of the world has for several centuries been steadily increasing and at an ever higher rate. Since 1650 it has grown approximately sixfold, reaching more than 3,300,000,000 as of 1964. Notwithstanding the Second World War, it gained about 175,000,000 between 1936 and 1946. The annual increase now is more than 60,000,000; and at this rate the earth will have at least 5,500,-000,000 people by the year 2000.

Through eliminating the more pressing evils of present-day society, and through putting into general effect already known measures of health and education, mankind can improve considerably both physically and intellectually. That is not all. For a scientifically induced mutation in man may well bring into existence a more advanced species, call it *Superman* or what you will, that will be as superior to us in brain power as we are to the anthropoid ape. Such an outcome is certainly within the realm of biological possibility. "For the most part the human cerebrum is regarded as a finished product. Its evolutionary history does not support this point of view, but makes it appear far more probable that the brain of modern man represents some intermediate stage in the ultimate development of the master organ of life." [54] Experimental science, we may recall, has already brought about mutations in organic forms such as mice and fruit flies.

In any case infinite possibilities remain of further triumphs for man in various realms, including, above all, the winning of adequate control over human nature itself. What I want to deny emphatically is the necessity of any ultimate doom for man, a fate often predicted today by pessimistic scientists rather than by theologians anticipating the Day of Judgment. I deny the *inevitability* at whatever distant date of this earth's becoming uninhabitable and a tomb for all the living creatures upon it.

Professor Harlow Shapley, former Director of the Harvard Observatory, has estimated that the sun will continue to radiate sufficient heat to maintain human life for at least ten billion years. Science in its efficacious modern form is only about 400 years old. What undreamed-of achievements may we not expect when this science is four thousand or four million or four billion years old? During such immense time spans man may well win such mastery over this whirling sphere that he will succeed in preserving this planet as a habitable abode indefinitely.

Surely the science of the distant future will be able to cope with, or even ward off altogether, potential Ice Ages and to overcome the danger of a fatal thinning out in the atmospheric oxygen that is so vital to living forms. Now that scientists have succeeded in unlocking the tremendous energies of the atom, it does not seem impossible that they will eventually gain such control over the sources of heat and energy that even the ultimate and probably inevitable cooling off of the sun will not prove to be a death warrant.

If the sun starts to become either too cold or too hot for the continuation of terrestrial life, one possible solution will be to utilize nuclear power to speed up or slow down the earth's revolution around the sun, so that our planet goes into a smaller or larger orbit respectively, taking it nearer to or further from the sun. This suggestion comes from Professor of Astrophysics Fritz Zwicky, who also proposes "a reconstruction of the planetary system" which would change the "orbits of Mars and Venus so as to bring them into a position . . . more suitable for human needs . . . Mars further in from the sun and Venus further out." [55] Assumed in this bold thrust of the imagination is man's eventual capability of emigrating to other planets in nuclear-propelled space ships, already foreshadowed by global satellites and rockets to the moon.*

There are two or three faintly possible cosmic accidents in the face of which man would in all probability be helpless. One would be a colossal explosion of the whole sun resulting in a blast of heat and light that would shrivel up every living thing on this planet and perhaps turn the earth itself back again into a flaming mass of gaseous matter. Another would be the disaster of some star's colliding with our solar system or coming so near to it that the movements of the sun and planets would be utterly disrupted. However, none of these events is likely to occur nor probably could occur for billions of years.

As for a collision, the multitudinous stars roam through the empyrean so extremely far apart that the stellar universe in general is comparatively empty. Sir James Jeans, the British astrophysicist, has estimated that an actual collision between two stars can take place on an average of only once in 600,-000,000,000,000,000 (six hundred quadrillion) years. Dr. H. Spencer Jones, Astronomer Royal of England, graphically pictures the situation in his fascinating book *Life on Other Worlds*: "Suppose we have a hollow globe the size of the earth, 8,000 miles in diameter, and that we put half a dozen tennis balls inside it and allow them to fly about in any direction, rebounding from the wall when they hit it. The chance

---

* Over billions of years human science will also, I believe, build up sufficient knowledge and power to deal with and counteract the so-called Law of Entropy, which holds that the sum total of matter-energy in the entire universe will ultimately be converted into non-useful, dissipated, stagnant heat diffused everywhere like vapor. The science of astrophysics is in such flux that this predicted "heat-death" of the whole mighty cosmos must remain, it seems to me, in the realm of speculation.

that two of these balls will collide is about equal to the chance that two stars will come into collision." [56] If, moreover, the current hypothesis of "an expanding universe" is true, so that stars and galaxies are in general getting farther and farther apart, then the possibility of collisions becomes less and less with the passage of time.

These various speculations naturally raise the question as to whether organic species exist or can exist elsewhere in the universe than upon our earth. Though living forms can adapt themselves to a very wide range of circumstances, as witness the history of plant and animal development upon this globe, there are certain conditions that are prerequisite for the birth and evolution of life. Stars and suns are automatically eliminated as possible abodes of life because they are all nothing more nor less than blazing furnaces, with average interior temperatures of about 20 million degrees centigrade. A planet like Mercury is ruled out because it is too near the sun and therefore too hot; a planet like Jupiter is ruled out because it is too far away from the sun and therefore too cold.

Jupiter, together with Saturn, is also too big, having retained on that account, through gravitational attraction, too much atmosphere, including so large a proportion of poisonous gases as to make life impossible. On the other hand, a planet very much smaller than the earth would be unsuitable for life because it would not have been able to retain *any* atmosphere. Hence we are forced to conclude that life can arise only upon planets that, like our own, are of a medium size and are neither too close to their parent sun nor too distant from it. In this class belong Mars and Venus, upon both of which some astronomers believe that living forms, at least of a vegetative nature, exist. This hypothesis, however, remains unproved.

If life is to be found outside of our solar system, the first necessity is of course a planet or a family of planets revolving about some star. In a cosmos of such tremendous dimensions it seems almost certain that every so often there has occurred the proper concatenation of stellar events for the creation of a planetary system. Professor Shapley estimates that scattered throughout the universe there are at a minimum 10 billion planets suitable for the birth and development of life, and that on at least 100 million of these some degree of organic evolution has taken place. For, as he writes: "Biochemistry and microbiology, with assistance from geophysics, astronomy and other sciences, have gone so far in bridging the gap between the inanimate and the living that we can no longer doubt but that whenever *the physics, chemistry and climates are right* on a planet's surface, *life will emerge and persist.*" [57]

We can make all sorts of conjectures as to what paths life might take on some other earthlike sphere: whether the highest forms might develop, for example, from some species not mammal in structure; whether thinking beings equal or superior to man in intellectual capacity have evolved; and whether, if creatures possessing mind do exist in other parts of the universe, man will ever be able to communicate with them. Considering our remarkable developments in the field of wireless telegraphy and radio, eventually some sort of communication would not be beyond the bounds of credibility.

I think I have said enough to indicate the broad imaginative vistas that seem to me a legitimate part of the Humanist philosophy. Of course I have been indulging in speculations; but they are justified *counter*-speculations, I believe, to the unduly pessimistic conclusions of many contemporary scientists and philosophers. Humanists dispute the doom-sayers and do not for a moment admit that man must necessarily be defeated in his career in this universe.

Whether or not mankind meets some crushing cosmic doom ten billion or a hundred million or a mere million years hence, the progress and well-being of the human race over such enormous tracts of time assuredly offers prospects of social significance that should provide sufficient satisfaction to all but the incurably egoistic. In any case, the value of man's happiness and achievement is not to be measured in terms of infinite duration. The philosophy of Humanism, with its conscious limitation of the human enterprise to this existence, sets us free to concentrate our entire energies, without distraction by either hopes or fears of individual immortality, on that building of the good society that has been the dream of saints and sages since the dawn of history.

CHAPTER IV

Humanism's Theory of the Universe

1. SCIENCE AND ITS IMPLICATIONS

Any complete philosophy of existence requires a carefully worked out theory of the universe, in technical terms a *metaphysics,* an ontology, or a world-view. As we have already seen, Humanism believes that Nature itself constitutes the sum total of reality, that matter-energy and not mind is the foundation stuff of the universe, and that supernatural entities simply do not exist. This nonreality of the supernatural means, on the human level, that men do not possess supernatural and immortal souls; and, on the level of the universe as a whole, that our cosmos does not possess a supernatural and eternal God.

Humanism's attitude toward the universe, like its judgment as to the nature and destiny of man, is grounded on solid scientific fact. The supernatural beliefs of Christianity were originally formulated in a prescientific era in which it was thought that the earth, with the sun and all the multitudinous stars revolving around it, was the center of the cosmos. In a temporal sense the earth and its forms of life were thought to be as old as anything else, since Nature in its entirety was supposedly created by God only a few thousand years before the birth of Christ. It is understandable how thoughtful persons, with such assumptions about the world, could come to suppose that man, as the highest of earth's creatures, was the darling of the universe; and that behind the visible creation dwelt an omnipotent, benevolent, and personal God, an all-seeing Cosmic Companion, whose chief concern was the care and guidance of human beings.

Modern science has completely and fundamentally altered the primitive picture of things that encouraged this particular religious view. Astronomers have proved that our little planet, far from being the center of the cosmos, is not even the center of the solar system, which is itself a mere microscopic blur upon the unimaginably vast canopy of the heavens. The earth revolves around a mighty sun more than a million times its size and nearly 93,000,000 miles distant. And this sun, with its retinue of nine planets, is only an average star in a local star cloud situated toward the edge of a great spiral nebula or galaxy containing altogether some 100 billion stars.

The larger part of this nebula or galactic system, as it is called, we see in the night skies as the Milky Way. The diameter of our galactic system is estimated at not less than 100,000 light-years. A light-year is the distance (about six trillion miles) that light, speeding through space at the rate of approximately 186,300 miles per second, travels in a year. Alpha Centauri, the nearest star outside of our solar system, is 25,000,-000,000,000 (25 trillion) miles away or 4.27 light-years. To reach this star in a spaceship hurtling through the heavens at a million miles an hour would take some 3,000 years.

It was the Copernican revolution of the sixteenth century that toppled the earth from its traditional position as the focal point of the cosmos. During the twentieth century the astronomers have brought about a second revolution in our conception of the heavens that dwarfs even more sharply the spatial significance of our planet. For they have shown that our galactic system is only one out of billions upon billions of similar galaxies scattered throughout the universe, each possessing an estimated average of ten billion flaming stars. The dramatically beautiful Andromeda Nebula, closest galaxy of the spiral type beyond the Milky Way, is 2,200,000 light-years from the earth. The distances of the farthest galaxies photographically visible run up to two billion light-years; while a new type of stellar objects called "quasars," identified through their emission of radio waves, are as much as six billion light-years away or

60,000,000,000,000,000,000,000 terrestrial miles. Beyond the limits of present photographic visibility countless galaxies, literally trillions in number, drift through the fathomless seas of space, which may well be infinite in extent. These stupendous facts point, as Professor Shapley suggests, to a universe that is essentially "galactocentric." That is why he calls it the Metagalaxy.

It is not important whether all these various estimates are precisely accurate, as of course they are not; the important thing is the staggering immensity of the cosmos. Sir James Jeans sums up the situation graphically: "At a moderate computation," he says, "the total number of stars in the universe must be something like the total number of specks of dust in London. Think of the sun as something less than a single speck of dust in a vast city, of the earth as less than a millionth part of such a speck of dust, and we have perhaps as vivid a picture as the mind can really grasp of the relation of our home in space to the rest of the universe." [58] If perchance the total aggregate of stars turns out eventually to be as numerous as all the specks of dust in the entire United States, I do not think our mental picture would become much altered.

The time spans of this cosmos in which we live are equally impressive. The average star, as for example our own sun, is probably about 5,000,000,000 years old. And what infinities of time had no doubt passed before the present array of nebulae made their appearance in the heavens! Competent geologists now put the age of the earth at not less than four billion years. Biologists estimate that living forms have been in existence on our planet anywhere from one billion to three billion years. While a generally accepted figure for the Age of Man, including the direct predecessors of Homo sapiens, is still in doubt, we know that it is at least one million years. This is to be compared with the assertion of theologians well into the nineteenth century that the supernatural creation of man had taken place some 6,000 years previously.

Thus the findings of modern science utterly blast the world

view of old-time religion. In terms of space and time, man and his tiny earth look extremely insignificant in relation to the rest of the universe. If there is a Supreme Being ruling over these billions of Milky Ways that roam through the unending corridors of the sky, he can hardly be the neighborly, fatherly God of Christianity. And if there actually is, in Tennyson's words, "one far-off divine event to which the whole creation moves," then what transpires on this earth is only an infinitesimal part of the trend; and such earthly evidences of Providence as theologians and metaphysicians purport to find can hardly be taken as applying to the universe in its entirety. Logically, a supernatural Mind or Purpose behind everything must include all those never-ending galaxies that extend into the farthermost regions of space and must cover all those untold billions of years in past and future that so stun the imagination. This is a point that the best of the religious philosophers neglect or overlook altogether.

Finally, what may be called the third revolution in astronomy has demonstrated that very likely there are highly developed forms of life in many other parts of the universe besides our earth.* The probability now is that creatures comparable in their capacities to man exist on millions or even billions of other planets in the cosmos. This deals another blow to the traditional assumption that a compassionate God looks upon the human race as his primary concern.

The scientific data we have been considering disclose the universe as incomparably more magnificent than anything ever revealed by supernatural religion; at the same time they strongly impel us to the conclusion that Nature at large is indifferent, *neutral* toward the welfare, the ideals, and the fate of man. They also suggest that our very imperfect race of men-creatures may be scarcely important or worthy enough to warrant immortality. This would hold true even if a cosmic God did exist, especially since there remains plenty of time

---

* Cf. pp. 113-14.

in which he might evolve a much higher order of being than Homo sapiens.

My earlier conclusions about the development of mind and the unity of the personality and body weightily affect the problem of God's existence. If mind gradually evolved over hundreds of millions of years upon this planet and if it is inextricably bound up with the complex and delicately adjusted kind of physical structure represented by the body and brain of man, then it appears conclusive that mind can exist elsewhere only if it has an intricate material base. But the God of the traditional religions is a supernatural, spiritual Being existing prior to and independent of matter; his mind is not dependent on physical structure, having created out of the void in the first instance every bit of matter there is. In any case we cannot conceive how there could possibly be a physical structure, a cosmic cortex, competent to sustain a Divine Mind functioning over the entire vast realm of space and time and busying itself with every last detail, such as man and the earth, throughout the infinite empire of Nature.

Latter-day theologians have claimed that the general theory of biological evolution proves the presence of a God working upon or within Nature. But the evolutionary upsurge that has culminated in man shows little sign of divine purpose or prevision. The processes of natural selection and survival of the fittest, with the many mutations that occur over hundreds of millions of years, adequately account for the origin and development of species. Though admittedly biologists have not yet discovered precisely how organic forms evolved from inanimate matter, this gap in knowledge can hardly be taken as proof of a guiding force. The existence of Deity cannot properly be deduced from any temporary ignorance of Nature's ways.

Of course the scientific concept of evolution, broadly interpreted as applying not only to living forms, but also to the earth as a material body, the solar system, and the endless stars and galaxies, effectively negates the old religious idea of a divine creation of the whole universe. Furthermore, if we take seriously the lessons of evolution, it would appear that God as a great cosmic Mind and Purpose, if he did exist, would have to be the end-product of a very long evolutionary process rather than its initiator and overseer.

Scientific progress in physics and chemistry, though having less obvious and spectacular consequences for religion and theism than the ideas I have been discussing, is of profound significance for the Humanist philosophy. To those sciences we owe the radical transformation in the accepted view of matter, so long looked upon as something base, uncreative, and inert. It may be helpful to review some of the elementary facts.

Modern research has demonstrated that matter, from its hugest aggregations down to its smallest particles, is made up of unceasingly active units of restless energy. This seemingly solid desk at which I sit and these seemingly well-knit hands with which I write are in the final analysis mostly empty space in which and through which there move at lightning speeds the basic molecules, of which science knows several hundred thousand different varieties. Molecules are a hundred-millionth of an inch in diameter; and in a single glass of water there are billions and trillions and quadrillions of them. A water molecule, for example, is built of two atoms of hydrogen and one of oxygen, which explains the familiar formula of H_2O known to every schoolboy. Every other kind of molecule is what it is because of its own special combination of atoms.

Atoms are constructed along the lines of miniature, though complicated, solar systems and in their turn have as ultimate components protons and neutrons. These make up the nucleus; and electrons revolve around this central "sun" at a velocity of over 100,000 miles a second. Each of the more than 100 different chemical elements or atoms is determined by the number of protons in its nucleus. The number of revolving electrons in each atom corresponds to the number of protons. In the lightest and simplest atom, that of hydrogen, there is only one proton, while in one of the heaviest and most complex atoms, uranium for example, there are ninety-two protons. It was experimentation with uranium that led in 1945 to the invention of the atomic bomb, with its revelation of the enormous energies that have always been latent in the heart of the atom. The consequent construction of the hydrogen bomb in 1952 disclosed even more dramatically the awesome possibilities of nuclear power.

Einstein's theory of relativity constitutes another scientific advance which strengthens the Humanist position that the universe is fundamentally a great system of matter-energy. For Einstein's discoveries render unacceptable the old idea of an Absolute Space and an Absolute Time through which the world moves, and show instead that space and time are both derivative from events and that they are, in fact, forms of relationship between events. Professor Sellars is right: "Time is but another term for the sequence of events. Time is change. . . . *Time is in the world, and not the world in time.*" [59] We can find the germ of this idea as early as Aristotle. G. W. Leibniz, German philosopher of the seventeenth century, suggested a similar view of time.

A simple analysis of how we calculate time leads to the correct interpretation. Days and months and years are measurements in terms of a relation between material events, that is, between the revolving earth and the sun or other stellar bodies. Similarly, watches and clocks tell the time in minutes and hours by means of hands moving at a set rate in relation to a stable dial. There is nothing subjective, as some commentators have thought, about relativity, since it establishes the velocity of light as an absolute standard of reference and sets up a general law that puts all measurements of time and space on an entirely objective basis. It is significant that Dr. Einstein called himself a Humanist.

Taking into consideration all of these scientific developments, we realize that matter, even at its most elementary level, is a thing of the most tremendous dynamism, complexity, versatility, and potentiality. It no longer seems mysterious that life and finally human beings should have arisen out of such altogether remarkable stuff. Moreover, science has found that matter-energy is absolutely indestructible and eternal. This point is summed up in what is known as the Law of the Conservation of Mass.

Thus creative matter needs no ultimate theistic Power to sustain it; no Prime Mover, as with Aristotle, to set it in motion and keep it active; no Divine Principle to impregnate it with the capacity of flowering as a whirling nebula containing billions of stars, as a warming and light-giving sun or as a fertile planet that produces all the wondrous forms of life, and at their apex man and his indomitable mind. Matter is self-existent, self-active, self-developing, self-enduring. It is auto-dynamic. Intellectually, there is nothing to be gained and much to be lost for philosophy by positing a supernatural Creator or First Cause behind the great material universe.

When the child asks, "Who made God?" he is unwittingly interjecting a comment that is both logical and philosophical. Similarly relevant is the old oriental myth that the world rests upon the back of a huge elephant that rests upon the back of a monstrous tortoise. For if everything has a definite cause, then God, too, must have a cause and so on ad infinitum. The fact is that regardless of how far we push our inquiries, at one point or another we are compelled to assume *something self-existent* that possesses certain powers and potentialities. Otherwise we become involved in a never-ending regress of explanations and assumptions. God as a First Cause simply constitutes a large-scale miracle gratuitously intruding at the alleged starting-point of everything.

Furthermore, the argument from a First Cause takes for granted that there must have been a beginning of the cosmos. However, no logical necessity forces us to the conclusion that there was a beginning in time; and indeed it would seem more sensible to accept Aristotle's opinion that the universe is eternal. In fact, those who postulate a supernatural God as

Creator or First Cause usually attribute to him eternal being and are therefore assuming, like most nontheists, an eternally existing reality.

Many persons consider the universe "mysterious" because they can get no satisfactory answer as to the *why* of everything. "Why," they ask, "should there have been a universe in the first place? Why is there any existence at all?" These questions assume in their very formulation that there must be a great over-all Purpose in the cosmos; and accordingly they expect an answer in terms of such a Purpose. The Humanist believes that these conundrums are essentially insoluble because actually no such Purpose can be found.

In specific scientific explanations as well as in ultimate philosophical questions a stage freqently ensues when it is profitless to keep on asking "Why?" At such a juncture we have to say: "Things are simply constructed this way or behave this way." The speed of light is what it is; the law of gravitation operates as it does; and the number of protons and electrons in each type of atom is what it is. In none of these instances can an intelligible answer be given as to *why*. "The scientist delineates the orderly and predictable interactions among the quantities; he never explains the quantities themselves." [60] In science as well as in philosophy, then, we eventually hit rock-bottom in the pursuit of certain inquiries.

Considerations similar to those we have evoked against the First Cause argument for the existence of God are pertinent to the argument from Design, which holds that the universe is so beautiful, splendid, and well-planned that a great Designer, a conscious God, must have worked it all out. Philosophically what the theists do here, besides assuming much more harmony than actually exists, is to treat qualities that were merely potential in matter and that appeared at a comparatively late stage in its development, as if they had always existed. The final result is to take mind, purpose, and other attributes of matter when organized in the form of human beings, and read them back into the original constitution of the cosmos. This conversion of eventual functions into antecedent forces, of potentiality into actuality, of ideas and ideals into independent powers, is one of the most persistent and harmful of philosophic fallacies. It is, in technical philosophic terminology, to *hypostatize*.

The primary meaning of potentiality is precisely that qualitatively new things can come into existence through fresh combinations and developments among the old. Hydrogen and oxygen possess the potentiality of eventuating in water, if they come together in certain proportions, without either of them *being* water to begin with. In an analogous way matter possesses the potentiality of eventuating in organisms that can think, without mind having existed in the first place as an attribute of matter or of a Divine Thinker behind matter. The ordinary theistic view, insisting that many of the most striking qualities that emerge in matter were already in God, implies an unacceptable curtailment of genuine novelty in the world.

Certain philosophers, of whom Aristotle is the prototype, have felt that it was impossible for matter to move continually from potentiality to actuality on its own, and have needlessly postulated a God whose prime function is to stimulate and direct this movement. In the twentieth century we may take as an example Professor Alfred North Whitehead, who defines God as "the principle of concretion." This God determines in each case that which is to become concrete reality; out of the infinite number of possibilities, he selects those that are to be actualized, concretized, as specific objects or events. Matter, of course, requires no such divine aid in its natural unfolding; and Dr. Whitehead's God of Concretion is as superfluous as the carrying of coals to Newcastle.

The modern metaphysics of the philosopher-statesman Jan Christiaan Smuts, one-time Premier of the Union of South Africa, repeats some of these same errors. Mr. Smuts developed a philosophy he called Holism, the central feature of which is an alleged whole-making tendency running through Nature, with the wholes becoming more homogeneous, more complex, and higher from the standpoint of value. Smuts says that we cannot account for evolution without this whole-making tendency as a principle of explanation. It is his God. Again, we see in Holism the common mistake of taking away from many-sided, infinitely productive matter the credit that belongs to it and interposing within it a special power from out of the blue.

This discussion leads us to a further examination of the very important law of parsimony,* which demands that any scientific explanation be based on the fewest assumptions necessary to account for all the facts involved. This cardinal principle of economy or simplicity of hypothesis developed during the late Middle Ages and became particularly associated, in the fourteenth century, with the views of an English philosopher, William of Ockham. The precise formulation, "Entities [of explanation] are not to be multiplied without necessity," was later given the name of Ockham's Razor. In 1687 Isaac Newton expressed the same idea when he wrote in his great book, *Principia:* "Nature does nothing in vain, and more is in vain when less will serve; for Nature is pleased with simplicity, and affects not the pomp of superfluous causes." [61]

This fundamental law of the simplicity of hypothesis has been a paramount intellectual tool in the advance of science. This law does not deny the truth that Nature often operates in a most complex manner; and under no circumstances can it override the observed facts of such complexity, as, for instance, in the organization of the human body. The law means only that we should not bring in unnecessary hypotheses to explain a situation, whether it happens to be comparatively simple or comparatively complex. The principle of parsimony expresses negatively the scientific rule that every hypothesis must meet the requirements of affirmative empirical proof before being accepted.

A good example of the significance of the law of parsimony

---

* Cf. p. 90.

is provided by a controversy that Galileo had regarding the mountains he discovered on the moon. A certain Ludovico delle Colombe attempted to refute him by maintaining that the apparent valleys of the moon were really filled with an invisible crystalline substance. Galileo replied sarcastically by saying that this suggestion was so excellent that he would apply it further and that, accordingly, it seemed probable that the mountains of the moon were, because this same invisible substance was piled on top of them, ten times higher than he had estimated! Galileo's mocking answer was particularly devastating because it showed that Ludovico had disregarded the principle of parsimony and that once this is done, the door is opened to a thousand and one absurd hypotheses and wild vagaries.

Applying this law to the question of Divinity, we can see that it rules out as superfluous the hypothesis of a supernatural God as Creator or First Cause or Prime Mover of the universe. It eliminates the God of monotheism as an explanation of the behavior of our vast cosmos just as it eliminates the hundreds upon hundreds of more limited gods of animism and polytheism, including all those attractive and picturesque deities of ancient Greece and Rome, as an explanation of natural phenomena. In the same way the law of parsimony makes a supernatural Soul for the universe at large as unnecessary and unsound, scientifically and philosophically, as a supernatural soul for each individual man and animal.

Again and again in the history of thought, specific scientific causes have displaced supernatural causes in man's understanding of phenomena formerly shrouded in mystery. And the extension of scientific law in general to realm after realm in modern times has made it harder and harder to conceive what God would do even if he did exist. The only function that Newton could find for the Deity was a sort of cosmic tinkering in adjusting certain irregularities in the movements of the more distant stars and comets—irregularities that soon afterward became fully accounted for by mathematicians and astronomers. As I have already shown, Newton's fellow Deists as a group held that there was no divine interference in the established order of Nature and that God had wound up the world, as it were, at the start and then let it go its own way as a completely self-regulating machine. Laplace, the French astronomer, took the logical next step and, when asked by Napoleon why he did not mention God in his *Mécanique céleste,* loftily remarked: "Sire, I had no need of that hypothesis." One can imagine what Laplace would have said in answer to a question seriously propounded recently by a British philosopher: "Is the eternal brooding of God necessary to keep space from disintegrating?"

Some philosophers and theologians accept the universality of scientific law, and then claim that scientific laws are the expression of God's mind and that through them he rules the cosmos. But this argument embodies a serious misinterpretation of the nature of scientific law. Scientific laws do not "govern" the universe as a king governs his subjects; nor does matter in motion "obey" laws as do the people in a functioning state. Scientific laws are the expression in intellectual terms of the way matter behaves, of its stable and enduring habits of action. Again, to utilize the law of parsimony, substances determine their own laws and require no Supreme Law-Giver to lay down or maintain their patterns of behavior.

In New York City in the year 1940, at a conference of philosophers, theologians, and scientists, Albert Einstein admirably summed up the Humanist standpoint when he stated: "During the youthful period of mankind's spiritual evolution human fantasy created gods in man's own image, who, by the operations of their will were supposed to determine, or at any rate to influence, the phenomenal world. . . . The idea of God in the religions taught at present is a sublimation of that old conception of the gods. Its anthropomorphic character is shown, for instance, by the fact that men appeal to the Divine Being in prayers and plead for the fulfillment of their wishes. . . . In their struggle for the ethical good, teachers of religion must have the stature to give up the doctrine of a personal God, that is, give up that source of fear and hope which in the past placed such vast power in the hands of priests." [62]

It is evident, then, that God, once imagined to be an omnipresent force throughout the whole world of Nature and man, has been increasingly tending to seem omniabsent. Everywhere intelligent and educated people rely more and more on purely secular and scientific techniques for the solution of their problems. As science advances, belief in divine miracle and the efficacy of prayer becomes fainter and fainter. Certain popular sayings have long recognized this situation, such as Benjamin Franklin's "God helps those who help themselves" and the more recent "Praise the Lord and pass the ammunition." Today the prevailing tendency in a culturally advanced country like America, regardless of what formal tributes may be paid to traditional faiths, is to retire the Almighty from his former role in this-earthly affairs and to look upon him as a sort of Honorary Chairman of the Universe.

Needless to say, many scientists would not agree with the philosophic implications I have drawn from various branches of science; and many scientists have arrived at conclusions that are the very opposite of mine in regard to the questions of God and immortality. It is to be remembered that a scientist, expert and competent in his own department of knowledge, does not necessarily carry over an objective attitude of mind into philosophic and religious issues any more than into economic and political ones. It is an acknowledged fact that again and again in the history of Western thought scientists have lent their prestige to the most far-fetched cosmological theories. Johann Kepler, one of the founders of modern astronomy, believed in astrology and sun worship. The incomparable Newton himself went astray in his philosophical peregrinations; while in our own day well-known scientists talk loosely of how the telescope or the test tube has at last led to the discovery of God and how the long conflict between science and religion has finally come to an end. No matter how brilliant the scientist, we must always ask him for his credentials and subject his views to the most rigorous examination when he wanders into fields that are not his own.

It remains to note that ideas of God, as well as ideas of immortality, have symbolized the ethical values and the ethical progress of mankind. In the West a God of cruelty and vengeance gradually evolved, in the thought of the more advanced religious groups, into a God of love and forgiveness. As Robert Ingersoll once remarked, "An honest God is the noblest work of man." The traditional religions have continually "materialized the terms of their moral philosophy into existing objects and powers." [63] And some philosophers have been so impressed by the beauty and aptness of supernatural religion as metaphor that they regard the criticism that it is contrary to fact as an illiberal practice of the literal-minded.

Now it would be very pleasant indeed if all religious persons adopted the attitude of George Santayana and like-minded philosophers that concepts of God and immortality are to be interpreted as poetic symbolism instead of truth.* The fact is, however, that comparatively few of those who are affiliated with the supernaturalist religions are as emancipated as was Santayana. In all ages religious convictions have had real and moving efficacy for the masses of men only when they have been taken quite literally. Such convictions, of course, have been closely bound up with colorful rituals that appeal more to the emotions than to the mind. Yet while it is true that religion is much more than a system of beliefs, it is also true that a definite set of beliefs is necessary to any religion.

What sheer objective evidence compels us to take literally is the literalness and tenacity with which men have held to religious dogmas throughout history. I think, therefore, that philosophy has the duty of pointing out the falsity of outworn religious ideas, however estimable they may be as a form of art. We cannot act as if all religion were poetry while the

---

* Cf. the literary quip, "God is the greatest character in all fiction."

greater part of it still functions in its ancient guise of illicit science and backward morals; we cannot smile upon religion as mere metaphor when the most powerful sections of it still teach the metaphor as dogma; we cannot nonchalantly assume that supernaturalism is a dead issue when it is still one of the predominant influences in the United States and most countries of the globe.

Professor William Pepperell Montague of Columbia University suggested as a step toward the recovery of philosophy in America that its teachers abandon "the 'genteel tradition' according to which controversial religious questions are politely evaded; and that instead they face those questions and discuss them *pro* and *con* fairly and courteously but frankly. . . . All too often the members of a class in philosophy get the impression that the subject is artificial and remote from their lives just because the teacher has politely refrained from connecting his thoughts about ultimate and important matters with the religious frame of reference in terms of which the student formulates the questions that are ultimate and important to him." [64] Though Professor Montague did not happen to be a Humanist, his comment is most appropriate and fits in well with the Humanist's determination to take religious issues seriously, whether he is functioning within academic walls or in the larger world outside.

2. THE REJECTION OF DUALISM AND IDEALISM

It is obvious that the Humanist metaphysics or theory of the universe, in line with the traditional Naturalisms and Materialisms, leaves no room for world-views in which supernaturalism plays any part. Thus it rules out the metaphysical Dualisms which divide the universe into two separate realms, a material one and a spiritual one; and which also divide man himself into two separate entities, hence making inevitable a dualistic psychology and a dualistic ethics. Representative philosophic or theological Dualisms are those of orthodox Christianity and of the outstanding Catholic philosopher, Thomas Aquinas; of Plato and Plotinus, with their emphasis on eternal Ideas rather than God; of René Descartes, who, despite his supernaturalist metaphysics, so notably advanced the cause of science; and of Immanuel Kant, who shattered through rigorous logic the so-called rational arguments for the existence of God and immortality only to re-establish these two central concepts of supernaturalism as categorical demands of man's faith in the worth-whileness of moral effort.

Dualism of one type or another has ever been a refuge for supernatural religion. Much of what I have already said in this book has aimed at refuting this philosophy, with its belief in a personal God and a personal immortality, and I shall spend little more time upon it. I do want to give, however, some special consideration to the dualistic system of Descartes, who made such great contributions to scientific thought in the seventeenth century that we still talk about the Cartesian revolution. Descartes conceived of the whole physical world, including the human body, as a vast machine describable and explainable in terms of mathematical and mechanical laws. "Give me extension and motion," Descartes boasted, "and I will construct the universe." And he proceeded to synthesize, popularize, and develop the burgeoning new science of his era.

In working out the full implications of the cosmos as a huge and intricate machine, Descartes banished all purpose and spiritual significance from material Nature. Such categories held true only for that supernatural realm in which God and man's immortal soul and mind operated. Since this God did not interfere with the functionings of the physical universe, that universe and this earth were left open for science to explore as it would. On the other hand, since Descartes reserved a place in his system for God and immortality, he could not rightly be accused of being impious or irreligious. There is some reason to believe, however, that the almost absolute divorce that Descartes postulated between the realms of Nature and super-Nature was a conscious device to free science from religious controls without offending the Church. In any case the Church was continually condemnatory of Descartes, put his books on the Catholic Index and at one time wanted to have him executed on the charge of atheism. Descartes felt that he was in such grave danger that he suppressed or left unfinished much valuable work.

Though Descartes greatly stimulated scientific progress and thereby the Humanist spirit, his drastically dualistic metaphysics brought confusion worse confounded into philosophy. The particular view of the material world that he and his followers expounded "ushered in a new process of the denaturalization of man and human experience. It transformed the conception of Nature into a purely mechanical system of tiny billiard-balls following the laws of dynamics. . . . Thus human experience was removed from Nature and made 'subjective': its locus was in man, in a separate substance, 'mind,' not in Nature at all. It was the mechanical effect of Nature upon and in man's 'mind,' not a co-operation of natural powers. The varieties of human experience, religious, moral, even intellectual, became quite literally supernatural—they were in no sense natural processes. Man's 'mind' was no longer a natural function, but an independent substance with an extra-natural status." [65]

Descartes's insistence on the primacy of consciousness, which he epitomized in his famous words, "I think, therefore I am," started a strain of subjectivism that hypnotized modern philosophy for almost 300 years. It resulted in a lamentable overemphasis on theory of knowledge (epistemology) and led straight to the long, fascinating, yet often far-fetched argumentation of John Locke, George Berkeley, David Hume, Kant, and Hegel. Hume, whose brilliant skepticism cut so deep that mind as well as matter seemed to dissolve in his analysis, reveals in a frank moment his misgivings about it all: "I dine, I play a game of backgammon, I converse and am merry with my friends; and when after three or four hours' amusement, I would return to these speculations, they appear so cold, and strained, and ridiculous, that I cannot find in my heart to enter into them any further." [66]

The chief effect of modern subjectivism was to bring forth

a bewildering series of idealistic philosophies rashly asserting that everything that exists is in the last analysis mind or idea. This type of philosophy ought rightly to have called itself *Idea-ism,* but instead adopted the world *Idealism,* which in the field of ethics is a perfectly clear term meaning the pursuit of high moral ideals. Thus it has become necessary always to distinguish between idealism as an ethical concept and Idealism as an inclusive philosophical system.

Extreme subjective Idealism argues that objects exist only as and when perceived by the individual human mind. This position leads straight to that form of madness known as solipsism, in which for each human being his own self is the whole of reality, with all other persons and the entire universe merely ideas in his consciousness. The more common and influential variety of Idealism is objective Idealism, which holds that the whole cosmos, from the remotest nebula down to every last atom, exists by virtue of being in the all-perceiving mind of God. Every human individual, every stick and stone, every planet and star, is a thought, more or less complex, in the Divine Consciousness. A limerick fashionable at Oxford, long a stronghold of the idealist philosophy, expresses this notion quite well:

> There was a young man who said, "God,
> How very remarkably odd
>   That this int'resting tree
>   Should continue to be
> When there's no one about in the quad."
>
> "Dear Sir, your inquiry is odd,
> For *I'm* always about in the quad;
>   And that's why the tree
>   Continues to be,
> Since observed by yours faithfully, God."

The two most important representatives of objective Idealism were the eighteenth-century English churchman, Bishop

Berkeley, and the nineteenth-century German philosopher, Georg Wilhelm Friedrich Hegel, who renamed his God the Absolute. Hegel's ponderous and comprehensive system created a powerful tradition of its own and for the larger part of the nineteenth century became the dominant academic philosophy in both Europe and America. Professor George H. Howison, who taught his own special brand of Idealism, well summed up the prevailing temper of American philosophy at a symposium in 1895 when he said: "We are all agreed [on one] great tenet, [which is] the entire foundation of philosophy itself: that explanation of the world which maintains that the only thing absolutely real is mind; that all material and temporal existences take their being from Consciousness that thinks and experiences; that out of consciousness they all issue, to consciousness they are presented, and that presence to consciousness constitutes their entire reality." [67]

In the United States, Hegelianism was in the ascendant in the eastern universities during the last decades of the nineteenth century and flourished in the Middle West in what was known as the St. Louis School. In the early years of the twentieth century Josiah Royce at Harvard became the leader of American Idealism, while more recently another Harvard professor, William Ernest Hocking, has perhaps been its ablest exponent. Otuside of academic circles the idealist doctrine had a powerful effect on Ralph Waldo Emerson and his fellow Transcendentalists; and it found somewhat eccentric expression in both the health-centered cult of Christian Science and the naïve religion of Spiritualism centered around the hope of immortality. Hegelian Idealism also influenced profoundly many thinkers who later broke away from it, among them Karl Marx and John Dewey. There can be little doubt that Hegel, as the greatest spokesman for one of the main philosophic positions, will go down in history as one of the outstanding figures in philosophy.

Dr. Samuel Johnson gave the classic common-sense answer to Idealism when, in discussing Berkeley's philosophy, he declared, "I refute it, *thus*," and kicked a large stone so hard that he rebounded from it. More seriously, we can state that Idealism repeats the mistake of other anthropomorphic philosophies by ascribing to the universe at large a purely human or organic attribute such as mind or consciousness. The idealistic fallacy can be further exposed by analyzing the intriguing suggestion of Sir James Jeans and others that God is the Master Mathematician. Jeans, being a notable astronomer and mathematician himself, was impressed by the extent to which the behavior of everything in the cosmos can be expressed in mathematical terms. From this scientific truism he took a dizzying leap and concluded that mathematics, as applied by a Divine Mathematician, is the very foundation of the universe.

But mathematics merely expresses the *relation* between things or symbolizes them; numbers are not the things themselves, nor do they constitute a higher reality. All men drafted under the United States Selective Service Act are assigned numbers. In certain connections and for certain purposes the conscripts are referred to by these numbers. This does not mean that they suddenly become mere mathematical symbols or that those symbols become somehow more real than the flesh-and-blood persons they represent. The same considerations apply to automobiles and the registration plate each of them is required to display. Though under certain circumstances a car will be referred to by its registration number, the solid materiality of the machine remains just the same.

Now ideas in general, of which numbers are only one class, likewise express and symbolize the relations between definite material objects and events. What the idealist does in essence is illegitimately to identify the things that are symbolized with the symbols used; magically to transform objects and events into symbols or ideas, and then the whole universe itself into Idea. This unwarranted metaphysical abstraction he proceeds to call God or the Absolute.

On the ethical side, the worst feature of Hegel's Idealism is that since the entire universe, including all human life and activity, emanates from God's own omni-creative consciousness, evil becomes unreal. For if every act is the expression of the Absolute Mind, the Universal Goodness, then everything that exists and everything men do must be good; the most excruciating physical pain and the most devastating mental anguish become negligible throbbings within the Divine Experience. So there is left no genuine distinction between good and bad; and the nerve of morality is cut. In fact the idealist philosophy was widely used as a system of apologetics for the *status quo;* and because for Hegel the state was the highest embodiment of the Absolute, the logical consequence was the attitude that the state can do no wrong.

The most valuable element in Hegel was his recognition of the fundamentally dynamic and evolutionary character of the universe and human society; and his emphasis on the interrelatedness of things. Hegel saw the whole of existence as a great complex dialectical movement, meaning that contradictions, identified as thesis and antithesis, continually work themselves out and merge in a higher stage identified as the synthesis. Idealism, however, turns things completely upside down by attributing this dialectical movement to conscious mind instead of matter.

It was Hegel's dialectical view of reality, corrected and revised through the elimination of his idealistic metaphysics, that Marx and Engels appropriated and used as one of the foundation stones in their philosophy. They were wise enough to combine what was valuable in Hegelianism with what they found true in the existing materialist tradition. What they did, in effect, was to take the dialectical part of Hegel's *dialectical* Idealism and the materialistic part of the old, mechanical, *undialectical* Materialism and weave them together in the new synthesis of Dialectical Materialism. In so doing they turned Hegel's cosmology right side up by making, in their system, matter instead of mind the basic stuff of the universe.

A contemporary of Hegel in Germany was Arthur Schopenhauer, pessimist-in-chief of philosophers, who, deliberately scheduling his lectures at the University of Berlin at the same hours as Hegel's, retired in a huff from teaching when he was unable to lure away the latter's students. Schopenhauer minced no words in commenting on his rival: "The height of audacity in serving up pure nonsense, in stringing together senseless and extravagant mazes of words, such as had previously only been known in madhouses, was finally reached in Hegel, and became the instrument of the most barefaced general mystification that has ever taken place, with a result which will appear fabulous to posterity, and will remain a monument to German stupidity." [68]

Yet Schopenhauer then proceeded, in *The World as Will and Idea,* to present a philosophic system that was just as mystifying as Hegel's, and even more extravagant. For Schopenhauer the world as Idea was the material, external side of existence; the world as Will was the internal, dynamic, most fundamental aspect of existence. In place of Hegel's all-embracing cosmic Mind as the basis of everything, Schopenhauer put an all-embracing cosmic Will—a Will definitely malignant, irrational, inhuman. Schopenhauer, then, was one of the very few notable philosophers who was clearly pessimistic in his interpretation of the universe. Thus his philosophy serves as a partial corrective to the false optimism of most philosophers, who have read their hopes and ideals into the structure of reality.

In his own way, however, Schopenhauer was as anthropomorphic as anyone else. For he ascribed to the cosmos the human attributes of mind, will and evil. Instead of postulating a good Mind or an all-inclusive God at the very heart of things, he postulated an evil Will, in essence an all-inclusive Devil. The excellent lesson that Schopenhauer's pan-Satanism teaches is that if we indulge in the pathetic fallacy of imputing to the universe qualities that emerge only in living forms, there is at least as much of a case for imputing the bad qualities as the good.

Friedrich Nietzsche followed Schopenhauer in regarding Will as the activating principle at the heart of the cosmos.

Bracing himself with crude interpretations of the Darwinian theory of evolution, he defined this Will as a brutal, assertive, and amoral Will to Power. In the human race this Will to Power manifests itself, according to Nietzsche, in the survival and superiority of the strongest, the most ruthless, the most masterful. Nietzsche had an extreme contempt for women. He was militantly opposed to democracy and bitterly attacked Christianity, primarily on the grounds that it encourages the democratic way of life. His ideal man was the tough and aristocratic hero recklessly engaging in strife, danger, and adventure and boldly setting himself up above all current views of good and bad. In his most brilliant book, *Thus Spake Zarathustra,* Nietzsche wrote, "A good war halloweth any cause."

This fierce philosophy, paradoxically enough produced by a constitutional invalid, later became a stimulus and inspiration for the German Nazis under Adolf Hitler. The Nietzschean Will to Power was equated with the Will to Dominate the World; the Nietzschean stress on biological superiority and eugenics, with the right of the master race to rule mankind. Nietzsche's wild and turbulent outpourings carried the individualistic, the romantic, and above all the egocentric note in modern philosophy, especially as evinced in the German versions of Idealism, to a frightening culmination. When philosophers start to take seriously the fantasy that the whole vast panorama of existence is spun out of our own thought, they are embarking on a course of colossal and perilous conceit. And no matter how much they attempt to cover up or escape from the original subjective assumption, they are bound to wind up in the most dangerous extremes.

Yet even Nietzsche, much of whose work appeared in the form of startling epigrams and a kind of prose-poetry, sometimes yields insights and speculations of real Humanist value, such as the vision of an eventual Superman who will surpass present-day man as much as man does the highest species of animals. One is repelled by the cruel, egoistic, hard-boiled sort of Superman that Nietzsche had in mind, but the idea of a new species beyond man is invigorating. Let us listen for a moment to the voice of Zarathustra himself:

> *I teach you beyond-man.* Man is a something that shall be surpassed. What have ye done to surpass him?
>
> All beings hitherto have created something beyond themselves: and are ye going to be the ebb of of this great tide and rather revert to the animal than surpass man? . . .
>
> Beyond-man is the significance of earth. Your will shall say: beyond-man shall be the significance of earth.
>
> I conjure you, my brethren, *remain faithful to earth* and do not believe those who speak unto you of superterrestrial hopes! Poisoners they are whether they know it or not. . . .
>
> What is great in man is that he is a bridge and not a goal: what can be loved in man is that he is a *transition* and a *destruction*. . . .
>
> I love him who worketh and inventeth to build a house for beyond-man and make ready for him earth, animal, and plant; for thus he willeth his own destruction.[69]

Closely associated with the different types of philosophic and religious Idealism is Pantheism. The God of Pantheism is impersonal and is immanent throughout the material universe; he is not independent of, apart from or above the cosmos, but identical with it. Therefore this God is not a Creator or First Cause in the Christian sense, but an indwelling, purposeful, omnipresent Power carrying things onward in the direction of higher values. For the Pantheist all matter, from the highest living organisms down to the tiniest inorganic particles, is somehow imbued with spirit or consciousness. In ancient times the Stoics constituted the most important school of Pantheists; and in the East, Buddhism contains obvious pantheistic elements.

In modern philosophy it was Giordano Bruno, an ex-friar of the Dominican order, who in the sixteenth century re-kindled the pantheist tradition. Bruno thought God could be found in no particular place precisely because he is every-where—alive and creative throughout the whole infinite uni-verse that is his glorious body. Pantheism has always been a favorite haven for mystics who wish to feel themselves com-pletely absorbed in the All or the One or the Infinite; and for poets who seek to find a pervasive cosmological and aesthetic background for the beauty and grandeur that they see in the natural world. In truth, Pantheism received its consummate expression in the English Nature poets of the early nineteenth century, especially in William Wordsworth. This passage from his "Lines Composed a Few Miles Above Tintern Abbey" is a superb rendering of the pantheistic conception:

> . . . . . . And I have felt
> A presence that disturbs me with the joy
> Of elevated thoughts; a sense sublime
> Of something far more deeply interfused,
> Whose dwelling is the light of setting suns,
> And the round ocean and the living air,
> And the blue sky, and in the mind of man;
> A motion and a spirit, that impels
> All thinking things, all objects of all thought,
> And rolls through all things.

The sum and substance of Nature, as interpreted for exam-ple by Spinoza, is not equivalent to the God of Pantheism. For that God is a value-bearing Being with a strong upward trend toward what men consider good, and to that extent is anthropomorphic. Spinoza's God, however, is a synonym for Nature and neither promotes nor opposes human values. It is therefore a mistake to classify Spinoza as a Pantheist.

The fact that Spinoza constantly used the word *God*, even

though he was not a theist, leads us to the general question of the redefinition of religious and philosophic terms. This procedure has gone on throughout the history of thought and is surely legitimate if it remains within sensible bounds. It becomes philosophic double-talk, however, if the redefinition violates the integrity of language; or if it is made in order to avoid an issue or to escape public disfavor. Unfortunately, much of the redefining that has taken place in religion and philosophy has been, it seems, primarily for the purpose of appeasing clerical, academic, or political authorities. And there is some indication that even the greatest of philosophers, such as Spinoza and Aristotle, felt constrained, by reason of social and political pressures, to compromise in the matter of phraseology.* Many of the old semantic taboos have continued, of course, right down to the present day.

Besides the questionable redefinitions of God that equate him with the totality of Nature, we find today a number of redefinitions that transform God into simply another name for well-known ethical tendencies in men which we all acknowledge to exist and which most of us wish to encourage. For instance, Professor Durant Drake writes that "God is the universal self in each of us, our good will and idealism and intelligence which binds us together and drives us on by inner compulsion toward that ideal life for which in our better moments we strive." [70] Professor Jesse H. Holmes describes God as the unifying element within that moves men to unity in a brotherly world. Dr. Henry Nelson Wieman, who produces a new concept of Deity every time he puts pen to paper, says: "God is that interaction between individuals, groups and ages which generates and promotes the greatest possible mutuality of good." [71] And a Rumanian Humanist, Dimitrie Draghicesco, defines God as the more or less complete omnipotence, omni-

---

* There is in America today a group of essentially Humanist clergymen and philosophers who call themselves "naturalistic theists," a phrase I find self-contradictory.

science, and benevolence to which man as a race can approximate in the long run.

It is my opinion that these types of redefinition engender considerable intellectual and philosophic confusion. If our supreme aim is to achieve on this earth the good society and the brotherhood of man, together with as close an approach as possible to human omniscience and omnipotence, then we shall get much further by describing our goal as precisely that than by befuddling people through labeling it *God*.

An old Chinese proverb avers: "The beginning of wisdom is calling things by their right names." This means in part that for the sake of clarity and truth there must be a line drawn somewhere, beyond which a word cannot properly be used. My own proposal for a minimum definition of God is Matthew Arnold's, "a Power not ourselves that makes for righteousness," with that Power understood not merely as the magnetic quality of ideas and ideals, but as an active force working for the good, independent of human beings and prior to their evolution. This suggestion identifies the differentiating characteristic of God as some type of powerful purpose at the heart of things pushing toward the higher values.

Unless we insist on limiting in some manner the acceptable meaning of God, it is easy, as Professor Otto maintains, to prove the existence of God by "dilution into vagueness"; through reducing the definition of the term "until it means no more than everyone, even the confessed atheist, will have to admit to exist. Thus the definition of God virtually proves his existence. . . . The word *God* is made to stand for so much that it loses all distinctive meaning. . . . Belief bought at this price costs too much. It not only impoverishes the religious life . . . but it tends to dissipate the mental discipline so laboriously and slowly achieved by men." [72]

The ethics of words is also involved in the many redefinitions of other terms such as *immortality* and *religion* itself. I think that current redefinitions of religion are particularly confusing, since they bring under it such very different and in some cases positively irreligious phenomena as nationalism, communism, and even atheism. Some of these redefinitions would by implication assign the name of religion to any socially organized enterprise that succeeds in winning the devotion and emotions of men. On this basis baseball, trade unions, political parties, armies, and poetry societies all become forms of religious endeavor. One of the broadest contemporary definitions of religion that I have come across occurs in the *Humanist Manifesto* issued by the religious Humanists. This document states that "Religion consists of those actions, purposes and experiences which are humanly significant." It is evident that the *Manifesto* makes religion cover practically everything of import that men do, think, or experience. It is only by means of this exceedingly loose interpretation of religion that the *Manifesto* group is able to classify Humanism as a religion.

Traditionally religion has involved appeal to, reliance on, or faith in supernatural powers, elements, or states of being. However, my minimum definition for a functioning religion is that it must be an over-all way of life (including a comprehensive attitude towards the universe and man), to which a group of persons gives supreme commitment and which they implement through the shared quest of ideals. Under this definition Humanism qualifies as a religion. Nonetheless, I prefer to call Humanism a philosophy or way of life.

The religious Humanists, whatever their faults in the use of language, reject the metaphysics and the Gods of Dualism, Idealism, and Pantheism. All three of these major philosophies represent, at their best, a steadfast search for a great good purpose in the universe as a whole; but in this quest all of them, to one extent or another, interpret the cosmos in its inner essence or its essential origin as patterned after the model of man himself. They all have their source, no matter how impressive their superstructures or how elaborate their ideologies, in a generous measure of wishful thinking. Humanism, on its part, reiterates that Nature considered as a totality, has no purpose, no preferences, no prevision of the future, no awareness of the past, no consciousness or mind.

3. THE UNIVERSE OF NATURE

Humanism is an *affirmative* philosophy. It is essentially yea-saying. It says: Yes, this mighty and abundant Nature is our home; in it we ever live and move and have our being. This Nature produced the marvel of life and the race of man. It sustains us with its varied goods and stirs us with its wonderful beauty. Yes, this is a good earth and upon it we can create a worthwhile and happy existence for all humanity. Yes, we men possess the glory of mind and the power of freedom; we know the grace of body and the splendor of love. We are grateful for the many simple pleasures that are ours, for the manifold enjoyments which art and culture and science bring. We mortals delight in the sweetness of living rather than lamenting over its brevity. And we rejoice in being able to hand on the torch of life to future generations. Yes, this life is enough; this earth is enough; this great and eternal Nature is enough.

These affirmatives imply a number of negatives. There is no place in the Humanist world-view for either immortality or God in the valid meanings of those terms. Humanism contends that instead of the gods creating the cosmos, the cosmos, in the individualized form of human beings giving rein to their imagination, created the gods.

The central pillar in the Humanist metaphysics is that the underlying and continuing foundation of the universe is not mind or consciousness, but matter in its multiple and changing modes. The truth of this position is not dependent upon the definition of matter in terms of any particular stuff. Our position is based simply on the proposition that objective reality—an external world—call it matter, energy, substance, events, electricity or what you will, exists antecedent to and indepen-

dent of the human mind, a Divine Mind, or any other conceivable mind.

The Humanist is, of course, opposed to tricky redefinitions
of the physical world that dissolve it into complete non-
materiality; and therefore to the tendency of some thinkers to
swing from the former extreme of conceiving matter as altogether inert and without motion to the opposite extreme of
conceiving motion as altogether vacuous and without any
tangible substance that moves. Even radiant energy, such as
light, X rays, and the electromagnetic waves that make the
radio possible, manifests itself in definite particles, or *quanta*
in the technical language of science, however infinitesimal in
size.*

The universe of Nature shows no favoritism toward man or
any other of its creatures. Nature is no more interested in
Homo sapiens than in the tiger, the rat, the extinct dinosaur,
or any other form of life; and it is no more interested in living
forms as such than in rivers, stars, atoms, or any other kind
of inanimate phenomena. As Santayana says of Nature: "Like
Polonius's cloud, she will always suggest some new ideal because she has none of her own." [73] "If we impute to Cronos any
intent to beget his children, we must also impute to him an
intent to devour them. . . . The universe can wish particular
things only in so far as particular beings wish them; only in
its relative capacity can it find things good, and only in its
relative capacity can it be good for anything." [74]

Nature's neutrality toward the human race does not mean
that man is an alien in this world. Despite its more turbulent
and untamed moods, Nature as manifested upon this earth
has provided, though without prevision or intent, conditions
sufficiently favorable for life to flourish and develop for at
least a billion years. Nature has made possible the evolution

---

* Unless otherwise indicated, I use the term *matter* in the broad
sense of including the various types of radiant energy.

of the species Man and his conquest of our planet from pole to pole. During the long evolutionary progress the mellower, life-encouraging aspects of Nature have on the whole outweighed its harsher, life-threatening aspects. And it is reassuring to feel that beyond our kinship with our fellowmen, which sometimes tends to wear thin, we can have a real sense of kinship with the natural world that is the source of our being and the locus of whatever happiness we attain.

The Humanist view that Nature is indifferent to human aims, that from it all calamities as well as all blessings flow, by-passes the so-called "problem of evil" with which theologians and philosophers have wrestled throughout the centuries. This problem revolves around the question of how an infinitely beneficent and omnipotent God could have created a world that has within it so much misery, cruelty, and stupidity. The theists have invented many a myth to explain this situation, such as the original sin and fall of man, and the existence of a supernatural Satan who fights the Lord and is responsible for bringing evil into the cosmos. In this interpretation evil becomes an important element in the very constitution of things. Another, more sophisticated myth is that evil is nothing but a human illusion, an error of mortal mind; or that it is a god in disguise, coming from God himself, and with the function of testing and strengthening men's souls for eternal life.

For Humanists, however, there is no deep and inscrutable theological or metaphysical problem connected with the presence of evil in experience. For them there is no evil except in relation to human life, strivings, and aims. Even disease germs and droughts are evil only as they interfere with human well-being. Most evils are man-made; all evils must be man-solved. There is, in a deep-going philosophical sense, no more a problem as to why evil should exist than as to why good should exist. Philosophers who attribute to the universe categories like good and evil, which are applicable only to human

conduct and evaluations, are not merely guilty of anthropomorphism; they also involve themselves in new problems that
are by their very nature insoluble.

The traditional Christian attitude toward evil is, from the
Humanist standpoint, itself an evil, because that attitude
ascribes to evil a fearful cosmic importance that bears down
on men psychologically and has positively bad moral effects.
Walter Lippmann's comments are illuminating: "Things are
neutral," he affirms, "and evil is a certain way of experiencing
them. To realize this is to destroy the awfulness of evil. I use
the word 'awful' in its exact sense, and I mean that in abandoning the notion that evil has to be reconciled with a theory
of how the world is governed, we rob it of universal significance. We deflate it. . . . It may be said that the effect of the
modern approach is to take evils out of the context of superstition. They cease to be signs and portents symbolizing the
whole of human destiny and become specific and distinguishable situations which have to be dealt with. . . . They are then
seen to be of long duration and of short, preventable, curable,
or inevitable. As long as all evils are believed somehow to fit
into a divine, if mysterious, plan, the effort to eradicate them
must seem on the whole futile, and even impious." [75]

Take the matter of physical pain. Many lengthy and learned
treatises have been written in an attempt to reconcile the
existence of pain with the justice or kindness of a divine
Creator. The orthodox Christian explanation is that no such
thing as pain marred the original Garden of Eden and that
pain came into the world only as a result of Adam's sin. If,
however, we turn to a scientific analysis of pain in terms of
biology and psychology, there is no mystery at all.

The animal ability to experience pain has definite survival
value, because it warns the animal, including the species Man,
of what is dangerous to health and life. If human beings were
unable to feel pain, they would be far less capable of coping
with disease and warding off death. Pain usually indicates that
something is wrong with the organism and that something

should be done to cure the trouble. The fact that the reduction of pain to a minimum is one of the important Humanist aims does not contravene this analysis. We have a classic example of religious bewilderment over an artificially conceived problem of pain in the Book of Job. Job, a virtuous and holy man who believed in divine retribution for human wickedness, worked himself up into a very agitated mental state because he found it difficult, if not impossible, to understand why he was chronically afflicted with agonizing boils.

The Humanist runs into no such dilemmas, since he does not expect the universe or any nonhuman power to care about his pains or his pleasures, his goodness or his good. The difference between good and bad is of crucial importance in human living, but that is not a sufficient reason for extending the import of good, or of both good and evil, to the whole cosmos. Again, there is a real distinction between life and nonlife, between the animate and inanimate; and between man and all the rest of Nature. These natural dualisms within Nature cannot be denied, but they by no means justify the setting up of a super-Nature in addition to the one we know, which is exactly what the traditional philosophic Dualisms do.

Most misunderstood of all and most likely to lead into philosophic error is the difference between thinking as a process and any other process in either man or Nature. The faculty of reason lifts man so far above all other known things in the world that philosophers have tended to elevate reason itself, apart from man, into a cosmic principle. Thus the theists have held that a Supreme Intelligence is guiding the universe; the Platonic dualists that eternal Ideas are the archetypes, the original models of all that exists; and the idealists that Mind is the actual stuff of existence.

In opposition to these various misinterpretations of the place of mind in the world, naturalistic Humanism reasserts that mind is a function only of living creatures organized in a certain complex fashion; and that to widen the functioning and locus of mind beyond the activities of such creatures is bad logic and bad philosophy. It is possible that in time experimentation will show that, in addition to man possessing the power of thought, some of the higher animals such as apes or horses can carry through elementary processes of reasoning. This will not alter the basic philosophic situation. Humanists, while they view mind as of far less importance in the universe as a whole than do the supernaturalistic philosophers, ascribe to it considerably more importance on the human level than do those philosophers. For Humanists contend that the use of reason in place of religious faith or intuition or authority is far and away man's best reliance.

Humanism believes that human thinking is as natural as walking or breathing, that it is inseparably associated with the functioning of the brain, and that ideas, far from existing independently in some separate realm, arise and have reality only when a complex living organism such as man is interacting with his environment and is intellectually active.

It is most essential to note that this statement placing ideas and thinking in their natural context does not mean that ideas themselves are tiny material particles whirling about inside the brain. It means simply that when ideas, which are nonmaterial meanings expressing the relations between things, occur in human thought, they always do so as functions or accompaniments of physical events or action patterns in the cerebral cortex of the brain. And they are always transmitted in human communication through some sign or symbol that is likewise of a material nature, however attenuated.

Activity within the brain is necessary for a man to have a new idea or recall an old one. Thinking, physiologists tell us, even emits electrical charges. When a man has an idea, the idea itself is not stored away inside the cortex as if one were putting something in a box; what is stored away is a certain inner pattern among the multitudinous cerebral nerve cells. When that pattern, which may become a habit, is reawakened or re-excited, the idea or ideas previously correlated with it leap into being again. The mind of an individual is the whole system of ideas or meanings he has acquired; but only a small portion of this system comes into use at any one time. The rest functions only as it is elicited by the proper stimulus.

For the individual who is thinking to himself ideas are private and to that extent subjective. But ideas are also objective in that human beings can communicate them to one another and can understand one another's meanings, when these are adequately defined. The fact that ideas can be objective and yet are nonmaterial has been a strong factor in impelling philosophers, especially those of a dualist bent, to set up a realm of ideas or mind apart from and above Nature. For the Humanist, ideas, whether simple or complex, trifling or noble, true or untrue, are not apart from but are *a part of* Nature. The experience of thinking or having ideas is *distinguishable* from men's other activities, but not *existentially separable*. Since ideas are always the ideas of thinking beings, there could be no ideas at all without such beings. There can be no thought without thinkers. Yet without thinkers there can be the *potentiality* of thought and ideas. Before the species Man evolved, Nature possessed the potentiality of producing both thinkers and ideas; but that potentiality did not mean that mind was already real. The manifest truth that the mental processes of men are germane to Nature, that Nature is intelligible to a very large degree, does not imply, as in the idealist tradition, that Nature itself is a mental process or has intelligence.

One of the chief motives in the philosophic tendency to set up a supernatural sphere of influence has been the endeavor to escape from the constant change, precariousness, and impermanence of the world around us. To offset these qualities of everyday existence, philosophers have sought to establish a realm where everything of value would be absolutely stable and secure. Thus the Christian heaven enshrines permanently, beyond all danger of decay or blemish, what are considered the major human values. The Platonic realm of eternal Ideas serves the same purpose, while the diverse supernaturalist

Gods hold in their own minds the special values that their respective worshipers cherish. Socially the effect of these compensatory metaphysical schemes has usually been conservative and has helped to preserve the traditional forms and structures of society. As Dr. Howard Selsam has acutely observed, the conservatives try to prevent change in practice and then abolish it *in theory* as well.

Humanism, on the other hand, recognizes change as a fundamental element in the universe and society. As the ancient Greek philosopher Heraclitus taught, all things are in ceaseless flux. Solid structures like mountains are only relatively permanent; in time they, too, will be worn away and their substance become part of other phenomena. It is useless to deny change or to attempt to suppress it. Much more fruitful for human beings is the policy of controlling and channeling intelligently the changing course of events.

A perennial question relevant at this point is whether any particular cosmological outlook logically leads to any particular socio-economic viewpoint such as that of conservatism, liberalism, or radicalism. My answer is decidedly in the negative. We cannot with certainty deduce any individual's socio-economic attitude from his attitude toward the universe, or vice versa. Today many Christian supernaturalists are radical in their politics and economics, and freely quote the Bible to support their opinions. On the other hand many antisupernaturalists are conservative or even reactionary on political and economic issues.

During the French Revolution, Robespierre, one of the most radical leaders, was hostile towards atheists and asserted: "Atheism is aristocratic. The idea of a Supreme Being who watches over oppressed innocence and punishes triumphant crime is essentially the idea of the people." [76] Furthermore, it would be possible for leftists to reconstruct the idea of immortality so that heaven would be regarded as the due reward of those who worked for the achievement of socialism, and hell as the deserved destination of all capitalists. Despite these considerations, the history of thought shows that on the whole the unorthodox in religion and philosophy have likewise been prone to break away from orthodoxy in other fields. There is undoubtedly a psychological connection here, but no binding logical one.

A repeated mistake that system-building philosophers, especially those of the idealist school, have made is to assign to the universe a fictitious unity. The great Cosmic Mind of Idealism binds together the entire universe in a unified totality, an all-encompassing monism. Humanism rejects this conception. We speak loosely of the universe to designate the whole of reality; but when we come to analyze the matter closely, we find that the infinitely diverse world of Nature is a many rather than a one, a multi-verse rather than a universe. Here Humanists, in supporting the idea of pluralism instead of monism, have taken a cue from William James, though they disagree with other aspects of his philosophy. James wrote: "Things are 'with' one another in many ways, but nothing includes everything or dominates over everything. . . . The pluralistic world is thus more like a federal republic than like an empire or a kingdom. . . . Monism, on the other hand, insists that when you come to reality as such, to the reality of realities, everything is present to *everything* else in one vast instantaneous co-implicated completeness." [77]

There are complicated and far-reaching interrelationships throughout Nature, but there are also constant cross-currents and conflicting forces. There are partial unities, to be sure, but no one, vast, overarching unity. The different entities that make up the world enter temporarily into identifiable systems, like that of the human body itself; but there is no one system, completely unified, that fuses together tightly all the sub-systems. Through the law of gravity every particle of matter has, of course, a physical effect, however infinitesimal, on every other particle of matter in the universe; but this does not entail such a close interwelding of material units that a universal monism results.

While all material entities are related to one another in respect to gravity, most of them are totally unrelated at any one time to most others in most ways. On the other hand, no entity is independent of all other entities. Every thing has some relations with other things; events overlap, interpenetrate, intermesh like the teeth of a cogwheel. Relationships greatly vary, as Dewey makes clear: "Some things are relatively insulated from the influence of other things; some things are easily invaded by others; some things are fiercely attracted to conjoin their activities with those of others. Experience exhibits every kind of connexion from the most intimate to mere external juxtaposition." [78]

No matter how far back, in our analysis, we push the cause-effect sequences of the universe, we are certain to discover a plurality of event-streams that can be accurately described only in terms of a plurality of principles. There was no *one* event that started the universe going, and in fact no beginning at all. For Humanism, matter is ever active in individual, discrete forms. Individuality in this sense is an ultimate principle of the universe. The constant activity in the world radiates from many different centers. This radical pluralism of Nature means that the cosmos is a vast, complex multiplicity and makes impossible the absolute and universal determinism expounded by certain religions and philosophies.

The abstract term *universe* designates all of Nature as one subject of discourse; but this does not turn its infinite many-ness into an all-embracing oneness. The pluralism which I am suggesting eliminates the old metaphysical problem of the One and the Many: the philosophic riddle of how the obvious many-ness of the world could arise and persist when all is supposedly One. This insoluble conundrum does not exist for the Humanist, who holds that the universe always was a Many.

4. CONTINGENCY, DETERMINISM, AND FREEDOM

The metaphysical pluralism which I have been discussing indicates that what we call *chance* or *contingency* is not merely a word for expressing subjective human ignorance of cause and effect, but that chance exists objectively outside of and regardless of the human mind. This idea was a favorite one of James and goes back as far as Aristotle and Epicurus in ancient Greece. Professor Kallen voices the same idea when he asserts that Nature possesses "*a surgent spontaneity* which can be referred to no ground, must be taken for its own ground and could as well not happen as happen." [79] [Italics mine— C. L.]

Chance does not *do* anything; it has no causal efficacy. It is the name we give to a specific type of occurrence. This interpretation of chance does not contradict the concept of scientific law. For scientific laws are the expression of if-then relations: if H_2O, then water; if water at 212 degrees Fahrenheit, then boiling water. But Nature does not guarantee or issue a command that at any particular time and place two parts of hydrogen will merge with one part of oxygen or that water will reach a temperature of 212°. Nature proceeds according to necessity only in the sense that when a certain *if* is actualized, a certain *then* accompanies it or will follow.

The initiation of the *if* is a matter of contingency. A scientific law always refers to a system of events that is to a greater or lesser degree isolated; events may and do intrude from outside any such determinate system and prevent the occurrence of a particular if-then, cause-effect sequence that otherwise would have occurred. In the Humanist metaphysics both necessity (or determinism or mechanism) and chance (or contingency or fortuity) are fundamental, pervasive, and permanent characteristics of the universe; and neither necessity nor chance can ever swallow up the other.

Professor Sterling P. Lamprecht sheds useful light on these points: "Contingency is often regarded as an alternative to mechanism. In fact it is a correlative aspect of Nature's ways. In our world we find that forces, once initiated, work out to their inevitable consequences. But the initiation of forces is not itself decreed. The laws of Nature are statements of the mechanical phase of Nature. They state the uniformities of correlation and sequence which events manifest. The laws of Nature are not, however, dictates that compel procedure— they are not statutes or prescriptive enactments. The presence of contingency in Nature is not evident at a glance because it is not effectively exploited by inanimate agents. Inanimate agents react to the actual stimulus of the moment; they react, it might be said, to the superficial. Intelligent agents react to more than the actual stimulus; they react to the potentialities of the actual. And these potentialities are always plural. . . . The alternative possibilities were present in Nature from the start even though they received no notable exploitation until intelligent creatures came to pass." [80]

In his book *Nature and History*, Professor Lamprecht amplifies: "We say, and we are entitled to say, 'If this is done, then such-and-such will ensue.' But the *if* of this statement is as metaphysically evident as the *then*. The *if* is as truly a recognition of the contingency of the efficient factor of which the law does not even try to give an account, as the *then* is a recognition of the necessity of the outcome. . . . Necessity and contingency, so far from being unconnected ideas to be taken, one wholesale and the other retail, are supplementary ideas which belong together in the analysis of every separate event." [81]

Humanism takes the position that human life, like Nature as a whole, is shot through with contingency. When chance manifests itself in human affairs, we frequently describe it as accident or coincidence or luck—good luck or bad luck. The approximately 500 persons in the United States who are struck dead by lightning each year are victims of chance in the form of very bad luck. On the other hand, if you are walking along any street, road, or path and unexpectedly find a purse containing $100, that is an illustration of objective chance in the form of good luck. Chance events are an everyday occurrence in the life of the average human being. Men often go to considerable pains to guard themselves against the possible bad results of chance happenings, as when they take out fire insurance. However, I do not mean to imply that every outbreak of fire is a matter of chance, since the crime of arson, which some people apparently consider a major sport, is still a considerable worry for police and fire departments. Many of the events that were formerly considered miracles were instances of chance. And it is interesting that contemporary law should classify as "acts of God" extraordinary and unpredictable events in Nature that occur without human intervention, most of which also properly come under the heading of contingency.

The most readily discernible instances of chance are to be seen in dramatic accidents in which independently initiated causal series or event-streams meet at a specific point in time and space. When a stroke of lightning kills a man playing golf, there is no common, relevant cause to be found that brought the man and the lightning into conjunction at that particular moment. Or consider the terrible collision on April 14, 1912, when the White Star liner *Titanic* on its maiden voyage ran full speed in the middle of the night into an immense iceberg in the North Atlantic. Since there were lifeboats for only half the passengers, more than 1,500 persons were lost when the steamship sank about three hours after the crash.

If we could chart the respective chains of causation that led the *Titanic*, sailing from Southampton, to its fatal encounter with the iceberg, drifting inexorably south, we should discover that in the background there was no conjoint, initiating cause that set both event-series in motion and impelled them to their rendezvous in the Atlantic Ocean. It was clearly a chance happening. Even if a team of scientific experts had been able somehow to trace back the two causal streams and ascertain that the collision was predestined from the very moment when the *Titanic* departed from England on the afternoon of April 10, that conclusion would not have upset my thesis. For the space-time relation of the iceberg and the *Titanic*, as the ship started on its voyage, was itself a matter of contingency, since there was no relevant cause to account for that precise relationship.

Professor Dewey has generalized the principle of chance for the scientific enterprise as a whole: "Science is bound to assume, no matter how far back it goes, a given distribution of material particles for which no reason can be assigned; these are just brutely so and so; moreover all scientific explanation is selective; laws must limit themselves to a small number of variables; and this fact is identical with recognition that for law (and the sum of laws) facts excluded as irrelevant are contingent. . . . Contingency is final because things in the universe have individuality, as well as having relations which are necessary, universal and invariant." [82]

An old argument against the existence of objective chance is that if there were an all-knowing mind in the universe, that mind could predict, from its knowledge of the complete state of affairs throughout the cosmos at any moment, everything that would happen everywhere, down to the minutest detail, for all future time. On the face of it this argument has an air of plausibility, but it is fallacious in that the very assumption of an all-knowing mind amounts to an assumption of the deterministic, anti-chance thesis that has to be proved. Such a mind could have an all-embracing preview of the future only if all existing entities gave rise to cause-effect sequences that swept unendingly ahead in rigid uniformities undisturbed by any chance encounters or deviations.

In short, universal omniscience, as distinct from specific scientific predictions concerning a limited or isolated segment of existence, definitely implies universal determinism. The Humanist claim that the existence of objective chance rules out universal determinism constitutes, therefore, another argument against the omniscient Gods of traditional supernaturalism. That the Humanists are not merely erecting a straw man here is easily seen in the fact that certain religions of inexorable determinism, like Calvinism and Mohammedanism, recognize and indeed insist upon the deterministic character of their supernatural God. God as pure determinism also appears in certain religious forms centering around human crises like that of death. Thus the well-known Protestant ritual includes the words: "The Lord gave, and the Lord hath taken away." And death notices sometimes begin: "Whereas God in his infinite wisdom has taken our dearly beloved. . . ."

It follows from our chain of reasoning that if an omniscient, omnipotent, all-determining God exists or if the material universe in itself adds up to complete determinism, then there can be no real human freedom. For in either case all human actions, decisions, and thoughts are predetermined just like all other events. The great cosmic juggernaut rolls on and nobody can alter its course in the slightest. The Humanist proposition that both pluralism and chance are characteristics of Nature is of portentous significance for our analysis of the nature of man, because that proposition opens the door to freedom of choice for human beings.

Personal freedom of choice ("free will" in traditional terminology) means the capacity of conscious men to make real decisions in situations where significant alternatives exist. Obviously, physical, economic, social, and other factors always condition and limit human choices. Our mental and physical inheritance, the extent and type of our education, our income and kind of job, in fact, our total environment past and present, all influence our current behavior. Professor Paul Tillich of the University of Chicago Divinity School expands on this thought: "When I make a decision, it is the concrete totality of everything that constitutes my being which decides, not an epistemological subject. This refers to body structure, psychic strivings, spiritual character. It includes the communities to which I belong, the past unremembered and remembered, the environment which has shaped me, the world which has made an impact on me. It refers to all my former decisions." [83]

By no means all human functioning is the result of deliberate free choice. Much of our internal functioning is fortunately automatic—indeed, deterministic—such as breathing and the circulation of the blood. Undoubtedly, too, many human actions are purely impulsive or governed by long-established habit. It is my firm opinion, however, that in a large proportion of our conscious actions there is an element of indeterminateness at the moment of choosing; and a decisive residue of freedom in the act of willing or volition at that moment which the weight of the past, great as it is, does not offset.

Human freedom always operates within certain definite limits, including those laid down by the conditioning of the past. Furthermore, man as an animal has a specific physical structure that can function and survive only if a number of environmental conditions are present. We cannot fly through the air like birds or swim under the water like fish. And in general men must conform to natural laws such as that of gravity. In this sense human life can aptly be compared, to take a cherished example, with the game of chess. There are stated and established rules of chess, representing determinism, that every player is required to follow. Yet within that broad framework an enormous variety of individual moves are possible; and the moves actually made exhibit freedom of choice. Of course the same principle holds true for all competitive games and sports.

Freedom of choice is inextricably bound up with the capacity of thought. The word *intelligence* comes from the Latin *inter* (between) and *legere* (to choose). Choosing means making up one's mind. In most cases, when confronted by a problem, we do not have to take action instantly. We are able to propose to ourselves various hypothetical solutions and reason out the implications of each one. Professor George H. Mead, who taught for many years at the University of Chicago, has described the process: "It is the entrance of the alternative possibilities of future response into the determination of present conduct in any given environmental situation, and their operation, through the mechanism of the central nervous system, as part of the factors or conditions determining present behavior, which decisively contrasts intelligent conduct or behavior with reflex, instinctive, and habitual conduct or behavior—delayed reaction with immediate reaction." [84]

In other words, the enterprise of thinking, with its manipulation of ideas that symbolize things and events, enables men to stand aside temporarily from the flux of existence or at least that sector of it with which they are immediately concerned. Meanwhile, during a typical unit of reflection, they examine imaginatively and rehearse mentally the different possibilities or options that are open to them, and finally choose the one they wish to see actualized. It is the ever plural potentialities in Nature and in human life that give us the opportunity to make choices that count among alternatives that are real.

In the intellectual process that leads to a decision, the individual almost always uses general concepts. According to Professor Charles Hartshorne of the University of Texas, ". . . our very power to form general conceptions (in a sense in which these are beyond the reach of other animals) is the same as our being not determined by irresistible impulse, habit or antecedent character, to but one mode of acting in a given case. The openness to alternatives, the flexibility, of our response is the behavioristic aspect of our knowledge of the universal, as that which can be indifferently instanced by this particular *or* by that. Such instancing, by its very meaning, must have wide ranges of freedom. Freedom in the indeterministic sense is thus inherent in rational understanding as such, understanding through universals." [85]

Suppose that I wish to spend a month's vacation in travel. "Travel," then, is my general conception, and almost innumerable possibilities can be subsumed under it. I might go to

Europe, to the Far East, to the Rocky Mountain area of the United States, or to a thousand other places. My trip of course is limited by the amount of money and time I can spend on it. To make more explicit Professor Hartshorne's meaning, my ability to think of the general idea of "travel," to explore mentally many alternative plans and finally pick out one to carry through—all this is not mere play-acting for the selection of an itinerary that was predetermined prior even to my thought of traveling. It is a serious exercise in deliberation that in itself all but implies freedom of choice.

The determinist answer to all this is that the different solutions to a problem which come to mind, and our reasoning regarding them, are completely determined by our past thinking. The cause-effect sequences in our brains are just as determining, just as inescapable, as anywhere else in Nature. If we produce a genuinely new thought, that too follows from a definite cause-effect pattern in the cerebral cortex. The human will is simply the dynamic urge to carry out wishes and ideas that have become part of our being through the impact of the total cause-effect necessities both within us and without us. True freedom, according to this view, is the capacity for acting according to one's true character, to be altogether one's self, to be *self*-determined and not subject to outside coercion. In the words of Professor Gardner Williams, "Preference plus power contain the essence of freedom." [86]

This doctrine deserves careful consideration owing to the intelligence and consistency with which it has been formulated. The majority of naturalist and materialist philosophers have supported it. But I do not think it is a view to which Humanists should give their assent. The sounder position is that we human beings possess the freedom, as Professor Montague phrases it, "to modify and supplement our past by a spontaneous effort not predetermined by that past"; [87] that we are free either to improve upon that past or to fall below its standards. Most men, I am convinced, have an unmistakable feeling at the final moment of significant choice that they are making a free decision, that they can really decide which one of two or more roads to follow. This powerful intuition does not in itself amount to knowledge, yet cannot be disregarded by philosophers and psychologists.

The more extreme deterministic philosophies, like certain other world-views, have provided a psychological escape for harassed man. They have set up a supreme authority that either automatically or otherwise arrives at and enacts all decisions down to the very last detail of human conduct, and so relieves men from the trouble of solving their own difficulties and from worrying over a future whose course is already predestined.* Yet most of those who have purported to believe in some form of fatalism or universal necessity have *acted* as if they had freedom of choice; and this indicates, in my judgment, that the dynamic of freedom runs so deep in human nature that no mere theories can succeed in negating it.

The common-sense reaction of the average person is surely that what he does or does not do makes a real difference in the outcome of his affairs. The Humanist pushes this idea further by asserting that human thinking in particular makes a difference. The hard-core determinist gets himself into a peculiar quandary here. For he is compelled to admit that his own determinist philosophy and all his brilliant arguments in favor of it, including every phrase, word, and punctuation mark, were from way back bound to emerge in the exact form that they finally took; and that the iron law of cause and effect likewise led me inevitably to my conclusions and statements concerning freedom of choice. This is a self-stultifying position; if it were true, man would be a species of robot.

Cosmic determinism also robs the concept of potentiality of most of its meaning by reading back present actuality into the primordial state of things. For the determinist position is

---

* When, in Dostoievski's *The Brothers Karamazov,* Jesus returns to earth, the Grand Inquisitor proposes to burn him for the crime of having placed upon man "the fearful burden . . . the great anxiety and terrible agony" of deciding for himself "what is good and what is evil."

that at any one moment in the history of the universe every event that happens in the future is then and there somehow contained or implied. Thus there has existed only one universal potentiality throughout all time, namely the potentiality of the one actuality that necessarily occurs. There are no plural or alternate possibilities; each thing has, and things as a whole have, only one possible line of development. The present unfolds from the past as automatically as a motion picture is projected onto the screen from a roll of film, and the future is all settled in advance.

One reason for the specious appeal of absolute determinism is a rather common misunderstanding of the principle of cause and effect. Thus some educated people, among them even scientists, conceive of the present as merely the effect of preceding causes and neglect the fact that the present is itself an active cause. Every effect becomes a cause in its turn. The *present* present, as the spearhead of activity in the world, is always working upon, transforming or conserving what has been handed down to it by *former* presents that are now past. The past *as* past has no efficacy; it is dead and gone. It is efficacious only as it is embodied in present structures and activities.

Everything that exists—the whole vast aggregate of inanimate matter, the swarming profusion of earthly life, man in his every aspect—exists only as an event or events taking place at this instant moment which is now. To exist means universally to be a form or quality of activity in some temporal present. Whatever exists must possess immediacy.

The activity which took place in the irrevocable and irreversible past builds the foundations upon which the immediate present operates. What happened in the past establishes many limitations as well as potentialities; it always conditions present activity, and present activity conditions the events of the future. *But conditioning is not the same as determining.* And each day's present in its onward sweep creates fresh patterns of existence, maintains other patterns, and destroys still others.

The past and future are both imaginative concepts. They

assume, however, the status of concrete present existence upon our calendars where time is represented in terms of space and is therefore *mis*represented. Our calendars preserve the old notion of the world being *in* time and moving through it. We know, on the contrary, as the theory of relativity has helped to make plain, that time is a quality of activity or process, a relationship between events.

Human beings and their actions, like everything else, constitute the advancing front, the surging crest of an on-going movement that never stops. Living, doing, thinking men, together with the natural forces under their control, are an unceasing wave of the present. This dynamic, creative present, however conditioned and restricted by the effects of previous presents, possesses genuine initiative; as it moves forward, it pushes into the past the transformations it makes in the malleable substance of the already existent. Professor Woodbridge further clarifies the situation: "The past is not the cause or beginning of the present, but the effect and result of history; so that every historical thing leaves, as it were, its past behind it as the record of its life in time. . . . For each career is the producer, but not the product of its past." [88]

This brings us to the distinction, crucial for our discussion, between the existing subject matter—what Aristotle called the material cause—and the agent or force that acts upon it—what Aristotle called the *efficient cause*.* To quote Professor Lamprecht again: "Subject matter and agency are both actualities of the present. But their roles are different. The former is that which is acted upon; the latter is that which acts. That which is acted upon may also be agent, because the interactions of Nature are highly complicated. And that which acts may well also be subject matter for some other agent. We cannot, therefore, pick out any actuality of the present and regard it as either subject matter or as agent in any absolute sense. . . .

---

* In his philosophy Aristotle distinguished four different kinds of cause. *Efficient cause* in his terminology has come to mean plain *cause* in modern usage.

"A physician who heals is agent and his patient is subject matter, even though, simultaneously with the healing activity of the physician, the patient also acts in various ways upon the physician. The wind is agent, and the bending elm is subject matter, even though, simultaneously with the impact of the wind on the tree, the elm diverts the wind somewhat from the course it would, in the absence of the elm at just that spot, have taken. But the physician and the wind, in their roles as agents, are not subject matter; and the patient and the elm, in their roles as subject matter, are not agents. The distinction between subject matter and agent is absolute, even if the actualities to which the distinction can be applied are complexly interrelated and continually changing in those interrelations." [89]

This distinction holds for a human agent putting into effect a present choice that affects his own body as subject matter or his own mind (as it exists up to that point) as subject matter. In the thought process it is always the mind functioning in the immediate present which is the initiating agent. The intellectual activity of the past has of course built up a complex of ideas, recallable through the memory mechanisms of the nervous system, that both conditions and aids a man's present thinking. But the individual thinking *now* and deciding *now* is a free agent, and his past accumulation of knowledge is subject matter that he utilizes and adds to. Only in his role as active agent does a man have freedom of choice; insofar as he is subject matter, what happens to him is determined by the agents that act upon him.

The determinists in their analysis tend to reduce everything to subject matter, ascribing to it all the powers of causation, that is, of bringing about change. But it is Aristotle's efficient cause alone that initiates change and that constitutes the creative process. Theologians borrow this thesis when they describe their God as the First Cause; they never talk of a first *effect*. It is God as agent, as efficient cause, who has the power, the initiative, and the freedom to be the First Cause and Creator.

Confusion concerning subject matter and agency comes to

the fore again in the *genetic fallacy* of viewing men's actions merely in terms of their causal antecedents. This "container" theory of causation repeats the old mistake of supposing that there must be an inclusive similarity between a cause and its effect, so that all the properties of the effect somehow pre-exist in the cause. But each individual thing that exists is what it *does* rather than what it is caused by; its antecedents cannot negate its specific characteristics and activities.

The lovely blossoming of a rose is just as real as the lowly roots from which the flower sprung. To cite a favorite example once more, water is caused by the interaction of hydrogen and oxygen. But water behaves in a way that you could never deduce from a study of hydrogen and oxygen separately; it would be absurd to claim that water cannot run downhill or satisfy a man's thirst because neither hydrogen nor oxygen does. With water there emerge new qualities and kinds of behavior quite dissimilar to those of its causal antecedents. Thus every phenomenon possesses a certain irreducible quality that is at least as important a factor in its behavior as the prior causes that bring it into being or the external causes that later affect it.

Since man is a rational animal and has succeeded in acquiring considerable knowledge about the world around him, he is able, in his role as efficient cause, to manipulate, change, and control subject matter to a remarkable degree. One of the most significant types of choice that a human being can make is to take advantage of established scientific if-then laws by initiating a specific event from which a certain desired result will flow. He is able to put into effect the necessary *if*.

If a man with diabetes takes insulin, the specific for that disease, he can control the diabetes. *If* a housewife lights a gas range and boils meat and vegetables over the flames, she will soon produce a nourishing meal. *If* I want to go out in my automobile, I start the engine by means of the self-starter and then use the accelerator, the steering wheel, and the brakes to direct the car. These contrivances all function and interact deterministically; but it is *I* who decides where I shall go. Whenever I drive a car, I count on its built-in determinism, although I realize that it may break down occasionally.

The same principles apply to the numberless machines and mechanical devices that modern man is able to utilize. Thus in a multitude of ways human beings make excellent use of a determinism of means: it is in this way that a knowledge of necessity leads to increasing human freedom and control. The determinists illegitimately extend this determinism of scientific if-then sequences to the human choices and actions that initiate them.

My analysis ought to have made plain that to phrase the central issue under discussion "freedom of choice *versus* determinism" is quite misleading, because it assumes at the outset that the two concepts are mutually exclusive. On the contrary, there is in human life a constant, interlocking pattern of *both* freedom and determinism. It is not, then, the role of human freedom in general to combat determinism, but to work with it, tame it and employ it for the achievement of worthwhile purposes.

Interacting everywhere with freedom and determinism is contingency, the chance event, the conditional happening. The fact that human freedom is inextricably linked with the pervasive contingency in our world shows that free choice is a perfectly natural phenomenon and not an inexplicable exception to Nature's ways. As an intrinsic characteristic of Nature, contingency not only makes freedom of choice possible; such freedom in its very operation is a prime example of contingency impinging upon the course of things. For "the efficient cause is the contingent factor in events." And when an individual is functioning as agent or efficient cause, his choices themselves become contingent factors as they are translated into action.

We see this more clearly when we realize that a contingent cause, whether in the form of a man or of something nonhuman, is always the immediate stimulus for a chance meeting, at a definite location in space-time, between itself and some other event not previously related to it in a causal sense. In a spectacular occurrence like that of the *S. S. Titanic* crashing into an iceberg, it is comparatively easy to grasp that two separate causal sequences were intersecting. More important to understand is that such conjunctions take place all the time, even in respect to a person's everyday life, when he is exercising his capacities as efficient cause.

For instance, since I follow no regular pattern in going out in my automobile, it is a matter of contingency as to precisely when I use it. Whenever I drive my car, the particular event-stream represented by myself meets and takes charge of the altogether different event-stream represented by my sedan. Thus, in this familiar type of action, contingency and freedom of choice clearly coalesce.

Every free choice is equivalent to a *free cause*. In short, *you* —a thinking, initiating, choosing agent—can be and frequently are the free cause of your own actions. Human freedom of choice provides a firm foundation for the creativity of man; and the more conscious you as an individual are of that freedom, the more creative you are likely to be.

Finally, if my position on freedom of choice is correct, we must discard as untrue all systems of religion and philosophy that are fundamentally deterministic or fatalistic. Also erroneous are those theories of history—materialist, Marxist or otherwise—that are based in essence on economic determinism or assert that some particular outcome for society is inevitable. For if men are genuinely free in the way I have indicated, it follows that groups, communities, nations and civilizations— all of which are composed of human individuals—likewise in the large possess freedom of choice.

5. THE ULTIMATES OF EXISTENCE

Perhaps the best way for me to sum up Humanism's theory of the universe is to outline, from the Humanist viewpoint, the irreducible traits of existence as such, those ultimate categories of reality that constitute one's metaphysics or ontology. In formulating a metaphysics, Humanism fulfills its philosophical function of synthesis on the grand scale and is able to present itself as an inclusive way of life.

Aristotle calls metaphysics First Philosophy and describes its task in these words: "There is a science which investigates being as being and the attributes which belong to this in virtue of its own nature. Now this is not the same as any of the so-called special sciences; for none of these others treats universally of being as being. They cut off a part of being and investigate the attributes of this part. . . . All these sciences mark off some particular being—some genus, and inquire into this, but not into being simply nor *qua* being." [90]

To follow through with Aristotle's analysis, we find that each science, astronomy or biology, for instance, concentrates on its own carefully defined and limited subject matter. Metaphysics, on the other hand, seeks to identify those relatively few basic characteristics which are to be found throughout astronomy, biology, and every other field of factual knowledge; it specifies those features of existence that are omnipresent. The term *galaxy* is important in astronomy, but there are no galaxies in biology; the term *mammal* is important in biology, but it is hardly relevant to the behavior of galaxies. However, the term *causality,* one of the most obvious metaphysical categories, is fundamental in both astronomy and biology.

Metaphysics, then, deals with the lowest common denominators of everything that exists, whether it be animate or inanimate, human or nonhuman. These lowest common denominators, such as substance and activity, supplement one another and must be consistent with one another; but they cannot be deduced from one another or from any conception common to some or all of them. We can find no intelligible explanation of *why* these particular generic traits exist; they simple *are.* Precisely because they are ultimate principles of explanation and intelligibility, they themselves are not susceptible of explanation. To demand a reason for them is like asking the cause of causality.

These universal categories apply to all *existential* subject matters, but not to abstractions from existence such as mathematics, logic, and other ideological systems, or to ideas as such. Although ideally the categories ought not in any sense to overlap, I have not strictly held to this procedure. It is important to note that the majority of the categories I have listed are paired, because they signify *polar* or correlative traits. That is, they are complementary counterparts which imply each other and involve a reciprocal relation comparable to *north* and *south, left* and *right, hot* and *cold*. Thus I have put into effect the principle of polarity, so designated by Professor Morris R. Cohen in his discerning book *Reason and Nature*.

Without suggesting that I have drawn up a final or complete metaphysical prospectus, I submit the following sixteen categories as the most significant—the foundation stones—in the Humanist metaphysics:

1. *Substance* (Matter-Energy). While there have been many different definitions of *Substance,* I am using it as a convenient over-all term for the infinitely varied manifestations and modes of matter and energy throughout the universe. It is to Substance, as the totality of subject matter encountered, that all the other metaphysical distinctions pertain.

2. *Activity* (Motion, Process, Event). Substance is always in movement, in flux, no matter how stable or inert it may appear. Just as all activity is the activity of something concrete, so every something, from the smallest subatomic particle to objects such as men and stars, manifests unceasing activity. It is especially important for human beings to be aware of Change and Becoming as modes of Activity.

---

* Polar trait.

*{ 3. *Form* (Structure, Organization). Every manifestation of Substance or Activity possesses a certain determinate form or pattern definable as a stone, a tree, a man, or something else. Form never exists apart from matter or energy, or by itself in any Platonic or other supernatural realm beyond Nature.

4. *Quality* (Attribute). Every existent has a certain combination of qualities. Primary qualities such as solidity shape, and texture are operative at all levels of existence. Secondary qualities such as color, sound, and smell are also objective; but as Professor Woodbridge states, they "require the intervention of some special structure if their appropriate causality is to be effective." Such structures are, for example, the complex sense organs of human beings, or cameras that use color film.

5. *Quantity* (Dimension). All varieties of Substance possess spatial and temporal quantitative aspects expressible in such terms as size, mass, speed, intensity, and location in space-time.

6. *Duration* (Time Span). Every object or event endures for a determinate period of time, no matter how infinitesimal. Duration is a quantitative dimension, but is of such import that it must rank as a separate category.

7. *Presentness* (Nowness, Immediacy). It follows from the fact that every entity is in essence an event and from the correct analysis of causation that all things exist in the present, and *only* in the present. The present is the sole locus of reality and is, as Professor Lamprecht explains, "metaphysically privileged."

8. *Causality* (Causation, Cause-and-Effect). Everything that exists is subject to causation and functions as both cause and effect. An existent functions as cause when it is operating as an active agent; as effect when some other agent-cause is acting upon it.

---

* Polar trait.

Causality is to be broken down into two polar categories:

9. *Necessity* (Law, Regularity, Determinism). Scientifically established cause-effect laws or functional relationships constitute if-then regularities, predictable patterns, in Nature. Such laws are deterministic only in the sense that the *then* surely occurs *if* the necessary and sufficient conditions are present. This conditional necessity leaves room for Contingency and accident, and opens the door for human freedom of choice.

10. *Contingency* (Chance). This category represents the type of Causality that exhibits no regular pattern and that initiates a unique and unrepeated cause-effect relation. Contingency points to the frequent and pervasive intersections and criss-crossing of independent causal sequences in both human affairs and in Nature at large. As Professor Randall observes, these meetings of unrelated causal series are unpredictable, but not—after we have analyzed their occurrence—inexplicable.

11. *Individuality* (Distinctiveness). Every existent, be it animate or inanimate, is a distinct individual, set off in its discreteness and particularity from all other entities and possessing an irreducible character of its own. Every entity not only occupies a unique position in space and time, but also thereby has unique relations with the rest of the world.

12. *Relation* (Connectedness, Relatedness). Every individual event or entity in the cosmos is related in some manner to some other thing or things. Nothing exists in absolute isolation. The dynamic aspect of Relation is *interaction*. Relation also includes the concept of *continuity* in both space and time.

---

* Polar traits.

13. *Potentiality* (Possibility, Power). Every object that exists has certain inherent possibilities of activity, adaptability, interaction, change, and development. Just which potentiality or potentialities will be realized depends on all the relevant circumstances.

14. *Eventuation* (Outcome, Culmination). This category denotes the continuous process of events in terms of successive results, culminations, and effects. The acorn eventuates in an oak tree, or in nourishment for an animal. Eventuation in itself does not imply evolution or upward development, for outcomes may connote retrogression as well as advance in the light of human values. But human beings, adapting means to ends, utilize foreseen eventuations for the fulfillment of desires, purposes, and ideals.

15. *Unity* (Oneness). Every object or event in its very nature and as an identifiable entity possesses some degree of unity.

16. *Plurality* (Pluralism, Multiplicity). Every existent exhibits plurality, either because it constitutes a functioning whole made up of different parts, or because it at least enters into plural relationships.

This brief summary of Humanist metaphysical categories is just as significant for its omissions as for its inclusions. It of course excludes many categories which other philosophies have enthusiastically incorporated. Thus Humanism, while recognizing the great significance in human life of concepts like mind, purpose, and goodness, does not consider them basic traits of the universe and refuses to elevate them into controlling forces in the cosmos as a whole. There follow eighteen categories, all familiar in the history of philosophy, which Humanism rejects as irreducible ultimates or as final principles of explanation for existence as such.

---

* Polar traits.

1. Mind (Reason, Intelligence, Consciousness)
2. Idea
3. Truth
4. Spirit (Soul)
5. Personality
6. Will
7. Purpose (Design, Providence)
8. Love
9. Good (Value, Morality)
10. Evil
11. God
12. Devil (Satan)
13. Beauty
14. Freedom
15. Life (Life Force, Élan Vital)
16. First Cause
17. Time } As Absolutes
18. Space }

Commenting on the last three of these categories, I wish to reiterate that Humanism, in ruling out a First Cause in its philosophy, holds with Aristotle that Nature is infinite in duration as regards both past and future. This eternity of the cosmos is implied both by the Law of the Conservation of Mass, which means that no iota of matter or energy can either be created or destroyed; and by the Law of Causation, which means that something cannot result from nothing and that there cannot be a *last* effect. Humanism does not, of course, accept the notion, once quite general, that space and time are self-existent absolutes through which the world passes. The Humanist regards space as derivative from and relative to Substance and its extension; and time as derivative from and relative to Substance and its activity.

Humanism's sixteen metaphysical categories are not nearly so romantic, so exciting, so pleasing to the human ego as those of the supernaturalist philosophies and religions. Yet a disciplined philosophy, alert to all relevant scientific advances, must eliminate as metaphysical ultimates those attributes that belong to man alone. Such a philosophy inspires a sense of exhilaration from its steady pursuit of the truth and sober analysis of metaphysical traits which are in all probability eternal.

Naturalistic Humanism, taking the facts and implications of modern science as its point of departure, yet not unmindful of the claims of religious and artistic genius, definitely repudiates the supernaturalist or anthropomorphic bias running through most philosophies of the past. For Humanism the universe of Nature is all that exists; and man's greater good within this Nature is man's be-all and end-all. This-earthly human achievement is a worthwhile goal in itself and not a means to salvation in another life. Whatever salvation man can find from evil must be in this world.

The great supernaturalist and idealist philosophies have always insisted on some sort of cosmic and metaphysical guarantee for the ultimate triumph of man or his values; they have postulated the existence of a benign Providence or a great Friend behind phenomena guiding the complicated affairs of mankind to an inevitably successful conclusion. Humanism, however, never loads the dice by reading the actualization of its ideals into the stars, the drift of history or a Divine Mind that underwrites the future. The universe does not care whether good or evil, or any other human value, prevails. Yet man can be proud that in the whole vast cosmos he is, at the least, one of the highest forms of being. Confronted with the measuring rod of value, the immensities of time and space shrink mightily when compared with a single human mind.

Humanism is a philosophy for mature people and grows increasingly influential with the maturity of the race. It is honest and realistic in holding that man cannot romantically expect that his story is necessarily going to have a happy ending; it is tough-minded and firm-hearted in teaching that we should not unsportingly demand any advance promise of ultimate victory. But the Humanist philosophy, though granting that man may lose and lose permanently, is convinced that he has the ability and intelligence and courage to win through. While it diminishes our cosmic pretensions, it augments our earthly hopes.

So Humanism encourages men to face life buoyantly and bravely, relying upon their own freedom and reason to fashion a noble destiny in a future that is open.

6. THE APPRECIATION OF NATURE

The Humanist tenet that Nature constitutes the universality of existence does not detract from the appreciation of natural beauty and indeed should sharpen it. Humanism gives ample scope to those reactions of awe and wonder that so many men have experienced when they gaze upon the unending array of stars, see a sun-streaked waterfall hurtling over a high precipice, or view the sweep and splendor of mountains, sea, and sky. Acute consciousness of the infinite loveliness of the external world can offset to a considerable degree any sense of human alienation or insignificance to which the naturalistic, humanistic metaphysics may give rise. There is a wealth of evidence to show that a keen responsiveness to natural beauty not only evokes in human beings experiences of the most intense and pleasurable kind, but also arouses in them a feeling of profound kinship with Nature and its myriad forms of life.

Here again I do not think that either of Humanism's allied philosophies, Naturalism and Materialism, has done justice to a theme that certainly is of importance for any well-rounded philosophy. There is very little in the writing of contemporary naturalists and materialists that develops the possibilities of Nature as an aesthetic object or that indicates the philosophic relevance of Nature appreciation. It seems to me that naturalists and materialists, in their perennial struggle against philosophies that erect false barriers between man and Nature, have neglected man's capacity to overcome cramping dualisms through a sense of oneness with our mother earth and the universe beyond.

In general it is the poets who have best described the multitudinous patterns of color, sound, and motion in the natural world and who have given most eloquent voice to the effect of Nature's beauty and grandeur upon the human heart and mind.* Among the poets of the English language it is, in my judgment, the Nature poets of the early nineteenth century, notably Keats and Shelley, Byron and Wordsworth, whose achievement is greatest in these respects. And of them all, Wordsworth stands out as pre-eminent in mastery of expression and variety of image. For the purposes of this discussion, however, I prefer to quote certain passages from Lord Byron that exemplify both virtues and defects in his attitude toward Nature. There was little of a religious note in Byron's work; and he frequently wrote quite naturalistically of absorbing the beauty of Nature into one's inmost being and of mingling in harmonious unity with the universe. Thus in *Childe Harold's Pilgrimage:*

> Are not the mountains, waves and skies, a part
> Of me and of my soul, as I of them?
> Is not the love of these deep in my heart? . . . .
> I live not in myself, but I become
> Portion of that around me; and to me
> High mountains are a feeling, but the hum
> Of human cities torture. . . . The soul can flee
> And with the sky, the peak, the heaving plain
> Of ocean, or the stars, mingle, and not in vain.
>
> Where rose the mountains, there to him were friends;
> Where roll'd the ocean, thereon was his home;
> Where a blue sky, and glowing clime extends,
> He had the passion and the power to roam;

---

* I am not attempting to cover here the extensive contributions to the appreciation of Nature made by modern prose writers, landscape painters, and composers.

The desert, forest, cavern, breaker's foam,
Were unto him companionship; they spake
A mutual language, clearer than the tome
Of his land's tongue, which he would oft forsake
For Nature's pages glass'd by sunbeams on the lake.

Now Byron, who during much of his career felt himself to be an outcast, was also, as these lines indicate, constantly thinking of Nature as a refuge from human society and from the hubbub of urban existence. While boredom and intolerance have not yet been eradicated from human intercourse and while the bustle and clamor of cities have enormously increased since Byron's day, I do not conceive of the normal appreciation of Nature in terms of escape from either men or machines. Rather it is an aesthetic pleasure, a spiritual delight, and a simple, rewarding way of recreation. Like any other kind of recreation, it of course often takes the form of a temporary withdrawal from the concerns of everyday life. For the mentally depressed or distracted, Nature appreciation can sometimes serve as a valuable therapy; it may induce tranquility and help restore the sick soul.

Byron's preference, as typified by the second stanza quoted, was for the wild, the remote, and the untamed in Nature. These melodramatic aspects of the natural world have their own appeal and can indeed be fascinating, but in the objective estimation of aesthetic value there is no reason for promoting them to a special position. The scope of natural beauty is as wide as the range of beautiful objects, large or small, near or far, wild or cultivated, static or in motion. Furthermore, in our philosophy of appreciation there certainly must be a place for the experience of beauty in Nature merging with that of human creation, as when we view the bridges of New York or San Francisco against their background of water, highland, and sky; or look upon London in the shining splendor of the morning sun, as described by Wordsworth in his sonnet "Composed Upon Westminster Bridge."

My reservations as to Byron's treatment of Nature lead to

the general observation that all the chief Nature poets of his period exemplified to one degree or another the obvious shortcomings of the Romantic movement. They were all inclined to overstate the case, to idealize Nature in a manner reminiscent of Rousseau and to overemphasize the good consequences for human character and conduct of closeness to Nature and sensitivity to its beauty.

Certain professional philosophers have made the same mistake. For example, Kant stated: "I maintain that to take an *immediate interest* in the Beauty of Nature (not merely to have taste in judging it) is always a mark of a good soul." [91] And Schopenhauer wrote: "A beautiful view is therefore a cathartic of the mind, as music, according to Aristotle, is of the feeling, and in its presence one will think most correctly." [92] To puncture such exaggerations, we have only to remember that Adolf Hitler was a great admirer of the fine mountain scenery in the Bavarian Alps where he had his retreat.

The thoroughly humanistic appreciation of Nature that I am suggesting does not share in the sentimentalities of Romanticism. It decidedly does not set up the nonhuman world as somehow more worthy of attention than man or as aesthetically superior to art. Nor does it indulge in the pantheistic and sometimes supernaturalistic overtones which Wordsworth, especially, was prone to bring into his poetry. So far as later British poets are concerned, both Swinburne and Meredith produced excellent Nature poetry that is Humanist in spirit.

In America of the nineteenth century we find much first-rate Nature poetry in Bryant and Whittier, Emerson and Whitman, with transcendental or idealistic influences markedly present in the work of the latter two. Among twentieth-century American writers, Arthur Davison Ficke has given notable expression to the warm and responsive Humanist attitude toward natural beauty, particularly in his fine sonnet-sequence, *Tumultuous Shore*. Consider these lines:

> And if he die? He for an hour has been
> Alive, aware of what it is, to be.

The high majestic hills, the shining sea,
He has looked upon, and meadows golden-green.
The stars in all their glory he has seen.
Love he has felt. This poor dust that is he
Has stirred with pulse of inward liberty,
And touched the extremes of hope, and all between.
Can the small pain of death-beds, can the sting
Of parting from the accustomed haunts of earth,
Make him forget the bounty of his birth
And cancel out his grateful wondering
That he has known exultance and the worth
Of being himself a song the dark powers sing?

In the field of philosophy itself Lucretius' superb descriptions in *On the Nature of Things* still remain the outstanding example of naturalistic appreciation of Nature. There is hardly a page throughout the entire volume that does not make reference to the ever-changing forms and qualities of the natural world. Of course the great philosopher-poet of antiquity included in his descriptive sweep almost everything that we now assign to the realm of natural science. I am not urging modern philosophers to imitate Lucretius in this respect. Nonetheless, in his general approach to Nature he established a pattern that could well serve as an example for present-day philosophers and their writing of readable work.

One of the most impressive sections in Lucretius is that in which he treats of great meteorological phenomena and extraordinary telluric manifestations. To a large degree his descriptions of earthquakes, lightning, thunderbolts, hurricanes, volcanoes, and the Nile in flood come under the heading of what Edmund Burke called the sublime. In depicting these turbulent moods of a Nature mighty and unrestrained, Lucretius makes us feel such a power and a glory in it all that we are ready to cry out: "Though Nature slay us, yet is it ever most marvelous and beautiful!"

Some years ago I had this precise feeling one summer's afternoon while walking along the Hudson River at the base of the Palisades during a brief but ferocious thunderstorm. The sky was inky black and poured forth torrents of wind-swept rain in slanting patterns; violent thunderclaps reverberated among the cliffs, and lightning flashes near and far lighted up the river in zigzag configurations. I had that exhilarating sensation of witnessing an awe-inspiring spectacle and knowing at the same time that there was a chance, however infinitesimal, of my being struck dead in my tracks at any moment.

As Lucretius tells us in a memorable passage:

> . . . At such a time the densèd clouds
> So mass themselves through all the upper air
> That we might think that round about all murk
> Had parted forth from Acheron and filled
> The mighty vaults of sky—so grievously,
> As gathers thus the storm-clouds' gruesome night,
> Do faces of black horror hang on high—
> When tempest begins its thunderbolts to forge. . . .
> . . . . Then the thunderbolt,
> Now ripened, so to say, doth suddenly
> Splinter the cloud, and the arousèd flash
> Sweeps onward, lumining with forky light
> All places round. And followeth anon
> A clap so heavy that the skiey vaults,
> As if asunder burst, seem from on high
> To engulf the earth.[93] *

The experience of finding Nature full of wonder and fascination even when it directly threatens human life leads us to the threshold of religious mysticism. But it is not necessary to enter that door. Instead I would take the view that not a few of the reports of religious mystics can be legitimately interpreted in terms of a perfectly normal, this-worldly mysticism

---

* For a modern literary treatment of Nature on the rampage, see the two thrilling novels, *Fire* (1948) and *Storm* (1941), by the American writer, George R. Stewart.

stemming from a deep sensitivity to the beauties of our natural environment. Fortunately, one does not need to be a professional mystic in order to know at first hand the meaning of what I am loosely calling "normal mysticism" or what Aldous Huxley terms "mystico-sensuous enjoyment." Professor James H. Leuba quotes the following from a "mystic" who might be any one of us:

"Once when walking in the wild woods and in the country, in the morning under the blue sky, the sun before me, the breeze blowing from the sea, the birds and flowers around me, an exhilaration came to me that was heavenly—a raising of the spirit within me through perfect joy. Only once in my life have I had such an experience of heaven." [94] Similar statements are a fundamental motif in a classic such as Thoreau's *Walden*. For example: "Sometimes in a summer morning . . . I sat in my sunny doorway from sunrise to noon, rapt in a reverie, amidst the pines and hickories and sumachs, in undisturbed solitude and stillness, while the birds sang around or flitted noiselessly through the house, until by the sun falling in at my west window, or the noise of some traveler's wagon on the distant highway, I was reminded of the lapse of time." [95]

Now most nature-lovers are not literary people who make records of their experiences. But the fact is that many ordinary persons who enter into communion with Nature may in this process lose themselves in a veritable ecstasy of aesthetic delight, so that they forget the passage of time and are lifted out of and beyond the regular flow of day-to-day existence. As an element in responsiveness to Nature this can happen in a variety of ways, many of them of a familiar kind, such as walking along a sandy beach upon which ocean waves are breaking, treading a pine-needled forest path on which shadows play, smelling a fragrant violet or rose in a garden, watching the sun go down in a cloud-filled sky, or looking out upon the big swirling flakes of a snowstorm.

A contributing factor to this sort of aesthetic and spiritual experience is often simple, healthy activity, in fresh air and

under the open sky, that stirs the blood and causes a pervasive glow of physical well-being. Certain outdoor sports like
sailing and skiing are especially calculated to stimulate the
senses and to afford opportunity for the enjoyment of Nature.
Emerson was right when he remarked: "Give me health and
a day, and I will make the pomp of emperors ridiculous." [96]
Assuming that one has a desire for the appreciation of the
external world, the only essential equipment is sound and acute
senses, particularly a pair of good eyes. Actually any normal
person can participate in such apprehension of the beautiful.
And in the common man an active love of Nature inspires the
unwritten but deep-felt poetry of the heart.

What Robert Marshall, a leading conservationist, writes
about the wilderness applies, I feel, to external Nature in
general: "The wilderness is . . . unique esthetically in that it
stimulates not just the sense of sight, as does art, or the sense
of sound, as does music, but all of the senses that man has.
The traveler wandering at evening to the shore of some wilderness lakelet senses through his sight the pink sunset sky and
the delightful pattern which the deep bay makes among the
spruce trees which rise from its shores; senses through his
hearing the lapping of the water against the rocky shore and
the evening song of the thrush; senses through his smell the
scent of balsam and the marsh flowers at the water's edge;
senses through his touch the gentle wind which blows on his
forehead and the softness of the sphagnum beneath his feet.
The wilderness is all of these senses harmonized with immensity into a form of beauty which to many human beings
is the most perfect experience of the earth." [97]

Elementary and easily accessible as are so many of the
forms of natural beauty, a specific urge or inclination to appreciate Nature is not something innate in the individual or
native to human society. In the Christian West the widespread appreciation of Nature for its own sake came only in
modern times. The Old Testament writers displayed an occa-
sional awareness of the beauty of Nature; and in the Book of

Psalms this consciousness was quite marked. Psalmist mention of natural phenomena, however, was primarily for the purpose of demonstrating the power and majesty of Jehovah: "The heavens declare the glory of God; and the firmament sheweth his handywork." For the ancient Hebrews, as for the Christians of later eras, inanimate Nature was chiefly significant because of what it manifested about the Creator.

The ancient Greeks, on the other hand, with their developed feeling for the beautiful in every sphere of existence, deeply appreciated as such the sensuous qualities of the external world. Their complex mythology interfered but little with this appreciation, since their pagan deities were associated rather pleasantly with landscape and Nature. Also in China and India the established religions have been more favorable than Christianity to the love of Nature. For they have encouraged the people of those countries to consider the beauty of Nature as itself divine rather than, like traditional Christianity, to interpret it merely as revealing the divinity of a personal, transcendent God or as symbolizing the truths of supernatural salvation.

Needless to say, the Christian interpretation of Nature has not prevented magnificent descriptions of natural beauty such as occur in St. Francis of Assisi's "Canticle of Brother Sun" or Joseph Addison's famous hymn "Creation." Yet as late as 1929, concern over unduly encouraging Nature worship was one of the reasons why the Protestant Episcopal Church, in its official revision of the Book of Common Prayer, changed the King James version of the 121st Psalm, first verse, from "I will lift up mine eyes unto the hills, from whence cometh my help" to "I will lift up mine eyes unto the hills; whence cometh my help?" Turning the second clause here into a question turns the second verse of the Psalm into a clear answer: "My help cometh from the Lord, which made heaven and earth."

A further bar to the direct and simple love of Nature in the West "was the conversion, by early Christian teachers, of the ancient gods of wood and spring into evil spirits, and of Pan into the Devil. Whereas in China the holy men retired to the mountains to be closer to the divine beauty of Nature, in the West hermits who withdrew to 'deserts' were believed to be peculiarly subject to the forces of evil. Thus the forests and mountains and rivers of Europe were not only considered vaguely sinful, but positively dangerous." [98] This association of Nature with sin was also stimulated by the interpretation that Christian theologians gave to the consequences of Adam's fall and the great flood as recounted in the Bible.

The more orthodox Christian view was that prior to Adam's transgression and the later deluge the earth was a perfect paradise and that it became far less attractive and beautiful after these disastrous events. As Luther put the matter, " . . . we must speak of the whole Nature since its corruption as an entirely altered face of things: a face which Nature has assumed, first by means of sin, and secondly, by the awful effects of the universal Deluge. . . . All creatures, yea, even the sun and the moon, have as it were put on sackcloth. They were all originally 'good,' but by sin and the curse they have become defiled and noxious." [99]

A later and influential school of thought, culminating in the seventeenth and eighteenth centuries and including the English divine, John Donne, claimed that originally the earth was an unblemished sphere, smooth as an egg, "with not a wrinkle, scar or fracture." The flood shattered and crumpled this state of perfection and resulted in allegedly ugly and undesirable phenomena such as seas and islands, valleys and mountains. In the passionate controversy that raged over this theory, mountains became the center of attention and were variously interpreted as ". . . symbols of sin and decay, monstrous excrescences, pits and pock-marks in the fair face of Nature." [100] All mountains, it was freely predicted, would be leveled on the Day of Judgment, in conformity with Isaiah's well-known prophecy that "every valley shall be exalted, and every mountain and hill shall be made low."

According to the Christian tradition, man's terrible wickedness had been responsible for the earth's becoming a jagged, unshapely, repellent ruin in comparison with the original paradise, or at least much less lovely and well-proportioned. This attitude toward the environment was unquestionably a factor in the common man's attribution of evil and fearfulness to the natural world and in holding back a proper appreciation of its beauty. Of course other elements, especially those connected with the material condition of life, played a significant role in this situation.

Paradoxically, the advance of science and civilization, while clearing away certain fundamental impediments to the appreciation of Nature, brings new ones in its train. Freedom to travel near and far, to see fresh sights and explore little-known lands, has increased immeasurably during the past century through the development of the modern railroad, steamship, automobile, and airplane. Yet the industrial revolution and the machine age have resulted in such huge complexes of cities, such a psychology of haste and strain, such a host of new social-economic problems that many individuals forget the joys of hiking and picnicking under the open sky.

Close to 65 per cent of the population in the United States is urban. These 125,000,000 or more persons do not on the whole maintain a close and continual relationship with Nature. It is primarily the urban environment that enters vitally into their lives; and as individuals these metropolitan millions do not have much choice in the matter. Inevitably the city milieu moulds their likes and dislikes, their enjoyments and recreations. To a considerable extent urban cultural standards permeate the village and agricultural districts, so that even the American farmer is suburban in his tastes. Plainly, people who live in the country are not necessarily highly sensitive to the charms of Nature.

It is worth noting that the United States stands unsurpassed in scenic beauty and variety, and outrivals all other countries in the extent of public lands reserved for the outdoor enjoyment of the people. I refer particularly to America's great network of National Parks, National Seashores, National Forests, and State Parks. In 1964 Congress passed the Wilderness Act that sets aside in a National Wilderness Preservation System more than 9,000,000 acres of U.S.-owned property, including a large part of the Federal tracts just mentioned, to be forever protected from the encroachments of civilization.*

Science during the last hundred years has greatly expanded man's vision of the amazing scope of the universe in space and time and greatly enlarged his knowledge of the relationship between him and the rest of Nature. This recent science has opened up to man vast new regions of superstars and galaxies; it has made him realize that in his very flesh and blood he is one with the dynamic and multistructured matter that pervades the entire cosmos; it has demonstrated that he has evolved from most humble origins in the primordial substance and is cousin to all living things. The revelations of biology strengthen the basis for human kindness to animals and for a sympathetic attitude toward all sentient life. Meanwhile the increasing control that science has won over external Nature makes it clear that the most serious danger at present to man is man himself and not nonhuman Nature.

For the mature mind, then, the progress of modern science enhances and broadens the appreciation of Nature that I am urging. It adds depth and meaning to that appreciation by helping man to see more clearly the sources of his being and the intimate interrelations between him and his cosmic matrix. These observations bring out the point that Nature appreciation in and of itself, as a more or less isolated activity, does not meet the requirements of the philosophic approach. What I am seeking is the conscious integration of a deep-going awareness of natural beauty into an inclusive Humanist philosophy.

---

* The American Humanist Association is the custodian of the Lamont Nature Sanctuary atop the Palisades of the Hudson and overlooking the river. This Sanctuary was established in 1953 by my mother, the late Mrs. Thomas W. Lamont.

Philosophy as criticism has the obligation to analyze current values and to call attention to any serious lack in the lives of human beings. Today one such lack is a basic aesthetic and philosophic responsiveness to Nature's beauty among considerable sections of mankind and especially among the busy, hurrying city-dwellers so characteristic of our age and of America. For Humanism, on the positive side, there is in this situation a definite opportunity—to correct a lamentable one-sidedness in contemporary man by evoking in him a deep-felt awareness of nonhuman Nature. At the same time the detailed analysis of Nature appreciation can bring to Humanism a greater understanding of the meaning and scope of mystical experience; and also provide Humanists with essential background and wider vision in the field of aesthetics, for which the contemplation of natural beauty has many implications.

Finally, the wholehearted appreciation of Nature serves to buttress effectively the humanist outlook in general. Humanism, in its opposition to supernaturalism and Idealism, has necessarily become involved in numerous negations. By laying stress on the beauty of Nature, Humanism becomes able to make one of the most powerful and persuasive of all affirmations. Without yielding to animism we can suggest that nonhuman Nature, including the graceful and colorful forms of beast, bird, and fish, gives to those attuned to it a heightened sense of being alive and at ease in this world. There is no heavenly Father in or behind Nature; but Nature is truly our fatherland.

Dr. Haydon, one of the signers of the *Humanist Manifesto*, has given rhapsodic utterance to this viewpoint: "The Humanist rarely loses the feeling of perfect at-homeness in the universe. He is conscious of himself as an earth-child. There is a mystic glow in this sense of belonging. Memories of his long ancestry still linger in muscle and nerve, in brain and germ cell. On moonlit nights, in the renewal of life in the springtime, before the glory of a sunset, in moments of swift insight he feels the community of his own physical being with the

body of his mother earth. Rooted in millions of years of planetary history, he has a secure feeling of being at home, and a
consciousness of pride and dignity as a bearer of the heritage
of the ages." [101]

In the framework of the Humanist world-view the ever-
present glory of the visible natural takes the place of the
traditional glory of the invisible supernatural. This is a fair
exchange, and more; but its full advantages are lost unless
philosophers and men at large rejoice profoundly in the in-
exhaustible beauties of their earth and universe.

CHAPTER V

Reliance on Reason and Science

1. FIVE WAYS OF SEEKING KNOWLEDGE

In determining what ideas are true and what actions sound, Humanism depends upon human reason unaided, and unimpeded, by any alleged supernatural sources. We come nearest to living the life of reason when we approximate most closely the methods of science in our treatment of difficulties and in our solution or attempted solution of problems. During a large proportion of our waking careers, however, when we act according to long-established habit or are immersed in immediate experience, pleasant or unpleasant, we are not engaged in trying either to solve problems or to enlarge our knowledge. Hence it is only part of the time that we need to use reason and scientific method.

Historically there have been five chief ways of seeking the truth: through revelation, through authority, through intuition, through rationalism, and through scientific method. Traditional religion has relied heavily on supernatural revelation in its quest for knowledge, as when some revered prophet or religious leader receives the word of God more or less direct and proclaims his vision as the absolute and immutable truth that the Almighty has vouchsafed to man. Such a prophet was Moses as described in the Old Testament and such a truth was the Ten Commandments which Jehovah personally revealed to him upon a mountain top. The Bible in general is a book built upon the continuing and often dramatic disclosures of the Lord to his elect. In any religion the ideas and insights that a believer purports to acquire by means of prayer are also presumed to come through revelation from a supernatural power.

Another common manner of ostensibly obtaining revelation from divine sources, particularly among primitive peoples, has been by resort to pure and simple magic in the form of divination. We can identify more than fifty different varieties of miraculous divination that have been depended upon during the history of the human race. Types widespread in the ancient world were hieromancy or divination by the entrails of sacrificed animals; capnomancy or divination by smoke from the altar; and astrology or divination by the stars. According to the "science" of astrology, the character and career of every human being is foreordained by the position of the heavenly bodies at the time of his birth. It is a significant commentary on the degree of superstition still existent in this twentieth century that, according to competent estimates, there are still more than two million devotees of astrology in the United States. Another species of divination that many modern men take seriously is palmistry.

The method of supernatural revelation in acquiring knowledge is also that of the religious mystics, many of whom have remained outside the bounds of any official church. The mystics supposedly get in direct touch with God or the World-Soul through superrational and supersensuous trances, visions, or intuitions. However, it is the considered judgment of the best students of religious mysticism that the characteristic experiences of mystics are wholly naturalistic and humanistic in origin and content. Some of the most prominent mystics have plainly shown symptoms of epilepsy, hysteria, or neurasthenia; others have been the victims of frustrated ambition or frustrated sexual passion. The work of Sigmund Freud and his discovery of the profound influence of the unconscious on the life of men and women also throws much light on the reports of mystics. Moreover, scientific investigation has found that states of ecstasy akin to those of the professional mystic can be produced in individuals by certain drugs, gases, alcoholic stimulants, and foods (such as hallucinogenic mushrooms); and by certain physical ordeals such as fasting, flagellation, and intense or prolonged dancing.

Most important of all, it seems to me, in establishing a natural continuity between religious mystics and other men is the fact that the ordinary, healthy, life-affirming person himself has moments and periods of real ecstasy: when listening, let us say, to some great symphony or sonata, when reading some magnificent passage of prose or poetry, when stirred by the emotion of love, when deeply enjoying some aspect of Nature's beauty. These peak experiences and many others that touch upon the rapturous or dreamy, or lead to sudden glory or illumination, give rise to such an intensified sense of life that one indeed feels transported out of this world. Again, such moods of exaltation are akin to the visions of religious mystics in that no words seem adequate to describe them. They are simply ineffable. On these occasions we rightly dwell in the present, savoring to the full the joys of the immediate and saying inwardly with Goethe, "O moment stay, thou art so fair!"

Humanists do not doubt that famous mystics and prophets have had remarkable and soul-shaking subjective experiences, tremendous moments of exalted vision. What we doubt is the correctness of their interpretation of these experiences, the *meaning* that they give to them. Ecstatic states in which one feels a vastly heightened sense of happiness or importance, freedom or power, are human experiences and nothing more. They do not justify the subject's conviction that he is conversing with the Lord Almighty or is in communication with another realm of being altogether. William James tells about a man who was able to induce mystical experiences by taking laughing-gas. "Whenever he was under its influence, he knew the secret of the universe, but when he came to, he had forgotten it. At last, with immense effort, he wrote down the secret before the vision had faded. When completely recovered, he rushed to see what he had written. It was: 'A smell of petroleum prevails throughout.'" [102]

What is usually presupposed in the method of seeking truth through religious or mystical revelation is the existence of a supernatural faculty of knowledge in man, the existence of a supernatural God, and the intimate concern and acquaintance of that Supreme Being with human problems. All of these assumptions the Humanist of course considers unwarranted. The idea of a supernatural faculty of knowledge in human beings is tied up with the old dualistic psychology and its theory of a supernatural soul; it is altogether inconsistent with our monistic thesis of mind and body as a naturalistic unity. The Humanist, then, looks upon divine revelation in religion as simply what certain leaders of men, often wiser than their fellows, decide is the truth during periods of special inspiration and insight.

As a religion grows more mature and more firmly established, the need arises for constant determination of what is to be regarded as authentic revelation and how that revelation should be interpreted in relation to a multitude of concrete questions. Usually the central church body or its highest official, such as the Catholic Pope, with his alleged infallibility on matters of faith and morals, assumes this responsibility and authority. And the members of such a Church accept as unquestioned dogma the pronouncements of recognized authority.

It is not only in the sphere of religion that the method of authority carries undue weight; there are also political, artistic, and even academic faithful who, willing to subordinate their personal opinions or wishing to avoid the social risk of independent thinking, give their assent to whatever "truths" some self-perpetuating council or high functionary or imperious pundit hands down. This surrender of the mind to authority naturally favors the defenders of traditional views in the realm of knowledge and of the *status quo* in social and economic affairs. The methods of authority and of revelation both demand ultimately that those who accept them have invincible faith, like the early Church Father, Tertullian. It was he who, referring to the reported resurrection of Jesus, made the truly breath-taking statement, "The fact is certain, because it is impossible."

Closely related to religious and mystical revelation as a way of knowing, but with higher standing in philosophy, is intuition. This means the direct, immediate, and certain apprehension of truth by the human personality, sometimes by means of so-called innate ideas, without the intervention of any reasoning process or the mediation of sense perception. Intuition as the royal road to infallible and self-evident knowledge has ever been a favored method for the religious or mystical mind. The Humanist does not deny that men have the gift of something that can legitimately be called *intuition;* but insofar as intuition turns out to be reliable, it is simply very nimble sense perception or thinking that penetrates to the heart of a situation with more than usual speed. Much has been made of "woman's intuition," as if the female of the species possessed a special faculty of knowledge not present in the male. The kernel of truth in this myth is that in certain situations women's perceptions, due to training and conditioning, may function more swiftly and accurately than men's. Intuition at its best amounts to nothing more than making a good, quick guess—having a "hunch," in the popular idiom—which may prove to be correct, but which always requires verification.

The fourth unacceptable way of seeking knowledge is that of traditional rationalism. This method starts out with certain fundamental mathematical or logical assumptions and, through rigorous deduction from them, builds up a closely interrelated complex of ideas into a coherent whole. The rationalist approach to truth has had considerable philosophic sanction and was the primary reliance of even so great a philosopher as Spinoza. But brilliant as have been the achievements of certain thinkers who followed the rationalist procedure, it has grave shortcomings in that it submits to experimental verification neither the original propositions, which may be selected through intuition, nor the final conclusions. *Contemporary* rationalism, however, as I noted earlier, is thoroughly scientific in its methods.*

The fatal flaw in all four of the truth-seeking methods that

---

* See pp. 25-26.

I have just outlined is that they give no place to the empirical verification and controlled experimentation that are so absolutely fundamental in modern science. Actually modern scientific method does make a limited use of authority, intuition, and rationalism. Over a long period of time scientists gradually develop a central core of authority in the form of independently verified and generally acknowledged facts and laws. But this body of authority can and must be continually challenged and revised; any scientific judgment whatsoever is always subject to further appeal.

Scientists also depend on intuition, in the humanistic sense, when they draw upon their imaginations to suggest new hypotheses for the solution of a problem; and they utilize the rationalist method, insofar as it entails strict logical deduction from clear premises, throughout the scientific enterprise. Likewise scientists can accept rationalism's doctrine of an ultimate coherence among all ideas that are true. To attain such coherence, in the form of a system of propositions all of which are strictly consistent with one another, must be an ideal in any branch of science as well as for all of the sciences regarded as a whole. For example, every proposition accepted as true in biology ought to be entirely consistent with every proposition accepted as true in psychology; and vice versa. This principle holds among all the different fields of knowledge.

We see, then, that there is some element of soundness in three out of the four unacceptable ways of attempting to establish knowledge; and that many thinkers have overstressed one particular aspect of the quest for truth and thereby failed to make a fully rounded approach. The fifth way of acquiring knowledge, modern scientific method, embodies whatever is valid in past methods and adds its own distinguishing characteristic of empirical confirmation through accurate observation and experiment. It is this quality of modern science that has chiefly accounted for its enormous success in broadening the area of knowledge, accelerating the process of invention, and extending man's control over his environment.

2. MODERN SCIENTIFIC METHOD

The development, over the past four centuries, of a universally reliable method for attaining knowledge is a far more important achievement on the part of science than its discovery of any single truth. For once men acquire a dependable *method* of truth-seeking, a method that can be applied to every sphere of human life, then they have an instrument of infinite power that will serve them as long as mankind endures. Scientific method is such an instrument. And not only does it constantly revise and render more precise our present body of knowledge, but it also steadily improves upon itself. It is a method that is self-corrective and self-evolving.

Yet closely bound up as scientific method has been with technical procedures and laboratory experiments, it is, as T. H. Huxley once said, "nothing but trained and organized common sense." In an essay entitled, "We Are All Scientists," Huxley wrote: "There is no more difference, but there is just the same kind of difference, between the mental operations of a man of science and those of an ordinary person, as there is between the operations and methods of a baker or of a butcher weighing out his goods in common scales, and the operations of a chemist in performing a difficult and complex analysis by means of his balance and finely graduated weights. It is not that the action of the scales in the one case, and the balance in the other, differ in the principles of their construction or manner of working; but the beam of one is set on an infinitely finer axis than the other, and of course turns by the addition of a much smaller weight. . . . Probably there is not one who has not in the course of the day had occasion to set in motion a complex train of reasoning, of the very same kind, though differing of course in degree, as that which a scientific man goes through in tracing the course of natural phenomena." [103]

The process of trial and error, fumbling and success which

every man follows to some extent, constitutes scientific method in a rudimentary form. Every time you buy a suit, a pair of shoes, or a meal you are attempting to the best of your ability to solve a certain problem and to give yourself a certain satisfaction. To the extent that you succeed you are being scientific. You may try on three suits of varying fabric and color at the clothing store, viewing yourself in the mirror each time and conducting in reality three experiments of a semiscientific nature. You at last select a single-breasted dark grey that seems to look well on you. The final verification of whether your choice was a good one comes later when you find out how the suit wears and how your wife or sweetheart likes it.

Now let me present another illustration that brings out clearly the basic continuity between scientific method and plain, prosaic, everyday thinking. Some years ago during a ski trip I was trying to unlock the door of my car on a cold winter's morning, but could get the key only halfway into the keyhole. Quickly analyzing the trouble, I decided that there must be some water or moisture frozen inside the lock and immediately resorted to impromptu trial and error. First, I attempted extra strong physical pressure to force the key all the way in, but to no avail. Next, I breathed vigorously into the lock, with the intent of possibly thawing it out. This did not work either. My third "experiment," based on the none too certain memory of an anecdote I had once heard, was to place the key as far as it would go in the keyhole, light an ordinary match and apply the flame for a moment or two to the protruding end of the key. Then I pushed the heated key hard again. This time it went all the way in, apparently having melted or softened the ice, and I unlocked the door. In larger and more important problems, however, the simple trial-and-error method can be very costly. In the case of illness, for instance, the patient might well die while various random cures were being tried.

Let us take an example of reliance upon true scientific method that has had relevance for many a family. Suppose your twelve-year-old son wakes up on a windy March morning and says that he does not feel well. On questioning him, you elicit the information that he has a slight headache and no appetite for breakfast. You take his temperature and find that it is 100—not high, yet sufficient to call for attention. Is it a mere digestive upset, is it grippe, is it appendicitis, or is it the beginning of some serious disease? By lunch-time your child is feeling a little dizzy and complains of pains in the general region of his "stomach." You telephone the family physician and ask him to come in as soon as possible. He arrives later in the afternoon, thoroughly examines the young patient and is able to locate the pains as coming from the right side of the abdomen. The doctor says that the symptoms seem to indicate an inflamed appendix and recommends calling in a surgeon.

After supper your son's pain increases and his temperature rises a little. The surgeon arrives, reviews the whole situation and verifies the family physician's diagnosis that, yes, this is a bad appendix. He discusses the idea of keeping the boy in bed for a few days to see if the appendix will calm down and also the alternate possibility of operating to remove it. You decide to send your child at once to the hospital, where he can be under constant medical observation. Early next morning the surgeon checks carefully and advises an immediate operation to take out the appendix, with the family physician concurring. You agree to this drastic step and the operation takes place at noon. It is successful and the surgeon reports that the appendix was badly infected and in all probability would soon have ruptured. Your son makes a rapid recovery, comes home within a week, and is back in school at the end of three weeks.

When we break down this typical case in the field of medicine into its component parts, we see that it exemplifies the five main steps, formulated by Dewey in his book *How We Think*,[104] that usually take place in working out a problem according to scientific method. First, there is the occurrence of a perplexity or problem: your son is feeling unwell. Second, there is analysis and clarification through observation and reflection, in order to arrive at precise definition or diagnosis of the problem—in this case to determine exactly what is causing the trouble. You take the boy's temperature; two doctors examine him and arrive at the diagnosis of appendicitis. Third, there is the suggestion of different solutions or working hypotheses for the problem of the inflamed appendix: keeping the patient quiet for a while in hopes that the attack will pass away or removing the appendix through surgery. Fourth, there is the reasoning out of the consequences or implications involved in each hypothesis and its evaluation in terms of these consequences. Is there much danger in an operation? Can the family afford it financially? Is there more risk in following a wait-and-see strategy? With the advice of the surgeon and regular family physician you finally decide on the more radical procedure. Fifth, there is verification of the chosen solution in that the appendix is discovered to have been in a most dangerous condition and in that your son completely recovers from his illness.

Of course I have oversimplified in this account of the five steps and should mention in addition that the doctors' procedures were formulated and carried out in the light of their wide experience with other similar cases. I have assumed that the doctors are competent and that their diagnosis (step two) is correct, though often in medical practice the diagnosis is more difficult to work out than the cure, which may already have been well established through previous experiments. Also, step five in this case of appendicitis amounts to verification only against the background of numerous other cases of a like nature.

There are some problems which require or permit no fifth step, those of pure mathematics, for instance, in which the very tracing of the implications of an hypothesis, through mathematical deduction (step four), amounts to verification. Moreover, many scientific hypotheses are not susceptible to final proof through *direct* observation, but are proved true through empirical verification of the logical or mathematical inferences following strictly from the said hypotheses. No astronomer has ever been able to watch the earth revolve in its entire course around the sun. Astronomers have verified the heliocentric theory by showing that it implies and is implied by a number of observations that can be and have been made of the positions of the earth, the other planets, and the sun. Then there are the so-called scientific "nonobservables," the submicroscopic objects such as atoms, electrons, and nuclear particles in general. No physicist has ever been able to see these tiny bits of matter; their behavior and very existence have had to be deduced from their observable effects. The same holds true of the infinitesimal and multitudinous genes, which carry from parent to child the basic hereditary characteristics.

In the field of philosophy this indirect method of verification is extremely important, particularly in the sphere of metaphysics. For in analyzing the cosmos, philosophers cannot possibly observe or experiment with the universe as a whole. Our conclusions about it, therefore, must be painstakingly deduced from observed and proved facts.

I do not claim that all good scientists follow, consciously or in the order given, the five-step sequence I have described; what I do claim is that their successful solution of scientific problems can always be analyzed according to this formula. Of course the average man in the carrying out of his daily affairs is not aware that separable stages of thought are involved. Our thinking in relation to the more simple situations is likely to proceed so rapidly that it is difficult to draw any hard-and-fast line between the successive steps.

Another essential qualification is that in the progress of science the perception or formulation of a problem that was never recognized before has often been the most important step in effecting a new scientific discovery. As the saying goes, "To know what to ask is already to know half."

An outstanding historical example of scientific method concerns yellow fever, an epidemic tropical illness that once slew its victims by the scores of thousands and sent 70 or 80 per cent of those afflicted to the grave. In Cuba during the Spanish-American war of 1898, more American soldiers were killed by yellow fever than by Spanish bullets and shrapnel. After the end of hostilities the disease raged on amidst the Cuban people and the American army of occupation. Yellow fever rapidly became a fearful menace in the Cuba just emerging from Spanish rule.

Alarm over this situation constituted the first step in the scientific study of the enigma of yellow fever. Careful analysis of the disease, the second step, showed that it spread quickly, malignantly, mysteriously, striking here, there, and everywhere; claiming victims from families that had had no apparent personal contact with the malady; sweeping suddenly through a whole town or city and taking hostages from every sort of group—poor and rich, young and old, weak and strong. The most pressing problem became: how is this dreadful fever transmitted?

Coming to step three, we find that there were many ideas current about the transmission of the disease. But they boiled down to two main hypotheses: yellow fever was caused and transmitted by an identifiable bacillus or microbe which was carried by contaminated objects such as the clothes used by an infected person; or the fever was transmitted by the bites of mosquitoes carrying the infection from one person to another. The second hypothesis was that of Dr. Carlos Finlay of Havana, whom sensible people regarded as something of a crank.

Step four, the following out of the implications of these two hypotheses, was fairly simple. If the first hypothesis were true, then close exposure, for instance, to the bedclothes or wearing apparel of those who had contracted yellow fever should cause the disease in at least some persons so exposed. If the second one were true—and nearly everyone thought it was absurd—then a mosquito which had bitten a yellow-fever victim or fed upon his blood and which subsequently bit normal, healthy persons ought to cause the disease in the latter in a decisive number of cases.

Experimental verification here, step five in scientific method, required controlled experiments on human beings, since no available animals were susceptible to the disease. Major Walter Reed of the U.S. Army Medical Corps, a tough-minded and determined doctor who was head of the special Yellow Fever Commission in Cuba, did not hesitate to call for volunteers. And a number of American soldiers, who well knew they would be risking their lives, responded to his appeal. Dr. Reed, after some preliminary and unsuccessful work in trying to spot a yellow-fever bacillus, veered toward the mosquito hypothesis which almost all of the experts and authorities, including members of his own Commission, thought so foolish. His strenuous and persistent efforts to prove this hypothesis constitute one of the most exciting episodes in the history of medicine.

Dr. Reed had a small camp built near the town of Quemados; and there he isolated in separate tents seven volunteers, guarding them for days and weeks from all danger of accidental contact with yellow fever and tenaciously keeping away from them, through carefully constructed screens, any stray mosquitoes that might be flying about. Then he brought to the camp his own special mosquitoes, which about two weeks previously had feasted upon yellow-fever patients, and turned them loose on the seven human guinea-pigs to inject whatever lethal germs they had acquired into the blood stream of these men. Within a week after being bitten, six out of seven of the volunteers came down with typical cases of yellow fever; and one of them died.

That looked like fairly conclusive proof of the mosquito hypothesis. But Walter Reed was not through. He had to *disprove* the other hypothesis, to show that the fever was carried *only* by mosquitoes. So he took three more volunteers and put them in a stuffy little house at the camp. Then he sent in to them the soiled and well-used pillows, sheets, and blankets of persons who had died from yellow fever. The three volunteers made up their army cots with these filthy bedclothes and slept on these cots in the hot, stuffy house for twenty nights. Not one of them contracted yellow fever. Dr. Reed was not yet finished, however. He sent in three more volunteers to sleep for twenty more nights in new contaminated bedclothes and in the very pajamas of yellow-fever victims. But no yellow fever resulted. Finally, he sent in three more men to repeat the experiment, with the added refinement of sleeping on pillows covered with towels soaked in the blood of men dead from the fever. Still no yellow fever followed.

Dr. Reed and his Commission performed other experiments with fresh batches of volunteers, but I shall not go into the further details. The main problem had been solved; the means through which yellow fever was transmitted had been discovered. By waging a furious war of extermination against the species of mosquito concerned, known as the *Aedes aegypti,* American sanitary engineers soon almost completely stamped out yellow fever in Cuba. The disease has since been largely eliminated in the civilized regions of the globe. Its original cause—the poison which the mosquitoes carried—was finally identified in the late nineteen-twenties as an ultramicroscopic virus that can penetrate the finest filters.

Turning to another field of science, we can see the same pattern of scientific method exemplified in the astronomical discoveries of Copernicus which, in the sixteenth century, opened up the revolutionary era of modern science. Copernicus, as a thorough student of mathematics and astronomy, became troubled (first step) over the traditional and almost universal conception of a motionless earth as the center of the universe and over the description of the heavenly bodies as worked out by the Egyptian astronomer Ptolemy in the second century A.D. When (second step) he analyzed his feeling that something was wrong, Copernicus stated that the fearful complexity of Ptolemy's calculations, which required no less than seventy-nine separate assumptions, was for him inconsistent with the perfection of God, who, he believed, operated through simple and harmonious laws. Here Copernicus was adumbrating, in religious terms, the scientific law of parsimony.

He then proceeded (third step) to search for a hypothesis that would explain the motions of the heavenly bodies more simply. And he took upon himself, Copernicus says, "the task of rereading the books of all the philosophers which I could obtain, to seek out whether anyone had ever conjectured that the motions of the spheres of the universe were other than they supposed who taught mathematics in the schools. And I found first that, according to Cicero, Hiketas of Syracuse had thought the earth was moved.* Then later I discovered, according to Plutarch, that certain others had held the same opinion. . . . When from this, therefore, I had conceived its possibility, I myself began to meditate upon the mobility of the earth." [105]

The hypothesis that Copernicus finally developed was that the sun and fixed stars should be considered as at rest, with the earth in continual motion on its axis and making a regular revolution once a year around the sun. Working out logically and mathematically the implications of this heliocentric theory (fourth step), he found that it enabled him to give a far more simple and uniform representation of the known astronomical data than did Ptolemy's complex system. Since Copernicus did not possess any important new astronomical data, he was not able to go on to the fifth step of verification through experiment.

Copernicus' brilliant successors, Kepler and Galileo, did have at their disposal new and significant astronomical observations and were able to carry through the fifth step, confirming with fresh empirical evidence the heliocentric hypothesis. More than that, they improved on Copernicus' theory by eliminating a number of planetary irregularities that it permitted and by showing that the planets move around the sun in the figure of a simple oval, an ellipse, instead of the perfect circle which

---

* Hiketas was a Greek astronomer who lived on the island of Sicily about the end of the fifth century B.C.

Copernicus had assumed. Later, Newton put the finishing touches on this phase of astrophysics with his epochal law of gravitation, which held for all material bodies and thus linked together under one inclusive principle things both terrestrial and astronomical.

I could go on indefinitely giving important historical examples of the successful use of scientific method; but I shall now pass on to some necessary comments that apply to the scientific process as a whole. There are certain simple essentials that hold for every stage of scientific inquiry. These are sound observation, creative imagination, correct reasoning, and moral determination.

Sound observation is important particularly in step two, when we are analyzing and clarifying the problem, and in step five, when we are verifying empirically our hypothesis or hypotheses. Prerequisites of reliable observation include keen and normal sense organs and command of available tools, both intellectual—in the form of ideas which help us to recognize and define the elements of our experience—and mechanical, which improve upon our senses and often enable us to manipulate existing materials for experimental purposes.

Professor Emeritus Edwin A. Burtt of Cornell suggests that "the history of science could be written in terms of the progressive invention of more powerful instruments for exact observation. The story of modern astronomy is largely the story of the telescope." [106] The microscope in biology and bacteriology, and the mouth thermometer and X ray in medicine, have been similarly important.

Creative imagination is especially important in steps one and two, when we are becoming aware of and diagnosing a problem, and in step three, when we are trying to think up fruitful hypotheses. Obviously a wide-ranging and powerful imagination is of immense advantage in the apprehension of possible solutions to a problem; and here it is that the flash of genius as contrasted with mere random guessing counts perhaps more than anywhere else in the enterprise of science.

Are there any universal rules on the best way to bring out genius, or if you are not a genius, your own best intellectual efforts? I think not. Constant pressure may be a necessary stimulus to some individuals; a cocktail or two seems to help others. Plenty of relaxation appears to be one of the factors generally favorable to the emergence of great scientific hypotheses. The famous German physicist, Helmholtz, tells us that after prior investigation of a scientific problem "happy ideas come unexpectedly, without effort, like an inspiration. So far as I am concerned, they have never come to me when my mind was fatigued, or when I was at my working table. . . . They came particularly readily during the slow ascent of wooded hills on a sunny day." [107]

Correct reasoning, the process of inference or deduction, is absolutely necessary in all phases of scientific investigation, but is particularly important in step four when we develop the logical implications of our hypotheses. Objective reasoning is the subject matter of numerous textbooks in formal logic; but for the rules and details of that discipline I must refer the reader to some such work as Professor Burtt's authoritative *Right Thinking*, which gives an excellent exposition from the Humanist viewpoint of the entire process of scientific method.

The fundamental principles of deduction were enunciated by Aristotle 2,000 years ago, and since then there has been little improvement on his formulations. His three most fundamental axioms of logic are: (1) the Law of Identity (A is A, meaning that a definite thing is always that same thing); (2) the Law of Contradiction (A cannot be both B and not-B at the same time and in the same respect); and (3) the Law of Excluded Middle (A is either B or not-B, meaning that an assertion is either true or false).

Admittedly, since Aristotle's time signficant developments have taken place in logic and mathematics; and recently the new and formidable discipline of symbolic logic has come into being. But his simple laws of thought remain definitive for valid reasoning; and even those who, like the Dialectical Materialists, purport to prove these laws outmoded cannot escape relying upon them in their arguments and explanations.

It was Emerson who remarked that "a foolish consistency is the hobgoblin of little minds, adored by little statesmen and philosophers and divines." [108] The truth in this observation is that consistent reasoning or action on the basis of incorrect premises may lead to disaster, and that common sense and the direct appeal to experience should be continually invoked to check the conclusions of deduction. This is another way of saying that we should place our reliance upon the *complete* following out of scientific method and not merely upon that part of it which centers around correct deduction.

A part of the discipline of formal logic that has recently been receiving special attention is *definition*. A whole school of experts in the so-called science of semantics has been promulgating the theory that most of men's serious problems are merely verbal, that they stem from wrong definition, faulty syntax and the resulting misunderstanding of meanings. "Metaphysics," according to one semanticist, "is simply bad grammar." In the excessive claims of the semanticists we recognize once again an overemphasis on one valuable philosophic idea or method. In his *Dialogues* Plato established on behalf of philosophy the Socratic method of insisting upon a painstaking definition of words and ideas. Aristotle, in his presentation of logic, developed this method further. And it is along these same lines laid down in ancient Greece that semantics will presumably make its permanent contribution to philosophy.

The attribute of moral determination is of course essential for persevering in the pursuit of difficult scientific problems. In addition, the study of history shows plainly how intense and unremitting have been religious, political, and social pressures upon those who have dared to challenge some traditional dogma and to blaze fresh paths through the jungles of human superstition. Ever among the pioneers of intellectual progress have been scientists whose devotion to truth and truth-seeking has taken precedence over their personal well-being and fate.

Even in times and places where the avowal of unorthodox ideas has not actually endangered the lives of scientists, dissenters have constantly been subject to ridicule, public abuse, or loss of livelihood.*

In the early centuries of modern science it was chiefly the astronomers and physicists who suffered persecution, because the Church feared that their discoveries and the implications of those discoveries would undermine the old-time religious views of the world; and because the ruling class of that age felt that its continued domination was bound up with the ruling myths of feudal society. Today it is those whose field is the social sciences who are most in danger, because their findings often indicate the desirability of drastic changes in the social and economic system. Atomic scientists and others in the natural sciences also get into trouble, primarily when they express liberal or radical opinions on economic, social, or international issues of a controversial nature. Even in supposedly democratic America scientists in general have come under increasing pressure by both university administrations and government bodies to conform or remain silent; and they have need of profound sources of courage and endurance in order to maintain their intellectual freedom.

Though scientific workers, like men and women in other professions, must naturally undergo rigorous training and possess certain personal qualities, scientific achievement and the scientific habit of thought are definite potentialities of the average person. As Professor Frederick Barry writes: "It is no more necessary that every scientist should be an original thinker than that every executive should be so. This is one of the reasons why research is so productive." [109] He goes on to state that the bulk of the work in science is done by those *who follow the rules* and who, outside of their profession, hold varying philosophical, political, and other views.

---

* For a detailed historical account of dissent in the West, see Professor Barrows Dunham's admirable book, *Heroes and Heretics*, Knopf, 1964.

It is essential to note, too, that science in its most fruitful aspects is a cooperative venture. Says the eminent English chemist Frederick Soddy: "The results of those who labor in the fields of knowledge for its own sake are published freely and pooled in the general stock for the benefit of all. Common ownership of all its acquisitions is the breath of its life. Secrecy or individualism of any kind would destroy its fertility." [110] This scientific cooperation is not only a contemporary thing, but extends into the past and future as well. "If I have seen further than Descartes," once remarked Newton, "it is by standing on the shoulders of giants."

The statements by Soddy and Newton point toward the fact that scientific method is in essence a democratic method in which men seek and attain truth through free, independent investigation carried on by qualified individuals and groups throughout the world. This process entails an open ballot, as it were, as to which among competing ideas and hypotheses are sound; and finally results in the *social* verification of scientific concepts. By the same token science is international in implication, scope, and operation.

Humanism believes that the greatest need of our age is the application, insofar as it is possible, of the method and spirit of science to all human problems and that the acquisition of this method and spirit constitutes a training of the mind far more important than the assimiliation of any number of individual facts. Scientific method is embodied at the present time in hundreds of thousands of inventions, industrial processes, and medical techniques of which everyone is glad to accept the benefits. Yet the unfortunate paradox is that relatively few adopt for their own general use this method that has made possible the automobile, radio and television, electric power, steel and concrete, the printing-press, the X-ray machine, innoculation against various diseases, satellites in outer space, and the establishment of a multitude of basic scientific facts and laws.

The disastrous consequences of this inconsistency are revealed, above all, in the broad realm of political, social, and economic activities, as witness the unhappy ordeals of mankind during the war-torn twentieth century. In the world of public affairs the nearest approach to scientific method still remains for the most part the elementary trial-and-error, hit-or-miss improvisation which, even when it occasionally results in sound policies, proves extremely costly and time-consuming. For the Humanist, then, the more adequate development of the social sciences is far and away the most important scientific task of this generation.

Everyone acknowledges that it is a good deal more difficult to apply scientific method in economics and sociology, in government and international relations, than in physics or chemistry or astronomy. Human beings and human societies are much more complex than atoms or the solar system, and more subject to multiple causation. The most successful scientific experimentation demands both isolation of the problem and rigid control over subject matter so far as the purposes of an experiment are concerned. Neither of these prerequisites is easy to obtain in the social sciences. It is not possible to experiment with men and women and children as with chemical solutions in a test tube or some species of animal in a laboratory. Few human beings are willing to be treated as guinea pigs, even for the high ends of science. And if I am right in my contention that individuals possess true freedom of choice, that makes even more formidable the task of the social sciences in arriving at dependable laws and predictions.

Moreover, it is by no means easy for social scientists to maintain strict objectivity and eliminate all personal and subjective bias. This difficulty is complicated by the fact that new theories in the social sciences are likely, as I have indicated, to arouse passionate opposition on the part of individuals or groups who feel that they stand to lose by some alteration in the *status quo*. Thus it is that the discussion of economic, social, and international problems becomes pervaded with intense emotion, which prevents the public from considering reasonably the various solutions suggested and which reacts badly on the work of the scientists themselves.

Perhaps the most important guiding hypothesis that has come to maturity in the social sciences during the last century is that of the economic interpretation of history and contemporary events. This means ascribing to economic factors on the whole and in the long run, priority in the explanation of history, but it decidedly does not rule out the causal efficacy of other factors interacting with the economic yet in general playing less of a role. One of the first and clearest formulations of the economic interpretation, as applied to politics, was put forward in 1787 by James Madison, fourth President of the United States and justly called "the Father of the Constitution." Madison of course believed in the sacredness of private property and advocated a harmonization of the various class interests in society.

He explained in *The Federalist* that the first object of government is to protect "the diversity in the faculties of men, from which the rights of property originate. . . . From the protection of different and unequal faculties of acquiring property, the possession of different degrees and kinds of property immediately results; and from the influences of these on the sentiments and views of the respective proprietors, ensues a division of the society into different interests and parties. . . . The most common and durable source of factions has been the various and unequal distribution of property. Those who hold and those who are without property have ever formed distinct interests in society. Those who are creditors, and those who are debtors, fall under a like discrimination. A landed interest, a manufacturing interest, a mercantile interest, a moneyed interest, with many lesser interests, grow up of necessity in civilized nations and divide them into different classes actuated by different sentiments and views." [111]

Thus we see that the economic interpretation of history, usually associated with the Communists and Marxists, was enunciated many years before Karl Marx was born. You do not, then, have to be any sort of radical or Marxist in order to believe in *an* economic interpretation of history. In America some of our most able historians, such as Charles Beard, have followed a non-Marxist economic interpretation and do not support the cause of the working class or the goal of socialism. Curiously enough, even leading capitalists and businessmen, who spend much time seeking to refute Marx, often adhere to an economic interpretation without realizing it. Thus, they claim that human beings are motivated chiefly by the quest for profits and that capitalism, or the "free enterprise" system, has become the necessary foundation for human well-being in general and for democracy in particular.

The central issue concerning the economic interpretation of history is how far it is reasonable to push it. Humanists agree that economic factors are of primary importance in affecting the course of human affairs. But that does not mean, as the Marxists maintain, that economic activities, property relations, and class struggles are controlling in the determination of human motives and in the development of the complex cultural superstructures of art, law, literature, philosophy, and religion. It was physical and biological factors that brought about the sudden death of President Frankin D. Roosevelt in April 1945. Yet that distressing event, which took place outside the circuits of economic causation, unloosed a Pandora's box of errors and evils in United States domestic and foreign policies.

Beyond these considerations lies the fact that human freedom of choice enables men to rise above their economic conditioning and monetary self-interest. Individuals dedicated to some compelling ideal have time and again shown a contempt for economic security, domestic comfort, and life itself. Among the ideals I have in mind is the determination, which can become an overriding passion, to find and express the truth, regardless of personal consequences or the fate of some previously cherished idea.

Brand Blanshard, Professor Emeritus of Philosophy at Yale, analyzes both Freudian and Marxist explanations of motivation:

"There are such things after all as native intelligence and the pressure of evidence, and neither singly nor in combination are they the functions of anything economic. Indeed, as has often been pointed out, the very success of Marx or Freud in showing his theory true would render the theory itself incredible. If all philosophical theories are produced not by the pressure of evidence, but by irrelevant pushes and pulls, this theory itself must be so produced, and then why believe it? On the other hand, if the theory *has* been arrived at under the constraint of logic and facts, then there is no reason why other conclusions should not be arrived at in the same way, and the theory fails again.

"It may be suggested that the theory of Freud is more plausible than that of Marx because desire is more intimately bound up with thought than are economic conditions. Agreed. But the Freudian theory would hold only if the course of thought were under the complete control of some desire other than the desire for truth itself. Now the desire for truth may be more commonly diverted from its aim by these other desires than was realized before Freud wrote. But that intelligence never succeeds in following an argument where it leads, that it is invariably put off the scent by the seductions of some irrelevant desire seems to me false, and self-evidently false. And if it is, we must admit that intellectual insight is an independent factor which is neither an economic nor a psychological puppet." [112]

Concluding now our general discussion of the social sciences, I think we can say that, despite various handicaps due to their very nature, they have made rapid progress both in methodology and results during the twentieth century. As regards method, they have come to rely more and more upon statistics and functional correlation. It is needful to remember that the social sciences in the full sense of the term are still comparatively young. Whereas modern scientific method became thoroughly established and accepted in the natural sciences during the seventeenth, eighteenth, and nineteenth centuries, it achieved a commanding position in the social disciplines only during the last part of the nineteenth century and the first part of the twentieth.

3. SCIENCE AND THE MEANING OF TRUTH

Humanism's reliance on scientific method extends to the investigation of the nature of truth. A careful analysis of both the natural and the social sciences shows, in the first place, that we do not attain something that is to be called "absolute" truth, but rather what John Dewey cautiously describes as "warranted assertibility." At best, then, we achieve in our search for knowledge only varying degrees of probability, of approximation to the precise and complete truth. For all practical purposes the true is the very, very probable; yet as such it is a dependable guide for action and by far the best guide that we can find in science, philosophy, politics, or any other sphere of human affairs. This properly humble recognition that truth in the last analysis is based on probabilities leaves no room for dogmatism; it encourages tolerance and the growth of free speech.

Reliance on probabilism extends not only to the facts and laws of science, but also to those general and ultimate assumptions that are necessary to the whole scientific enterprise. These assumptions, which are presupposed in all scientific factual inquiry and induction, but which can never be absolutely proved, are known as *postulates*. The first one, that of the Uniformity of Nature, hinges upon the observable fact that there are orderly relations, statable in general laws, objectively obtaining among many events or groups of events in our experience. This postulate of the Uniformity of Nature, more accurately described as that of *predictive uniformity*, assumes that "our world is such that a given group of events will show in subsequent experience the same kind and degree of interconnection that they have shown already." [113]

In short, this postulate, without contradicting the conclusion that pluralism and chance exist, makes explicit the presupposition that our complex cosmos is by no means a chaos, but can be objectively analyzed and described in terms of regular spatio-temporal conjunctions that hold for the future as well as the past. Were this not so, no scientific laws would stand up as true and no reliable reasoning could be carried on. For the very heart of scientific law consists in the assertion of invariable connections between specified phenomena; and the process of deduction itself implies regular connections. From one set of premises a certain conclusion follows, from a different set another conclusion; and at least one of the premises must affirm an actual or supposed law of relation. Of course, the mathematical method and analysis which are so indispensable to science depend on the existence of regular relations. And though the Euclidean system of mathematics is not the only possible one, it is clear that any other conceivable system must likewise be based on the assumption of regular relations.

The second fundamental postulate of science is that of Causality. Not only are there orderly relations in the world, but also many of these relations are expressible in causal terms. This postulate assumes that every event which occurs has a definite cause and that the same cause always produces the same effect. The assumption of Causality, however, does not presuppose that the whole of Nature is bound together in a single, all-inclusive causal system. Such a system would imply that rigid universe of determinism the existence of which I was at pains to disprove in the last chapter. There I explained that there are independent chains of causation which may never intersect at all and which enter into a cause-effect relationship with one another only if they do intersect.

Though the postulates of the Uniformity of Nature and of Causality have been demonstrated as sound in an enormous number of instances and indeed during the entire history of science, they remain assumptions because we cannot be 100 per cent sure that they will hold for all future time. Those who follow scientific method as the surest path to the truth can be said to have *faith* in these two postulates. But it is a faith very unlike that of the supernatural religions, because reliance on these postulates has brought far-reaching success and progress to science, and because these postulates continue to be proved justified in every new scientific discovery and in the everyday life of mankind.

Faith in scientific method functions as a regulative principle of human action and as part of an experimental process in which the repeated questioning of *all* principles is encouraged. This attitude contrasts sharply with the burning, dogmatic, unalterable faith that has invariably been an element in traditional religion.

An objective study of science shows that all knowledge, even the simplest mathematical proposition, springs originally from human experience within this natural world. Scientific method operates without any dependence on or need for a supernatural mental faculty in man that gets in touch with a supernatural truth-giving Being or that draws ideas out of some mysterious realm beyond Nature. There is no ground, either, for alleging that "scientific" truth originates in the this-earthly experience of man, but that "spiritual" or "ethical" truth comes from on high in an altogether different way. It is the Humanist contention that *all* truth or knowledge has the same natural status and origin.

The procedures of science also indicate that no idea or group of ideas, regardless of how logical, brilliant, or seemingly self-evident, achieves the status of knowledge *immediately*. The establishment of knowledge in any field requires time and trouble in the form of observation, reflection, experimentation, and testing. This fact automatically rules out religious revelation or any kind of intuition as in itself a dependable method of arriving at the truth. The most dazzling flash of insight from whatever source cannot be trusted until it is thoroughly verified. There can no no *innate* knowledge either.

In order of time, then, knowledge is always secondary and

derivative, despite its crucial importance when finally ascertained. After any idea has been definitely established as an item of knowledge, we can then use it immediately in future situations. There are a multitude of well-tested conceptions about the common-sense world of experience that we have learned to take as a matter of course. Obviously, too, ideas that are once proven true can become instruments of quick and reliable human communication and the objects of pure aesthetic enjoyment and contemplation. These considerations do not run counter to my assertion that the *original* establishment of any item of knowledge is not a matter of immediate apprehension. Immediacy of *use* is not the same as immediacy of *proof*.

The impossibility of self-evident, instantaneous knowledge is closely correlated with the fact that sensations and sensory images *are* immediately had in human experience, but are not in themselves equivalent to knowledge. Past philosophies and psychologies have frequently confused sensations and ideas, claiming that sensations give an instant knowledge of things. Sensations or sense perceptions in their elementary, undiscriminated flow are simply noncognitive natural events that are neither true nor false in themselves. They are the immediately felt or sensed experiences which constitute by far the larger part of total human experience, but which are on a different level from the knowledge experience. This point becomes clearer when we remind ourselves that most subhuman animals feel pain and pleasure and have sensations, but do not reason and acquire knowledge.

Human sensations are stimuli to thought and knowledge, and also serve as checks and signs. For instance, a complex of sensations in which a certain shape and color predominate is not intrinsically a piece of knowledge; exactly what object it represents is at the outset a matter of doubt and becomes clear only when reflection and objective discrimination are able to assign to it a specific *meaning* in a specific context. Thus sensation or sense perception enters into a knowledge relation only when it stands for, becomes a sign of, something more than or other than itself, as when a perception of something round and red comes to signify "apple" in one connection and "stop light" in another. As Dewey sums up the matter, sensory qualities "are not objects of cognition in themselves," but "acquire cognitive function when they are employed in specific situations as signs of something beyond themselves." [114]

When for some human mind any object, event, perception, or mental image means, signifies, signalizes, symbolizes, indicates, suggests, represents, stands for, connotes, implies, or is a sign of another thing or event, then a person is having an idea. There are many directly sensory or perceptual meanings, as when a green light signifies "go" or smoke signifies "fire." But most of the established ideas or meanings that men use are conceptual ones and are embodied in and correlated with socially agreed-upon linguistic symbols, that is, in standardized words whose meanings are defined in dictionaries and other books of reference. Words seen or heard come to us in the form of sense perceptions and perform their cognitive role when we are conscious of them as visual or auditory signs bearing a certain meaning. We can listen for hours to a man talking in a foreign language, but unless we understand that language his words will be to us mere sensations of sound carrying no particular significance. Knowledge is always knowledge *of* things and events, as mediated through sense experience, *with* their meaning or meanings.

We attain the truth when we attribute to things or events their correct meaning or meanings, in terms of their precise behavior, of their causes and effects or of their other relationships. Every true idea must have an objective referent. An object or event may give rise to a number of meanings, depending upon its various functions and interrelations. Assigning the wrong meaning or meanings results in untruth or error and thereby in mistaken human actions that may have the most deleterious consequences. A sensation of round redness, an example I cited above, can be established as indicating what we call an apple only after some common-sense reflection, including checking and comparison with past experiences of a like nature. The sensation does not carry its true meaning on the face of it; the object might have turned out to be a tomato or a ball.

This theory of knowledge clears up many problems over which philosophers have wrangled perpetually. A straight stick thrust into water looks bent. Is this bent quality then only an "appearance" as compared with the "real" stick, which is straight? There is in fact no problem here if we accept the perception of bentness as a perfectly real natural event and proceed to work out its correct meaning. That meaning is that the refraction of light through the water causes the stick in this situation to look bent; if I did not see it that way, there would be something wrong with my eyes.

Or take the matter of hallucinations or apparitions, when a man thinks he sees someone or something that is not actually there. We need not necessarily doubt the occurrence of his illusion, but through intellectual analysis we are able to attribute to it its proper meaning. This is, first, that it is a purely personal and subjective phantasm and, second, that the individual in question is drunk or mentally ill or suffering from the effects of some other abnormal state. There is no objectively existing thing in the external world corresponding to the man's vision, but there *is* an objective cause of it. The existence of subjective experiences is an objective fact, and they are always bound up with objective events and structures.

Dreams are subject to similar treatment. Dreams are events that most certainly occur, as everyone can testify. It is the meaning given to them that so often turns out to be illusory. If I dream that I am talking with a friend who has died, I might interpret it as demonstrating his personal survival in an after-life; but if I am sensible, I shall attribute his appearance in my dream to grief over his death and a strong desire to see him again. I sometimes have such dreams about friends or relatives who have died, and doubt very much that I need go to a psychoanalyst for an explanation.

Our further analysis of science leads, finally, to the conclusion that a meaning or idea is to be judged true if, in acting upon it, we find that it accomplishes, in terms of concrete consequences, what it *purports* to accomplish; if the potential consequences claimed on its behalf actually take place and are verifiable. Conversely, its unreliability will be demonstrated if these consequences cannot be verified, if the idea *fails* to measure up to its pretensions. A doctor's diagnosis is true if it is so proved in tests applied to the patient; his idea of a proper cure is likewise proved true or untrue by its results.

This criterion of truth by which a theory or idea is pronounced correct according to whether it succeeds or fails in human verification and action is all-inclusive. It holds with equal relevance in the realm of physical science, of social science, of purely personal self-interest, of military tactics, of sports, or indeed of any branch whatever of human investigation or activity. A rough-and-ready formula that aims to express this *operational* conception of truth is: an idea or hypothesis is true if it works, or, negatively, an idea is not true if it does not work. To follow through with this double formulation, we of course must know the general context of the idea and all the relevant circumstances in relation to its working or not working.

In any case, practice or workability is the *test* of a truth, not the *source* of it. The truth of an idea does not lie *in* verification; we are able to prove it true *through* verification. An idea is true *if* it works, not because it works; for it already *was* true and corresponding to objective reality. New truths lie all about us waiting to be discovered by men wielding scientific techniques; but the process of discovering does not *make* ideas true.

With these necessary qualifications, the "Does it work?" standard, which has become more or less idiomatic for most

Americans, expresses fairly well in plain everyday terms the pragmatic theory of truth. Certain homely proverbs or maxims do likewise, such as "The proof of the pudding is in the eating"; "Handsome is as handsome does"; "Actions speak louder than words"; and the Biblical "By their fruits ye shall know them." Just as there is a significant continuity between ordinary common sense and scientific method, so there is between common sense and the pragmatic notion of truth. This pragmatic conception brings truth down to earth, where it belongs; and it is democratic in that it removes theoretical barriers to the common man's attainment of knowledge.

In current political life the pragmatic criterion means that public officials, whether elected or appointed, must finally be judged not in terms of campaign promises and public speeches, but in terms of their concrete accomplishments, of the results that they achieve on behalf of the people. "Let's look at the record" was the effective way in which Governor Alfred E. Smith of New York used to express this principle. The pragmatic standard also implies that men in any walk of life should be evaluated on the basis of what they *do* and not what they are *called*. This point takes on added importance in times of social crisis and tension when the tendency increases to discuss and dispose of the great questions of the day by means of epithets and smear words.

The insistence that theories, hypotheses, ideas, concepts, and programs must be proved correct in practice, strictly tested by means of empirical procedures controlled and carried through by human beings goes hand in hand with the conviction that truth is objective. Pragmatic proof is not a matter of mere personal, private experience or satisfaction, but an experimental process operating on the principle that reliable knowledge is socially verifiable. As Professor Abraham Edel phrases it, "To assert that a proposition is true means to predict its continued verification, its permanent presence within the body of accepted knowledge. . . . To speak of truth as eternal is not necessarily to locate it outside of the changing world. It means instead that continued testing of the proposition's consequences will continually confirm it." [115]

It is necessary to note that since ideas are meanings, the correspondence of truth to objective reality is not equivalent to a pictorial duplication of it, a photographic copy. The function of knowledge is to gain increasing control over existence on behalf of human purposes, not to reflect the objective world as in a mirror. A related philosophic error is to consider that human experience is primarily a matter of contemplation; to take the "spectator view" of knowledge, which derives to a large extent from an overemphasis on the role of vision.

Men are constantly changing and transforming Nature for their own ends. This transformation occurs not only through scientific controls and inventions as embodied in all sorts of economic and other familiar processes, but also in the very carrying out of scientific method in the laboratory and elsewhere. In their experiments scientists, in order to follow the lead and determine the consequences of some hypothesis, are continually manipulating physical materials, shifting the position and relations of objects, mixing things together in totally new combinations. Thus they experimentally alter some controlled and isolated sector of the environment as a way of discovering truth.

Completely exploded is the notion so long prevalent in philosophy and psychology that men acquire knowledge through the imprint of sensations upon the mind as if upon a photographic plate. "According to this theory, mental life originated in sensations which are separately and passively received, and which are formed, through laws of retention and association, into a mosaic of images, perceptions and conceptions. . . . Except in combining atomic sensations, the mind was wholly passive and acquiescent in knowing. . . . The effect of the development of biology has been to reverse the picture. . . . Experience becomes an affair primarily of doing. The organism does not stand about, Micawberlike, waiting for something to turn up. It does not wait passive and inert for something to impress itself upon it from without." [116]

The general conception of knowledge that I am supporting received its first detailed treatment in modern times during the late nineteenth century at the hands of the American logician and scientist, Charles S. Peirce, who called his doctrine *Pragmaticism.* William James further developed this theory under the name of *Pragmatism,* but pushed it to unacceptable and subjective extremes, as in his book *The Will to Believe.* John Dewey then took hold, corrected James' misconceptions and termed the result *Instrumentalism,* in order to avoid confusion and to bring out the instrumental, problem-solving character of human thought and knowledge. Clarence I. Lewis, former Professor of Philosophy at Harvard, has worked through to a similar position, although he uses somewhat different technical terms.

Not all Humanists go along with me in supporting the pragmatic conception of knowledge, and controversy continues to rage over it. Very often, however, those who criticize it and who say that Dewey's philosophy remains tainted by subjectivism themselves proceed on the basis of a pragmatic theory of knowledge. Like the logicians who cannot help using Aristotle's laws of thought in condemning those very laws, so the philosophers who condemn Dewey are prone to depend on the very pragmatic sanction that he upholds.

Among Dewey's severest critics today, for instance, are the Marxists. Yet Lenin once stated that "practice alone can serve as a real proof." And one of America's leading Marxist philosophers, Dr. Selsam, attributes to Engels, and himself avers, that "Practice lies at the root of all knowledge. . . . Practice is the test of truth. Just as knowledge begins with practice, so it is in practice that we prove the truth of our ideas." [117] Selsam's statement makes plain, I think, that the pragmatic view of truth as developed in American philosophy and especially by John Dewey comes close to authoritative Marxist thought.

This point is hotly denied by the Marxists, who have failed to judge Dewey's philosophy impartially because in his later years he became hostile towards the Soviet Union.

The fact remains that neither the possession of a philosophically sound theory of knowledge nor a correct understanding of scientific method, or both together, is a guarantee that anyone will arrive at the truth in regard to any particular question. Serious mistakes can be made in the application of scientific method. Agreement that all hypotheses must be verified does not necessarily result in agreement as to the exact type or degree of evidence required in a specific case. In the sphere of the social sciences, especially, scientific method is still so lacking in precision that first-rate economists and sociologists often differ radically as to the right solution for some important problem. Trained thinkers who have established themselves as experts in one field of knowledge may turn out to be most unreliable in some other field of investigation or habitually scatterbrained in the conduct of their personal affairs.

Scientific method as such is ethically and socially neutral. It has frequently operated on behalf of all sorts of antisocial ends such as organized crime, wars of aggression, and the suppression of racial minorities. The Nazis utilized scientific method with great success in the waging of mechanized warfare; and when they set themselves the problem of how to exterminate the Jews of Europe, they used scientific techniques very efficiently to advance their hideous end. Again, it is scientific method that has discovered how to harness nuclear energy to human purposes. Yet everyone knows that the most portentous question of the day is whether nuclear energy will be applied constructively for the welfare of mankind or whether it will become the most destructive Frankenstein in history by transforming, in a possible third World War, the chief centers of modern civilization into smoking charnel houses.

In short, reason and scientific method are not in themselves

enough to achieve a Humanist world. Wielded by cold and
cruel men in search of personal gain or by autocratic groups
disdainful of the common welfare, science can lead to a veritable hell on earth. Only in the service of generous and humane ends does it fulfill its highest possibilities. For the
Humanist, intellect and emotion, head and heart, must function together. In educational circles, at least, this ancient
principle has found wide acceptance. Thus the constitution of
the Phillips Exeter Academy reads: "Though goodness without knowledge . . . is weak and feeble, yet knowledge without
goodness is dangerous. . . . Both united form the noblest
character and lay the surest foundation of usefulness to mankind." The Platonic dictum, "Virtue is knowledge," is insuf-
ficient.

Behind the scientist's pursuit of truth there should be emotional drive; and once a man is sure of a truth, it is right that
it should command his emotional allegiance. To neglect either
head or heart is to overemphasize one of them at the expense
of the other. Here we come back once more to the monistic
psychology that sees man as a dynamic unity of body and
mind, feeling and thought. To conceive of human beings as
mere thinking machines is as artificial and dangerous as to
treat them as mere bundles of emotion. It is always the *whole*
man with whom we have to deal.

The best safeguard for the proper use of science is that it
should always go hand in hand with the methods and aims of
democracy; its own general advancement, as we have seen,
depends on democratic cooperation and verification. Humanism, then, firmly supports the use, development, and extension
of reason and scientific method, democratically conceived and
directed, as mankind's greatest hope for successfully coping
with its formidable problems; and as the only way of achieving that unity of theory and practice which has so long been
a goal of philosophers.

CHAPTER VI

The Affirmation of Life

1. THE ETHICS OF HUMANISM

In the Humanist ethics the chief end of thought and action is to further this-earthly human interests on behalf of the greater glory of man. The watchword of Humanism is happiness for all humanity in this existence as contrasted with salvation for the individual soul in a future existence and the glorification of a supernatural Supreme Being. Humanism urges men to accept freely and joyously the great boon of life and to realize that life in its own right and for its own sake can be as beautiful and splendid as any dream of immortality.

The philosophy of Humanism constitutes a profound and passionate affirmation of the joys and beauties, the braveries and idealisms, of existence upon this earth. It heartily welcomes all life-enhancing and healthy pleasures, from the vigorous enjoyments of youth to the contemplative delights of mellowed age, from the simple gratifications of food and drink, sunshine and sports, to the more complex appreciation of art and literature, friendship and social communion. Humanism believes in the beauty of love and the love of beauty. It exults in the pure magnificence of external Nature. All the many-sided possibilities for good in human living the Humanist would weave into a sustained pattern of happiness under the guidance of reason.

In this Humanist affirmation of life the monistic psychology again plays a most significant role. For this view means that in whatever he does man is a living unity of body and personality, an interfunctioning oneness of mental, emotional, and physical qualities. Humanism adheres to the highest ethical ideals and fosters the so-called goods of the spirit, such as those of culture and art and responsible citizenship. At the same time it insists that all ideals and values are grounded in this world of human experience and natural forms. As Santayana puts it in summing up his conception of human nature, "everything ideal has a natural basis and everything natural an ideal development." [118]

Much of the emphasis in supernaturalist ethics has been negative, calling on men continually to deny many of their most wholesome impulses in order to keep their souls pure and undefiled for that life after death which is so very much more important than life before death. In this ethics the prospect of supernatural rewards and punishments in the future overshadows present conduct; the values decreed by supernatural authority override those of the natural and temporal order in which man actually lives.

By contrast, the emphasis of Humanist and naturalistic ethics is *positive*.* It is an ethics in which conscience does not merely play the role of a vetoing censor, but is creative in the sense of bringing to the fore new and higher values. This system of morality recommends the greater and more frequent enjoyment of earthly goods on the part of all men everywhere; it repudiates ascetic other-worldliness in favor of buoyant this-worldliness; it is against all defeatist systems which either postpone happiness to an after-existence or recommend acquiescence to social injustice in this existence.

An excellent example of the typical religious defeatism that Humanism decries is the following consolation offered by Pope Pius XI in his encyclical of 1932, at the height of the Great Depression: "Let the poor and all those who at this time are facing the hard trial of want of work and scarcity of food, let them in a like spirit of penance suffer with greater resignation the privations imposed upon them by these hard

---

* Whereas eight of the Old Testament's Ten Commandments, for instance, are phrased in negative terms.

times and the state of society, which Divine Providence in an ever-loving but inscrutable plan has assigned them. Let them accept with a humble and trustful heart from the hand of God the effects of poverty, rendered harder by the distress in which mankind now is struggling. . . . Let them take comfort in the certainty that their sacrifices and troubles borne in a Christian spirit will concur efficaciously to hasten the hour of mercy and peace." *

Humanism sweeps aside the confusing and corrupting Dualism of the past in which "the natural life of man with its desires and pleasures became something to be shunned as evil and degraded, something to be forsaken for higher things. Man's true nature was of a different quality, his destiny lay in another realm. . . . It is this dualism running through all of man's actions that has left its impress on the commonly accepted moral codes of the West to this day, and seems even yet to make impossible that wholehearted and simply enjoyment of the goods of a natural existence that men now envy in the Greeks of old. It is not that men have ever refrained from action or from these pleasures, but that they have never been able to rid themselves of the notion that there is something essentially wrong about them." [119]

Humanist ethics is opposed to the puritanical prejudice against pleasure and desire that marks the Western tradition of morality. Men and women have profound wants and needs of an emotional and physical character, the fulfillment of which is an essential ingredient in the good life. Contempt for or suppression of normal desires may result in their discharge in surreptitious, coarse, or abnormal ways. While it is true that uncontrolled human desires are a prime cause of evil in the world, it is equally true that human desires directed by reason toward socially · useful goals are a prime foundation of the

---

* It is only fair to note that, since this statement was made, the Roman Catholic Church has become liberalized to some extent, particularly under the stimulus of John XXIII, Pope from 1958 until 1963, and of Paul VI, who succeeded him.

good. They provide the drive and energy that eventuate in individual and group achievement.

The reasonable self-restraint that Humanism favors has little in common with the constant sense of guilt encouraged by the traditional Christian ethics. A central proposition in that ethics is the original sin and inherent wickedness of man; and one of its special stresses is that the sex impulse in human beings is essentially base and bad. Adam's original sin, it would have us believe, is transmitted from generation to generation through the act of procreation. Thus the Christian Church, in order to establish the complete purity of Jesus, felt obliged to assume that he was born of a virgin in violation of ordinary biological laws. In 1854 the Roman Catholic Church took a further step when Pope Pius IX handed down the dogma of the Immaculate Conception. This doctrine means, to quote the Pope's Bull, "that the Blessed Virgin Mary, from the first instant of her conception, was . . . preserved from all stain of Original Sin." It was owing in large part to the influence of Christianity that immorality for most people in the West became synonymous with improper sex conduct.

Humanist ethics of course recognizes the necessity of high standards in relations between the sexes, but it does not regard sexual emotions in themselves as in any sense evil. Those emotions, far from being tainted because they stem from the the reproductive functions of the body, ought to have a preferred status because of that very association with the creation of life. And as Santayana observes, "Love would never take so high a flight unless it sprung from something profound and elementary." [120] Morally speaking, the sex life of an individual is no more important than his political or economic life. In fact, Humanism asserts that perhaps the most pressing ethical need of our time is the establishment of higher standards of action in the fields of politics and economics. A man can be an exemplary husband and at the same time be dishonest in business affairs or engage in political graft. Overemphasis on the sex aspect of morality has led to a neglect of its other aspects and a narrowing of its range.

The realm of ethics is pre-eminently social in scope and application; within its sphere lies all human conduct in which socially significant alternatives are possible. Many small everyday acts have no ethical significance, though any type of action may under certain circumstances carry such significance. In origin and development ethics is likewise social, the term itself coming from the Greek word *ethos*, meaning custom or usages. Ethical values and standards evolve in the interaction between individual and individual, between the individual and the group, and between group and group. The sympathetic impulses in human nature, such as the parental, the sexual, and the gregarious, become socially transformed and broadened in human association.

The advantages of mutual cooperation, support, and protection lead to the social functioning and utilization of basic instincts such as those of self-preservation and reproduction. Conscience, the sense of right and wrong and the insistent call of one's better, more idealistic, more social-minded self, is a social product. Feelings of right and wrong that at first have their locus within the family gradually develop into a pattern for the tribe or city, then spread to the much larger unit of the nation, and finally from the nation to mankind as a whole. Humanism sees no need for resorting to supernatural explanations or sanctions at any point in the ethical process. A divine First Cause or Sustaining Principle is no more necessary in the sphere of ethics than in that of physics or metaphysics. Human beings can and do behave decently toward one another without depending on the intercession of a third party known as God.

In making ethical decisions the Humanist relies, as in any endeavor to solve a problem, upon the use of reason approaching as closely as possible to the method of science, instead of upon religious revelation or any sort of authority or intuition. Since moral judgments, like judgments of aesthetic quality, are a species of value judgments, it is most difficult to obtain general intellectual agreement as to what is right and what is wrong. Nevertheless, the Humanist contends that a true science of ethics is possible and will yet be established.

For Humanism no human acts are good or bad in or of themselves. Whether an act is good or bad is to be judged by its *consequences* for the individual and society. Knowledge of the good, then, must be worked out, like knowledge of anything else, through the examination and evaluation of the concrete consequences of an idea or hypothesis. Humanist ethics draws its guiding principles *from* human experience and tests them *in* human experience. Since, as I pointed out in the last chapter, knowledge of anything is in the first instance never immediate, there can be no immediate knowledge of the right. However, once we have established or accepted a regulative principle of morality, we are able to *use* it immediately thereafter.

In Humanism's stress upon the need and value of intelligence in the ethical enterprise, its approach differs once again from that of the traditional Christian ethics. Though Humanism naturally incorporates certain of the generous social ideals voiced by Jesus, it finds little in the New Testament that can be considered as an appeal to reason. The appeal of Jesus was primarily designed to bring about a change in the heart of man; and this transformation was to be wrought by individuals receiving insight and inspiration from a personal God. Deeply imbedded in the Christian tradition was an antagonism toward the intellect, expressed originally in the myth that God punished Adam for disobeying the divine injunction against eating the fruit of the tree of knowledge. In St. Paul's matchless panegyric on love in I Corinthians 13 he concludes: "And now abideth faith, hope, love, these three; but the greatest of these is love." In his whole summation of the highest Christian virtues in Corinthians, there is not the slightest mention of intelligence as a primary human value. Some 1,500 years later

Martin Luther was insisting that reason is "the Devil's bride" and "God's worst enemy."

Supernatural religions in general have been very distrustful of human reliance on reason. The ethical tradition in which the human mind, unprompted by any supernatural agency, was regarded as able to attain moral truth came down from ancient Greek philosophy, notably that of Aristotle, and from modern thinkers like Spinoza.

The Humanist submits every ethical precept of the past to the searching analysis of reason, operating in the light of present circumstances. For the Humanist well realizes that all ethical laws and systems are relative to the particular historical period and to the particular culture of which they are a part. What was good for the Old Testament Hebrews some 4,000 years ago or for the Greeks in 400 B.C. or for Europeans only 100 years ago is not necessarily good for Americans living in the second half of the twentieth century. Furthermore, in the world today there are a considerable number of different nations and peoples, some of them in quite dissimilar stages of historical development. Ethical standards generally accepted in the United States today may be in their formative phases in less developed countries or consciously frowned upon among peoples with a different socio-economic system. These remarks do not mean, of course, that moral standards are merely subjective or that we cannot learn a great deal from the ethical systems of the past.

Clearly, however, ethical rules of conduct become out-of-date as conditions change and time marches on. In general the advance of science and invention has affected ethical philosophy to an immense degree. Modern medicine, for instance, has demonstrated that many undesirable human traits which used to be ascribed to original sin or bad character are actually attributable to glandular insufficiencies or deep-seated emotional frustrations. The discovery and dissemination of scientific birth control techniques are naturally of vital significance in the sphere of sex behavior. The growth of mechanized, urban civilization in recent centuries has both altered long-established ethical standards based on a primitive agricultural civilization and given rise to innumerable new ethical problems. A twentieth-century invention like the automobile demands a new and special code of ethics for the millions of drivers, more than 92,000,000 in the United States alone. Reckless driving that threatens life and limb has become one of the major immoralities. This is a field in which the law rightly steps in to regularize and enforce proper standards of safety.

The multiplication of fresh ethical problems of a complex character in our present-day society shows the need for the moral flexibility that Humanism advocates. The function of basic moral principles, expressing the funded wisdom of human experience, is not to provide absolute rules of conduct that will automatically tell men just what to do under all circumstances. Their function "is to supply standpoints and methods which will enable the individual to make for himself an analysis of the elements of good and evil in the particular situation in which he finds himself." [121] That analysis should always take into consideration the surrounding circumstances, the total context of a concrete problem.

Let us return for a moment to the appalling evil of automobile accidents, which in the United States now (as of 1965) bring death annually to more than 40,000 persons, almost five times the death toll from murder. The ethics of automobile driving has become a pressing problem for America in every section of the country. Should the careful, intelligent driver try to solve this problem by never driving over 40 miles an hour? No. It all depends on the circumstances. On the great modern parkways, the state Thruways with separated one-way lanes for traffic, the ordinary prudent man (to use a favorite expression of Aristotle) can drive his car safely at 60 miles an hour. But in the heart of a big city he must slow down to 25 or even 15. Thus the ethical driver, sensitive to his own safety as well as that of others, must ever be on the alert to the changing conditions he encounters, applying his *general principles* of good driving to each *specific* situation. So it is with moral problems as a whole.

Humanism teaches the formation of sound moral habits as well as of guiding moral principles, but believes that neither habits nor principles should grow too set or rigid. The highest ethical duty is often to discard the outmoded ethics of the past; it is a truism to say that the merely good is the enemy of the better. The Humanist refuses to accept any Ten Commandments or other ethical precepts as immutable and universal laws never to be challenged or questioned. He bows down to no alleged supreme moral authority either past or present.

This is one way in which the Humanist continually reasserts the moral freedom that is inseparable from moral responsibility. The act of willing this or that, of choosing among various courses of conduct, is central in the realm of ethics. As I said in Chapter IV, I believe firmly that in making ethical decisions, man has the prerogative of true freedom of choice. There are two main types of ethical decisions in which human freedom functions. First, we have the situation in which an individual is sincerely perplexed over what is the right thing to do and chooses a certain line of action after careful deliberation. Second, we have the situation in which a person quickly realizes, from past experience, what he ought to do, but is tempted not to do it because some insistent personal desire or temptation lures him in a different direction. In this kind of situation the *I ought* implies the freedom of *I can, but need not.*

In the first type of case one of the most difficult classes of problems to settle revolves around the proper relationship between means and ends. The enunciation of ethical ideals, be they ever so splendid, tends to become mere sentimentality or demagogy, unless intelligence can devise means to put them into effect. The good man is one who not only has good motives and acts according to reason, but who is also effective in the successful adjustment of means to ends. Efficiency in this elementary sense is, I think, an essential ingredient of the good life.

Does all this imply, then, that the end justifies the means? No, that is much too loose a generalization and is like asking "Is the object worth the price?" It is impossible to give a meaningful answer to this very general question, unless we know the precise object that is under consideration and the exact price that is being demanded.

No responsible person really believes that *any* object justifies *any* price any more than he believes that *any* end justifies *any* means. But we can say, and everyone with an ounce of common sense must agree, that *some* objects justify *some* prices and *some* ends justify *some* means. In getting at the ethical significance of a means-end situation it is always necessary to be specific and inquire, "Does this particular end or set of ends justify this particular means or group of means?"

Most tactful people do not hesitate to tell "white lies" occasionally in order to escape from the incessant interruptions of the telephone, the embarrassment of unexpected callers, or the overenthusiasm of friends or family in trying to draw them into this or that activity. Doctors also resort to white lies when they deceive a sick man as to the seriousness of his illness, in order to prevent worry and fear that might aggravate his condition, or simply to keep him from feeling unhappy. Sharp debates still rage in the medical world as to whether or not to tell the truth to patients in the terminal stage of incurable cancer. Thus white lies of one sort or another constitute a compromise with ideals of honesty and are an example of our allowing certain ends to justify means that are ordinarily unacceptable.

To take a more important class of cases, consider the matter of violence and coercion. Is it justifiable to use the bad means of violence in order to further an end generally recognized as good? Well, even a 100 per cent pacifist would no doubt grant that it is legitimate to shoot a mad dog which is about to attack a small child. And most persons would not wish to advocate the disbanding of municipal police departments, even though policemen sometimes abruptly kill robbers or murderers who are escaping from the scene of a crime. In fact, our entire legal system depends in the last analysis upon the state's coercive powers of enforcement. Plainly, then, in the present stage of civilization, force and the threat of force are ethically justifiable under certain circumstances.

In judging whether any particular means is ethically justifiable for the accomplishment of a certain end, we must in the first place endeavor to estimate impartially the *total consequences* of using that means, including possible deleterious effects on the end desired. A certain means may well alter the very end for which it was brought into play; the question is precisely how and to what extent. A particular means may have unfortunate by-products and yet be justified because it achieves the main end in view. Even when a drastic means completely negates the desired end, as when a severe operation results in the death of the patient, we cannot necessarily conclude that the means was not justified.

This leads me to state that we cannot fairly evaluate the ethical implications of utilizing a specific means unless we consider the possible alternatives, unless we determine the probable consequences of *not* using that particular means. In many a case the best chance of saving a sick man from death is to take the risk of having him undergo a major operation. When it comes to broad social problems, unhappily we are not applying our means in a society that is already perfect; and as long as the system under which we live remains imperfect, we cannot hope to change it through altogether perfect methods. Yet there are many amateur moralists in circulation who apparently do expect just that. With their extraordinary propensity for thinking in a vacuum, they set up an ideal standard of conduct and then condemn anything that falls short of it, regardless of consequences and alternatives, regardless of how the actions of both unreliable friends and unscrupulous enemies limit the means which individuals and groups can use with efficacy. Another way of expressing this point is to say that choosing the lesser evil sometimes results in the greater good.

What I have been saying implies a constant and close relationship between means and ends and a recognition that, in the main, means are just as important as ends. In fact, there is a continuous succession of means and ends; and a certain means is often so important that it becomes an end in itself, while an end achieved often becomes the means to another end beyond. A child goes to an elementary school as a means of becoming prepared for high school or private secondary school; but his work in the elementary school is of sufficient importance to make its successful conclusion a thoroughly worthwhile end in itself. The boy then goes to high school, which is a means to entering college but also a significant end in itself. The young man's years at college, too, are both means and end: a means to his successful career in mature life and a most important end in the training of his mind and the broadening of his education.

Means and ends, then, together constitute essential stages in an onflowing continuum of activity that is literally endless. Their artificial separation accounts for much that is bad in present-day society. Perhaps the worst of such separations, increasingly aggravated by the division of labor in modern industrial production, is between the average person's work and his life as a whole. Thus a worker may function as a specialized automaton in the assembly line of some big factory, so that his job becomes merely instrumental to making a living. Ideally, one's occupation should be significant and enjoyable in itself and thereby an end as well as a means. Much of the confusion regarding means and ends derives from the Christian tradition in which mundane life was regarded as a mere means, a toilsome pilgrimage, toward the supreme end of heavenly bliss.

We see a somewhat comparable split between means and ends when fanatics, frequently bursting with noble intentions, set up some far-off earthly end as all-important and try to persuade people to make literally everything they do subordinate, in the form of means, to this one goal. This leads to an extreme sort of future-worship and the neglect of men's present rights to happiness and their immediate opportunities for it. If human beings are to be happy and to enjoy life, it must always be during some period of time describable as *now*. What the future-worshipers do is to ask each succeeding generation to sacrifice itself in working exclusively on behalf of a distant Utopia that may or may not some day arrive. The Humanist asserts that, from the viewpoint of human happiness and the sum total of good, today is just as significant as tomorrow and the current year just as significant as any a decade hence.

Another common but unacceptable cleavage in traditional ethics, besides that between means and end, is the cleavage between motive and act. Kant is the prototype of those philosophers who overemphasize the matter of motives, since he sets up the possession of a good will, aside from the consequences of the acts for which it is responsible, as the test of goodness and makes the absolutely pure soul with pure motives the ideal of individual morality. This Kantian notion stems from a supernaturalistic, mind-body dualism and leads to the superficial doctrine that the remaking of society depends solely upon the moral regeneration of the individual as contrasted with systematic changes and reforms of an institutional character.

It would be likewise one-sided, however, to go to the other extreme from the Kantian ethics and claim that we can evaluate the ethical quality of a man through his overt actions alone. For intentions do enter as an important factor into the ethical significance of human conduct. The fact is that there is no sharp separation between motive and action; a total action consists of *both* the motive and the concrete act. This view is written into our accepted law. Thus an enormous difference exists, involving the death penalty, between first-degree murder, when a man kills with deliberate intent, and technical manslaughter, as when the driver of an automobile accidentally runs over and kills someone. On the other hand, by establishing the offense of criminal negligence, the law recognizes that absence of a bad motive is not always a sufficient excuse.

The animating and persistent dispositions of men, be these dispositions good or bad, lead on the whole to concrete actions and effects of a determinate nature. A person with the best of intentions may do something which accidentally injures others. But we do not judge him entirely in terms of this one act, because his motives in general are of a sort that result in other acts which, broadly considered, seem conducive to the social welfare.

The attribution of low motives to people whose ideas or conduct you do not like is a favorite pastime throughout the world. It should be obvious, however, that it is rather difficult to gauge with accuracy the complex subjective states that lead a man to this or that action or opinion. Humanists, therefore, are chary of passing sweeping moral judgments on other people. Even the wisest of men hardly possesses the knowledge and impartiality to render a Last Judgment on himself or anyone else. Nevertheless, increasingly during these trying times men adopt the attitude that those differing with them on some current issue are absolute scoundrels and utterly damned. Needless to state, it is possible for reasonable and morally worthy persons sincerely to disagree on the great controversies of the day. The human mind being a somewhat imperfect instrument, even outright inconsistency is seldom a sure sign of hypocrisy. Intellectual intolerance and moral arrogance on the part of those who may themselves ultimately be proved mistaken are at the opposite pole from the true spirit of philosophy.

The whole question of motivation is fundamental to the Humanist philosophy for another reason. One of the great aims of Humanism is the transformation and socialization of human motives. This is a sector where human nature can be drastically reconditioned and reshaped. What the scientific study of human motives shows is that human nature is neither essentially bad nor essentially good, neither essentially selfish nor essentially unselfish, neither essentially warlike nor essentially pacific. There is neither original sin nor original virtue. But human nature *is* essentially flexible and educable. And the moulding or re-moulding of human motives is something that takes place not only in childhood and youth, but also throughout adult life and under the impact of fundamental economic institutions and cultural media that weightily influence mind and character. The social development and conditioning of human beings, their training, direct and indirect, by means of all sorts of educational techniques, can be so extensive that the hoary half-truth, "You can't change human nature," becomes quite irrelevant.

Humanism believes that in ethical training, while sufficient attention must naturally be given to the process of self-cultivation, equal emphasis should be laid on the individual's relation to society, his unending debt to the collective culture of mankind and his corresponding obligation to serve the common good. Humanism holds that even highly developed intelligent self-interest, such as Plato discusses in his *Dialogues,* is not sufficient as an ultimate ethical sanction. For intelligence operating on behalf of an evil will is precisely the definition of Satan. A first-rate mind always acting at the behest of self-interest does not necessarily result in a person's furthering the welfare of the community. There may and do occur situations that ethically demand the very last measure of personal sacrifice and in which, therefore, no form of mere individual self-interest will be adequate. Neither the capable mind nor the good will acting alone and in isolation can be depended upon for genuine ethical achievement; both functioning together make the ideal partnership from the Humanist standpoint.

The theory that everyone invariably acts from self-interest, direct or indirect, is psychologically unsound. The simple fallacy behind that theory consists, as Dewey states, "in transforming the (truistic) fact of acting *as* a self into the fiction of always acting *for* self." [122] Now obviously a man does act frequently on behalf of himself alone; but also he can and does act on behalf of other people and large social objectives. He may well obtain personal satisfaction in so doing, even fame or glory,* but that satisfaction is likely to be a by-product and is not necessarily his original and primary goal.

There are many situations demanding courage or heroism in which a man has time to think through the main implications and consequences before taking action. If the final decision involves his risking or even giving up his life in a good cause, you may say that he is pursuing his self-interest because he is a believer in supernatural religion and expects to receive his reward in heaven. Traditional Christianity has indeed preached and encouraged a self-interest ethics in this sense of building up credits for an after-existence. But suppose the individual has no faith in immortality and yet follows a course that he knows is quite certain to end his earthly career. How can we possibly reduce to self-interest his decision to surrender what he considers his one and only life?

Throughout history and especially during modern times, there have been millions of men and women with some sort of Humanist philosophy who have consciously given up their lives for a social ideal. Of course they have wanted to devote themselves to that ideal and have been willing to make the supreme sacrifice for it. Yet because an individual desires to do a thing does not prove at all that he desires to do it from mere self-interest. In the case of dying for a cause, such as the defense of his country or the welfare of humanity, he may truly desire the good of country or mankind above everything else, even above his own self-preservation. Or in the narrower setting of close personal relationships a man may care for his wife, his child, or his friend literally more than he cares for

---

* I like Austin Dobson's line "Fame is a food that dead men eat," and the dictum of Goethe's Faust "The deed is everything, the glory nothing."

himself. Even animals far less advanced in the evolutionary scale than human beings manifest an instinctive disposition to protect their young at all costs.

Intense interest in other people or in society as a whole is, to be sure, an interest manifested by a self, but that does not make it synonymous with self-interest. To call genuine self-sacrifice or patriotism or public service forms of self-interest is to stretch the connotation of *self-interest* to cover its opposite, so that it loses its distinctive meaning. And there can be no doubt that much of the age-long controversy on this subject of self-interest has been due to verbal confusion and to the illegitimate practice of the self-interest school in trying to get rid of altruism by defining it out of existence.

The self-interest theory has been closely tied up in the history of thought with the ethical view that pleasure is and should be the goal of human endeavor. This pleasure ethics is founded on a false analysis of human nature. For psychology demonstrates that we do not in the first instance desire an object because it gives us pleasure, but that it gives us pleasure because we desire it. We enjoy a tender, well-cooked steak because we desire it in terms of bodily need and hunger; if we are already satiated with food, we have no appetite for a steak. It is really objects that we immediately desire, the accompanying pleasure being a welcome by-product and a sign that the object is one that we fundamentally want, something that is basically congenial to our nature. Feelings of pleasure cannot be automatically produced, since they are inseparably bound up with our experiencing of objects that are agreeable to us and that we positively desire only under certain conditions. This is a decisive reason why the direct and self-conscious pursuit of pleasure is not likely to succeed and bring lasting satisfaction. Herein lies what has long been known as the Hedonistic Paradox.

Applying this analysis to the larger problem of ethical reflection and decision in regard to the general good, we see that an individual certainly possesses the power of setting up social aims as among his primary objects of desire. The pleasure or happiness that may result from his furthering those aims is then secondary and derivative.* Thus Humanism affirms the psychological possibility and the ethical desirability of intelligent altruism. There is nothing more shallow than those sophisticates who insist on reducing all human conduct to personal self-interest † and who persist in saying that egoism is more "natural" than altruism. Neither egoism nor altruism is an original characteristic of human nature; both, however, are potential dispositions of the personality. Thinkers who claim that complete selfishness is an inborn quality of human beings are taking over and expressing in different language one of the great errors of Christian ethics, namely that man is inherently sinful and depraved.

The more extreme forms of self-interest are, in truth, equivalent to ordinary selfishness, in which there is little consideration for others and in which an individual frequently fulfills his needs and desires to the detriment of someone else. Obviously self-regard in the sense of keeping healthy, acquiring an education, earning a living, and finding a congenial life partner of the opposite sex is something to be encouraged. Self-cultivation in general and during youth in particular is by no means opposed to the social good; indeed, it helps to build a personality which can render greater service to society. Similarly a sense of personal pride in fine workmanship redounds to the advantage of the community. It is not Humanism's intent that an individual should belittle the value of his own self in affirming that of other selves. On the contrary, he must have a continuing sense of his own worth and a constant awareness of his own rights.

---

* Cf. p. 253.

† This is a good example of "the reductive fallacy," in which philosophers or others oversimplify by illegitimately classifying certain multiple phenomena under one category. In the United States today the most vociferous exponent of this self-interest fallacy is Ayn Rand, a popular novelist with philosophic pretensions and semantic naïvety.

Humanism, then, follows the golden mean by recognizing that *both* self-interest and altruism have their proper place and can be combined in a harmonious pattern. The individual who tries to serve his fellowmen must permit his fellowmen to serve him. His own welfare is as much a part of the welfare of mankind as that of anyone else. "Unless self-gratification were a valid aim, benevolence would not be a moral virtue, because there would be no sense or meaning in doing good to others unless they wanted good done to themselves." [123]

The significant thing is not the truism that it is always a self that has interests; it is the *kind* of interests that any self has. The self or personality is not a fixed, simple, and ready-made entity standing behind a man's activities and directing them; that idea is a holdover from the supernatural doctrine of a divinely created soul—complete in all essentials—entering the body from on high. The human personality is a fluid, developing complex of habits, impulses, and ideas that is never finished and is always in the making *through* its activities and interests.

The unity of the self is not something one starts with, but something one may achieve, and even then only in a relative sense. Of course the self can change for the worse as well as for the better. In any case the range and quality of an individual's interests come to define in large measure the nature of his self. A man *is* what he does and likes to do. The Humanist concept of a growing, expanding personality, which comes to include social aims and ideals as an integral part of the self, cancels out the false antithesis of the individual *versus* society.

The concept of an always selfish self is a cultural product and today goes hand in hand with a social system that sets up economic self-interest in the form of money-making and profit-making as the primary motive capable of stimulating men to productive effort. In philosophy the self-interest theory of ethics received its most precise and mature formulation in the writings of the nineteenth-century Utilitarians, Jeremy Bentham and John Stuart Mill. In this regard their work, though quite humanistic in its total effect, was the philosophic counterpart of the profit-motive theory of Adam Smith and other exponents of laissez-faire economics.

In America's present capitalist society, with its constant emphasis on the profit motive and competitive individualism, there is a tendency to look upon those who support a broader and more scientific view of human motivation as intellectual crackpots; and to consider those who try to practice altruism as impossibly naïve or afflicted with a martyr complex. Amateur psychoanalysts and half-baked Freudians are fond of explaining away manifestations of social idealism in terms of some obscure neurosis. They assume that normal people function on the basis of self-interest and that therefore militant social idealism must be due to peculiar quirks in the human personality. Yet it is obviously fantastic to maintain that a deep desire for social justice, any more than a passion for truth, ordinarily springs from some sort of personal neurosis or maladjustment.

Despite its criticism of the self-interest morality, the ethics of Humanism is cognizant of how deeply rooted in our economic and cultural situation are both the theory and practice of crude self-interest. Humanism is realistic in that it fully recognizes to what an extent men are bent in a wrong direction by propaganda and cultural conditioning which appeal to, reinforce, and spur on the selfish and violent impulses. Humanism is further realistic in understanding that in the last analysis "the refutation of egoism consists in the *eradication* of egoism, that is, changing the actual feelings, desires and atttudes of those who are egoists." [124] This clearly cannot be done simply by trying to preach, talk, and argue men out of habits and actions that run counter to the social good.

Hence Humanism considers it most essential to carry through a systematic and skillful program of training the motives and the emotions so that the social and sympathetic tendencies of human beings will be encouraged. Without exception the great thinkers on the subject of morality have agreed that a

cardinal aim of ethical education is to develop men and women
who find pleasure and happiness in doing right, and pain and
unhappiness in doing wrong. Social conditioning, working
upon plastic human nature with all the new techniques of
twentieth-century teaching, communication, and advertising,
can accomplish wonders either for good or for bad.

The role of reason in this situation is not to act as a force
contrary to the emotions and to assume the impossible task
of driving them out or suppressing them; that would be partly
to adopt the ethics of the old supernaturalism. The function
of individual and community intelligence is to guide and re-
direct emotional life; to replace antisocial passions, motives,
ambitions, and habits by those that are geared to the common
good. Even those deep-seated tendencies of hate and aggression that psychoanalysts say practically all human beings har-
bor within can be harnessed to a constructive purpose and
directed against such evils as poverty, disease, tyranny, and
war.

Emotion and reason are not, as popularly believed, opposed
to each other; they are complementary and inseparable attributes of human beings. Some degree of intellection is associated with every identifiable human emotion, for any definite
emotion has a consciously distinguishable object. Fear of being
blown to bits by an atomic bomb is not the same as the fear
of getting a ticket for illegal parking. The difference in the
quality and strength of these two fears depends upon the
cognitive recognition and estimate of what is being feared.
In general, the greater the measure of sound reasoning associated with the individual's emotions, the greater is the chance
of his attaining the good life.

A widespread misconception is that powerful emotions are
to be deplored. Professor V. J. McGill points out: "It is hard
to find a psychological text which does not warn against *intense
emotion* in general, as if it were deleterious to feel too strongly
about anything. The public takes the same view, disparaging
strong emotions, yet esteeming love and certain other passions

beyond anything in the world. It seems pretty clear, however, that whether a strong emotion is desirable or deleterious depends on its cognitive object, the attitude toward it, the rationale of the situation. It is perhaps sufficient to note that mother-love, love between the sexes, the passionate quest of the scientist or humanitarian, are praised only when they *are* intense." [125]

Returning once more to the role of the intellect, I wish to point out that in Humanism's general scheme of education nothing is more important from an ethical viewpoint than teaching boys and girls, men and women, how to reason correctly and to use their minds in dealing with the myriad problems of life. Such teaching must be aware that reason is "not a ready-made antecedent which can be invoked at will and set into movement. . . . It is the attainment of a working harmony among diverse desires . . . a laborious achievement of habit needing to be continually worked over." [126] The irrational impulses of human beings have played an enormous role in bringing recurrent disasters upon mankind and remain a sinister danger in contemporary affairs. For the Humanist, stupidity is just as great a sin as selfishness; and "the moral obligation to be intelligent" ranks always among the highest of duties.

2. THE SOCIAL GOOD AND INDIVIDUAL HAPPINESS

Humanists are clear and certain that the social good, both in the present and future, should be the supreme ethical goal. That goal is inclusive of all mankind and envisages the ongoing survival of the human race as intrinsically worthwhile. Logic alone will not win men's assent to the social good as the paramount aim in life; the desirability of that aim is not something that can be proved like a mathematical proposition. It is a sweeping ethical *assumption,* as important in its field as the scientific assumption of the Uniformity of Nature. Humanism consciously makes this ethical assumption, tries to persuade men in general to make it, and advocates the kind of education that will lead them to make it. Hence the Humanist ethic urges the development of those basic impulses of love, friendliness, and cooperation that impel a person to consider constantly the good of the group and to find his own happiness in working for the happiness of all.

As I have already pointed out, an individual's loyalty to the larger social good may under certain circumstances cost him his very existence or at least considerable suffering. We must frankly admit that a man's uncompromising dedication to the happiness of others may lead to unhappiness on his part. A pure conscience is not in itself sufficient to offset the persecution of governments or the cruelty of tyrants. As Aristotle sensibly observed in *The Nicomachean Ethics:* "To assert that a person on the rack, or a person plunged in the depth of calamities, is happy is either intentionally or unintentionally to talk nonsense." [127] "Virtue is its own reward" in the sense that the awareness of doing right always brings spiritual satisfaction; but such satisfaction is not sufficient to make the total man happy when he is suffering excruciating physical punishment. And if he is executed for his virtue, his "reward" quickly comes to an end altogether.

On the whole, however, a society in which most individuals, regardless of the personal sacrifices that may be entailed, are devoted to the collective well-being, will attain greater happiness and make more progress than one in which private self-interest and advancement are the prime motivation. This is so for three main reasons.

First, a society of cooperative and socially conscious individuals will be able to achieve and maintain those higher material and cultural levels that provide the broadest foundation for human happiness and progress.

Second, a cooperative society fits in with and fulfills some of the fundamental aspects of human nature. Man, like the higher primates from which he is descended, is a gregarious creature and, as Aristotle noted long ago, "a political animal." We are *social* beings; and though we can artificially set ourselves apart from the world, we are essentially and always part of human society. Generally speaking, people experience their deepest and most enduring joys, not as solitary hermits on some mountain top or desert isle, but in association with their fellowmen, their friends, or their family. Even simple sex love is primarily a social experience.

Third, loyalty to a worthwhile social aim can bring stability and harmony into men's lives. Such a loyalty gives them a central and absorbing purpose around which they are able to integrate their personalities and constructively organize their day-to-day and year-to-year existence. Allegiance to the social good serves as a beacon that illuminates to some degree most of life's problems. Such an allegiance widens an individual's interests and carries him beyond himself, leading him to subordinate or even forget petty personal desires and troubles in the cause for which he is fighting. It releases untapped energies and enables a man to feel success in the accomplishments of others as well as his own; to experience the warm glow of fellowship with like-minded men and women who share in the ups and downs of common struggle.

I cite here two authorities nineteen centuries apart. "This is the true joy in life," writes George Bernard Shaw, "the being used for a purpose recognized by yourself as a mighty one; the being thoroughly worn out before you are thrown on the scrap heap; the being a force of Nature instead of a feverish selfish little clod of ailments and grievances complaining that the world will not devote itself to making you happy." [128] And Jesus said: "He that loveth father or mother more than me is not worthy of me: and he that loveth son or daughter more than me is not worthy of me. And he that taketh not up his cross, and followeth after me, is not worthy of me. He that findeth his life shall lose it: and he that loseth his life for my sake shall find it." [129]

The individual, under whatever sky and no matter what his

work or where he stands on the ladder of achievement, infuses his life with meaning through his devotion and contribution to the larger social good. The vast complexities and impersonal functioning of modern society have led to a feeling of insignificance and impotence on the part of millions of people. The insane asylums are overrun with persons who try to boost their egos by imagining that they are famous historical characters. Contemporary psychiatrists and psychoanalysts frequently discover that the mental troubles of their patients are traceable to a persistent belittling of themselves. The average man has need of assurance that his activities are of some social usefulness and importance.

Humanism does not for a moment imply that *any* social goal which evokes loyalty in an individual is worthwhile, because then allegiance to an evil cause would have to be considered good. To guard against such confusion and to know what we really mean we must always assign concrete content to our social aims. While it is needful to use a shorthand term such as *the social good* or *the general welfare* to sum up Humanism's ultimate ethical objective, it is equally needful to break down that objective in terms of specific goods. Thus the social good surely entails such values for the individual as health, significant work, economic security, friendship, sex love, community recognition, educational opportunity, a developed intelligence, freedom of speech, cultural enjoyment, a sense of beauty, and opportunity for recreation. Here are twelve major goods that any rational society would presumably attempt to encourage and establish; and an inclusive list would contain many more. A knowledge of how different goods or values of this sort are interrelated is an indispensable factor in ethical analysis.

There often occurs a clash between acknowledged values in which one good must be temporarily sacrificed for another. Frequently tragedy turns out to be the conflict, not between right and wrong, but between right and right. Our interest in human progress may at times be at variance with our concern for the present happiness of men. And sacrifices in the immediate present by both the individual and the community are sometimes required for the sake of achieving a future goal. Conflicts between two compelling goods we must resolve as best we can by way of the broadest and most permanent synthesis of values that is possible.

Turning now to a more detailed analysis of individual human happiness, we can state that happiness is not properly definable in terms of the glorified heavenly rest home or passive contemplation so common to the supernaturalist tradition. Nor is it to be defined as withdrawal from the world in this life and retreat to some ivory tower of art or reflection. Such ideals of happiness are escapist dreams originating to a large extent in bad social conditions where most work is drudgery, where human living lacks aesthetic quality, and where in general the struggle to maintain life at a decent level is heartbreakingly difficult.

The fact is that men are inherently active beings and can therefore discover happiness only in some form of activity. The most pathetic sight on earth is not the tired businessman, but the *retired* businessman. He is restive and dissatisfied because suddenly he finds himself with nothing to do. No one can long remain content merely in contemplating past successes. As we know, the entire universe, from atoms to stars, is naturally and eternally active. Likewise the human character can never stand still, because continual change is part of its own nature and resides in the very constitution of things.

Happiness, however, does not consist in activity as such or simply in the attainment of one object of desire after another. This is why we so often have that empty feeling after accomplishing some difficult end upon which we have set our hearts; why the thrill of achievement can give way so quickly to the blankness of boredom. The Humanist conclusion is that the final goal of human striving is unity, satisfaction, equilibrium *in* activity. The path to happiness for the personality lies in harmony in worthwhile action; not a static, but a dynamic harmony that is achieved under the guidance of wisdom. In this way the mind, which is in essence a problem-solving instrument, keeps on meeting the challenges of the environment and stays alert to the end instead of sinking into semisomnolent quiescence.

Modern men may find "peace of mind" or "peace of soul" in calmly and successfully coping with problems as they arise, but not in imagining that they can eradicate all personal discontents. Dr. Karl Menninger, one of America's most eminent psychiatrists, asserts: *"Unrest of spirit is a mark of life;* one problem after another presents itself and in the solving of them we can find our greatest pleasure. The continuous encounter with continually changing conditions is the very substance of living. From an acute awareness of the surging effort we have the periodic relief of seeing one task finished and another begun. . . . A querulous search for a premature permanent 'peace' seems to me a thinly disguised wish to die." [130]

It is the Humanist view that if the individual pursues activities that are healthy, socially useful, and in accordance with reason, pleasure will generally accompany them; and happiness, the supreme good, will be the eventual result. This ethical doctrine goes all the way back to Aristotle and is called *eudaemonism* (from the Greek for *happiness*). It contrasts with hedonism, which holds that pleasure alone is intrinsically good, by putting primary emphasis on the sorts of activities that a person chooses; at the same time it assigns an important and pervasive role to pleasure. "Pleasure," as Aristotle said, "perfects the activities," yet remains secondary. The Humanist ethics, then, "recognizes that the intentional objects of human striving are, in point of fact, not pleasures, but pleasurable things. And by identifying the good with voluntary activities and preferred objects, which are publicly observable, it facilitates discovery, measurement and production of the good." [131]

The Humanist conception of happiness is grounded in a psychology that allows for the natural differences between individuals and for the manifold possibilities in each person.

Since no man can possibly fulfill the numberless potentialities of his being, particularly in our many-sided culture of today, he must select a consistent combination of activities upon which he centers his life. The well-rounded and maturely developed personality is not that of the dilettante scattering himself aimlessly and endlessly in different directions, but is one which attains a unified pattern. The role of the intellect in this process is most important since it serves to discriminate among the thousand and one impulses and desires of an individual, acting as a moderator. In this sense the mind is like the conductor of an orchestra and is able to coordinate an individual's life in terms of some predominant purpose.

The dynamic harmony that Humanism advocates does not imply a superstrenuous existence, though it has a place for excitement and adventure and zestful living. In brief, it does full justice to the varying aspects of human nature and fits in well with the monistic psychology of unity between the personality and the body. Thus it corrects the overemphasis on certain mental and spiritual qualities so characteristic of the dualistic and supernaturalistic ethics. Humanism is opposed to all philosophies that cut man in two, figuratively speaking, and so result in a truncated version of human nature.

It is likewise opposed to the general tendency of philosophers, even those whose metaphysics is naturalistic and humanistic, to put undue stress on the intellectual life to the neglect of the emotional. Western philosophy, for instance, has traditionally slighted the value of love between man and woman.* Humanist ethics, on the other hand, believes that sex love, a value that transcends class, racial, and national barriers, is not to be assessed less highly than intellectual achievement, artistic creation, or any other recognized good. In reference to sexual relations the monistic psychology again makes clear that there is no sharp separation in emotional life

---

* Bertrand Russell is one of the outstanding exceptions here. In my judgment his *Marriage and Morals*, first published in 1929, is the best book on sex relations ever written by a professional philosopher.

between the physical and the spiritual, and that love at its best represents a pervasive intermingling of the two.

The Humanist aim of harmony in human living includes the ancient ideal of "a sound mind in a sound body." Nobody has ever improved upon this classic formulation, though we might express the thought somewhat differently. "Mental and bodily health" or "mental and bodily normality" or "psychological and physiological health" all represent the same idea. While of course individual happiness is in the last analysis a subjective thing, we do know that it is furthered by a vigorous and healthy functioning of the whole organism. And for mental and bodily health we can set up relatively objective norms statable and measurable by science.

There are certain material conditions that must be considered minimum requirements for physical health, such as good food, good air, good housing, sufficient clothing, adequate medical care, and ample exercise and recreation. Obviously if we are to guarantee to everyone in the community, all the millions of workers in factory and field, the prerequisites of bodily health, we shall have to make extensive changes in our economic system. We shall have to eliminate economic depressions and mass unemployment, raise immensely the general standard of living, cut down on the hours of work, lengthen vacations, and rebuild most of our urban and rural areas on the basis of intelligent planning. Such great improvements demand far-reaching institutional reconstruction.

So it is that Humanism wholeheartedly gives assent to Thoreau's statement: "There are a thousand hacking at the branches of evil to one who is striking at the root." [132] And so it is that Humanists insist on the ethical relevance of good economic conditions. The abundant life for the individual goes hand in hand with an economy of abundance. Except for the infinitesimal part of its career represented by a few countries during the past century or so, mankind has always had to face the crushing hardships of an economy of scarcity and the ruinous blasts of a Nature mighty and untamed. Today, however, with our scientific techniques and machine civilization, there is little excuse for not adequately controlling Nature and making available to everybody a high standard of living. In the tremendous potentialities of a modern technology utilized on behalf of all humanity, the Humanist can glimpse the actualization of his forward-looking social program.

In general the first necessity for mental health is precisely the sound bodily health that I have already discussed. In addition, there are certain other essential or at least contributing conditions, such as satisfaction in one's work, psychological security, freedom from fear and anxiety, normal sex fulfillment, and an inclusive philosophy of life, of which Humanism itself is one type. It is in the broad field of mental health or normality that the infant sciences of psychoanalysis and psychiatry have their special part to play. These professions not only require considerable development in consistency of methods and exactness of standards, but also much widening of facilities so that their complicated techniques of diagnosis and cure can be made available at reasonable prices to all in need of them.

Again, if the masses of the people are to obtain the full prerequisites of mental health, we shall have to rebuild the very foundations of our existing society. There cannot, for example, be much feeling of psychological security in a world where economic crisis is an ever-present threat; or in a world where international war periodically engulfs mankind, with entire peoples subject to terrifying and devastating air raids, slaughter by the millions, and nationwide starvation. The current danger of a third world war, in which nuclear bombs and bacteriological warfare would probably play pre-eminent roles, makes the situation more alarming than ever before.

In the face of all the international misunderstandings and tensions of the present age, Humanism stands firm in its vision of the social good as including the entire human race. As my fifth point in the Humanist program phrases it, this philosophy "holds as its highest goal the this-worldly happiness, freedom, and progress—economic, cultural, and ethical—of all mankind, irrespective of nation, race, or religion." While the sincere Humanist strives to the best of his ability to further the good of his family, his local community—city, town, or village—his State and his nation, he is continually looking beyond his native land to the world at large and thinking about the well-being of all the peoples of the earth.

According to Plutarch, Socrates said that he was "not an Athenian or a Greek, but a citizen of the world." In the days of the American Revolution, Thomas Paine stated: "All mankind are my brethren; to do good is my religion." Later, in the Civil War era, William Lloyd Garrison declared: "My country is the world; my countrymen are mankind." These are all statements in the true Humanist spirit. On the other hand, I believe that Humanists should not become sentimental about humanity as a whole. I would reserve the word *love* for the intimate attachments of family and friendship, using the words *sympathy* or *compassionate concern* to express our feelings toward our fellowmen in general. There are many human beings who are guilty of such monstrous evil that we cannot honestly love or like them; but we may feel compassionate concern for almost anyone.

While there need be no inconsistency between the welfare of city and nation, or between that of nation and humanity, conflicts can and do arise between narrower and broader ethical ends of this kind. Certain forms of modern nationalism —fanatical, intolerant, militaristic, and contemptuous of foreign peoples—amount in essence to the large-scale organization of egoism. They clearly clash with the ideals of Humanism and put current meaning into Dr. Samuel Johnson's remark that "Patriotism is the last refuge of a scoundrel." To love one's country does not really imply that one must hate other countries or adopt the slogan "My country right or wrong." The principle around which the United Nations and the International Court of Justice are organized is that the scope of national sovereignty must be curtailed and that nations must be willing to accept, as against what they conceive to be their

own self-interest, the democratically arrived at decisions of
the world community.

Like all other influential religions and philosophies, Humanism reserves the moral right to disagree with or defy any
governmental or other authority. The final court of appeal for
the Humanist is his own conscience and intelligence, as developed in the light of Humanist ethics. The Humanist stands
ready to take the consequences and pay the price for his integrity and his ultimate loyalties. As the brave and militant
hero of Albert Maltz's novel *The Underground Stream* said
just before a band of Fascist terrorists snuffed out his life:
"Beneath all else is this: A man must hold to his purpose.
This—nothing less—is the underground stream of his life.
Without it he is nothing. I cannot yield! A man is nothing who
yields his purpose." [133]

Humanists are convinced that the struggle to build a better
world is likely to go on indefinitely. In whatever nation or
community we are functioning, our chief aim must be neither
to avoid trouble, nor to stay out of jail, nor even to preserve
our lives, but to keep on fighting for the ideals of Humanism.
Our central purpose is not a ripe old age, although that would
be gratifying, but the generous expenditure of our energies for
the good of our country and the advancement of mankind.
The important thing is that we should continue to resist and
combat evil men and evil institutions as long as we possess
the strength to do so.

I spoke earlier about ethical systems being relative to specific social and economic conditions. Notwithstanding this
relativity, Humanism takes over from past systems and adapts
to current situations significant elements that are still relevant
to human living today. The Stoic ethics, for example, with its
ideal of fortitude under all circumstances, is one of the noblest
in the history of thought and points to an essential value that
any rounded ethics should encourage. For both society as a
whole and the individuals within it must be prepared to go
through periods of stress and strain and to face emergencies
with a valorous spirit and resolute will.

Even during days that are relatively quiet and peaceful in a political sense the individual may have need of the Stoic attitude in confronting personal misfortune of one sort or another. Such might be a serious and crippling accident, sudden death in one's family, or one's own impending doom from an incurable disease. To express the Stoic idea in another way: "The one thing that really matters is to be bigger than the things that can happen to you. Nothing that can happen to you is half so important as the way in which you meet it." [134]

The Humanist ethics is, then, thoroughly realistic in recognizing the large amount of suffering and tragedy that has occurred in the past and that continues to afflict mankind in the present. And the Humanist knows, too, that in the second half of the twentieth century the possible extent of tragedy for mankind at large has been multiplied by the proliferation of nuclear weapons that could wipe out hundreds of millions of human beings in the space of a few days. In any case it is a long, long way to Utopia. Yet for all that, I think that the writer Max Lerner, in calling his philosophy "tragic humanism," stresses too much the traumatic aspects of life.

Humanism can also draw to some degree on a different kind of ethics—the Epicurean, which in ancient Greece of the fourth century B.C. was a rival to the Stoic viewpoint. Epicurus believed that present pleasure was the chief end of life, but taught the ethical desirability of seeking the more cultured pleasures, such as those of friendship, of the mind, and of art. He stood for the higher hedonism and for retirement from the world when things are going to rack and ruin. I have already criticized as unsound the ethics of setting up pleasure-seeking as the supreme human aim. Epicureanism does remind us, however, that the enjoyment of pleasure is one of the great values, in contradistinction to the dominating tradition in the West which has given pleasure a bad name and has associated it primarily with sensual satisfactions.

The Epicurean ethics, like the Stoic, was designed to meet the challenge of social breakdown and hard times; and so it is understandable why it recommended an individual quietism of minimizing desire to conform with the attainable. Humanism advocates the maximizing of social cooperation to expand the possibilities of individual fulfillment; its attitude is one of activism as contrasted with passivity. Without ever being submissive the Humanist can accept the general proposition that individual harmony, and social cooperation itself, demand the renunciation of some desires and the strict control of others. As to withdrawal from the world, that too can be a good if it represents a temporary move to refresh the spirit and restore the physique rather than a permanent attitude of disdain, disillusionment, or defeat.

Humanist ethics can profitably assimilate the deep ethical wisdom that is part of many other philosophies besides those I have specifically mentioned. In this section, however, I am not trying even to survey, much less to analyze in detail, the great ethical systems of the past and present. Rather, I am merely indicating the method of Humanism in adapting to its own ethical outlook what is sound and pertinent from thinkers who belong to both the non-Humanist and Humanist traditions. For a reliable and over-all treatment of the ethical enterprise, from a viewpoint that is generally humanistic and naturalistic, the reader must go to a classic such as *Ethics* by John Dewey and James H. Tufts.

To conclude our discussion of ethics, if a man really believes seriously in the Humanist goal of happiness, freedom, and progress for all humanity and keeps that ideal constantly in mind, he will never lose sight of the wide synthesis of values for which Humanism stands. That supreme synthesis can perhaps best be described as a greater and greater sharing of the good things of life on the part of more and more persons in every country. This means nothing more nor less than democracy in its most meaningful and far-reaching sense. For Humanists the familiar formula of "the greatest happiness of the greatest number" expresses the merging of an ethical and a democratic ultimate. Humanism implements its ethics, and meets the danger of mere lip service to noble-sounding professions, by offering a program of *action* in terms of the democratic way of life.

3. HUMANISM AND DEMOCRACY

Humanist principles demand the widest possible extension of democracy to all relevant aspects of human living. The Humanist conception of democracy naturally incorporates earlier contributions to the democratic ideal such as the guarantees embodied in the American Bill of Rights, and the stirring battle cry of the French Revolution, "Liberty, Equality, Fraternity." Also Humanists the world over subscribe to the internationally valid tenets of the Universal Declaration of Human Rights adopted by the United Nations General Assembly in 1948.

Democracy is of course a method as well as a goal. It is the most intelligent method of conducting political life, of carrying through social changes and of settling disagreements in the realm of public affairs. The life of reason, the appeal to the supreme court of the mind, for which philosophy stands, implies in its very essence peaceful persuasion through the free exchange and competition of ideas in the wide arena of social discussion. The philosophic ideal is the transformation of our bitter social and economic disputes into great Platonic Dialogues carried on in legislative bodies and the organs of public opinion—dialogues, however, that in due course have a definite outcome and therefore do not end as inconclusively as most of those in which Socrates took part.

Humanism's support of the democratic way is a matter of both idealism and realism. To quote Professor Reinhold Niebuhr's epigram, "Man's capacity for justice makes democracy possible; but man's inclination to injustice makes democracy necessary." [135] Democracy is a comparatively new thing in the world; and a very radical thing. Violence, bloodshed, coercion, and war—both civil and international—are the old, traditional methods of resolving deep-going conflicts of opinion and interest. Such methods have been wasteful, in terms of human life and economic dislocation, beyond all computation. Often they have succeeded in curing one evil only by substituting another.

Since Humanism as a functioning credo is so closely bound up with the methods of reason and science, plainly free speech and democracy are of its very lifeblood. For reason and scientific method can fully flourish only in an atmosphere of civil liberties. Humanism envisions a republican society where Humanists and everyone else can express unorthodox ideas on any subject without risking persecution, prosecution, execution, exile, obloquy, or loss of employment. As a minority position at present Humanism must defend democracy on the grounds of both the social good and sheer self-interest. Only if the channels of opinion are kept open can the Humanist viewpoint hope to win a majority in the nation and the world.

A true democracy welcomes differences and disagreements and cherishes, as a creative force in society, minority criticisms of existing institutions and prevailing patterns of thought. The democratic spirit is not dogmatic, for it recognizes the value of constant challenges to basic assumptions. The crackpot may turn out to be the trailblazer; the genius usually starts his career as a dissident minority of one; and many a leading statesman spent much of his earlier life in a jail or prison camp.

Humanism, then, urges complete democracy as both an end and a means; and insists that the idea of democracy has developed in history mainly in a humanistic way, needing no support or sanction in supernatural revelations or metaphysical guarantees. The Humanist requires no cosmic spokesman to inform or remind him of the dignity of man and the ideal of human brotherhood. The most democratic countries certainly are not and have not been those most steeped in supernatural religion. Humanist belief in democracy as the goal and in democratic processes as the method is not derivative from extrahuman sources; it stands on its own feet.

In the past Americans have been prone to think of democracy mainly in terms of political democracy and civil liberties. These basic forms of democracy are crucial because they provide the central mechanisms for orderly change and progress. But from the Humanist standpoint they are not in themselves sufficient, even when fully actualized, for a completely democratic society. Needless to say, such actualization has never taken place in the United States or any other country that professes to be democratic.

Humanists advocate the broadest possible application of democracy to the functioning of nongovernmental agencies and organizations and in extrapolitical fields such as those of economics, cultural activity, and race relations. Humanism recommends, too, affirmative Federal and State legislation in America to strengthen the enforcement of democratic rights throughout the country, with recognition of the principle that modern democracy in a complex industrial society demands not only safeguards against governmental tyranny, but also positive action by government to safeguard freedom.

Unfortunately, *democracy* has become one of those infinitely ambiguous terms that defy the dictionaries, confound the statesmen, and confuse the people. Yet it remains a good and useful word. An essential task of Humanism as a philosophy is to clarify the meaning of an important idea such as that of democracy. One way of doing this is to break down this very general concept into various categories, to think of democracy in its specific applications. Thus I find that there are at least ten different types of democracy, all interrelated and to some extent overlapping, but all susceptible to differentiation.

First, there is *political democracy*, that is, government of, by, and for the people under republican or parliamentary institutions. Political democracy establishes and enforces suitable regulations for free elections, majority rule, major and minor political parties, and the functioning of government. In a democracy the state is the servant of the people and is controlled by the people. Though a democracy must proceed on the basis of majority decisions, it has the obligation of fully protecting the rights of minorities. The principle of majority rule is unacceptable unless fair opportunity is given for the evolution of minorities, new or old, into majorities.

Second, there are *civil liberties,* under which all individuals and groups have the right to free speech, due process of law, and equality before the law. In the United States our basic civil liberties are outlined in the Federal Constitution, primarily under the first ten amendments known as the Bill of Rights. These original guarantees have been greatly broadened and complicated by the development of new and potent media for the transmission of ideas, such as motion pictures, radio, television, and newspapers with a mass circulation; by the growth of monopolies in these same fields of communication; and by the increasing strength and scope of the labor movement. The movies and TV underscore the point that the right to see is now one of the most important of civil liberties. The freedom of people to see, hear, and read—for acquiring knowledge or for enjoyment—is as essential as the individual's right to speak, write, or create as an artist.

In my judgment civil libertarians have stressed too much the undoubted fact that freedom of expression is the best way for men to arrive at the truth. The justification for free speech goes deeper than that. For the realm of significant meaning and cultural creativity is far wider than the realm of truth. Novels, poetry, and art do not need to be true in a factual or scientific sense; the human imagination cannot permit itself to be fettered by fact. Moreover, human thought at all levels is bound up with language and communication, which is necessary for men's intellectual development and training in the use of reason. Communication is also necessary to learning and mastering the processes of democratic self-government.

After World War II a dangerous and widespread movement developed in the United States to abrogate or abridge the ordinary civil liberties of individuals and groups who did not conform to prevailing patterns of opinion.* Reminiscent of the repressive years following World War I, this antidemocratic campaign made headway under the guise of fighting communism and Communists. True to form, government officials and government bodies have encouraged this campaign and in many ways have led it.

For example, various Congressional committees have run wild over the past two decades. The House Un-American Activities Committee, the Senate Subcommittee on Internal Security, and the Senate Permanent Subcommittee on Investigations (at one time known as the McCarthy Committee) have consistently flouted the Bill of Rights. Legislation repressing free speech and association has been passed, such as the Smith Act, the Internal Security Act, the Communist Control Act, and a spate of State laws—all ostensibly aimed at Communists, but also intended to silence criticism by frightening the nonconformist. Hand in hand with such legislation have gone harsh administrative strictures on the part of Federal and State governments. Widespread loyalty programs, blacklists of organizations and individuals, and denials of passports have been the order of the day.

The drive against freedom has extended to every field of cultural activity. Education, book publishing, newspaper reporting, religion, the movies, radio and television, drama, painting, music, and the other arts have all been seriously affected. Pressure groups such as the Daughters of the American Revolution and the American Legion have joined enthusiastically in the attempt to suppress heterodoxy or even mild liberalism.

At the very height, however, of the repressive movement

---

* For a detailed survey of the civil liberties crisis in the United States from approximately 1946 to 1956, see my book *Freedom Is as Freedom Does,* Horizon Press, 1956. This study includes the story of my successful battle against the McCarthy Committee in its attempt to have me jailed for alleged contempt of Congress.

known as McCarthyism the judiciary of the United States began to reassert the rights of the individual. This return to constitutional principles in the realm of law became particularly marked in 1957 when the U.S. Supreme Court, under the leadership of Chief Justice Earl Warren, handed down a number of far-reaching decisions favorable to basic civil liberties. These decisions drastically curtailed the sweeping powers which had been assumed by Congressional investigating committees; insisted that government loyalty programs and criminal prosecutions of Communists, labor leaders, and dissenters in general must conform to the Constitution; and upheld the traditional principle of academic freedom. The Supreme Court continued, with some qualifications, to make rulings in support of the Bill of Rights; and by the early sixties there had become evident in America a definite turning of the tide toward freedom.

Third in the Humanist inventory of democracy there is *racial* or *ethnic democracy,* commonly known as *civil rights,* wherein all racial or national groups and minorities stand on an equal basis with other ethnic groups and are not subject to discrimination in any sphere of life. In the international sphere racial democracy has made rapid strides since World War II through the winning of liberation and nationhood by many colored colonial peoples in Africa and Asia. In the United States race prejudice is concentrated against the Negroes, more than 22,000,000 in number. It also operates against other minorities such as Indians, Jews, Orientals, and Puerto Ricans.

The epoch-making Report of President Truman's Committee on Civil Rights, *To Secure These Rights* (1947), devotes the major portion of its space to recounting the extent and seriousness of racial inequality and injustice in America, from the brutal and violent lynchings of Negroes to the quiet ostracism of Jews through the "gentleman's agreement" and the pervasive rule of "restricted clientele" or "Christians only." The legal and extralegal discrimination, segregation, and general humiliation which America's minorities are compelled to suffer relegates them in effect to second-class citizenship.

The close relationship between ethnic and political democracy is seen in the barriers against Negroes' voting in the South during the more than 100 years since President Lincoln's Emancipation Proclamation. This situation has recently improved somewhat. Complete racial democracy is impossible without economic and cultural democracy, a fact demonstrated, again, in the eleven Southern States of the Old Confederacy where the acknowledged aim has been to keep the Negro "in his place" at a low economic and cultural level. The 1954 decision of the U.S. Supreme Court outlawing racial segregation in the public schools of America constituted a portentous step in the direction of educational and ethnic democracy for the Negro.

The nationwide disregard and defiant flouting of that decision, however, demonstrate up to the hilt that the enforcement of Supreme Court rulings in the United States does not take place automatically. It is dependent on both the posture of public opinion in a State or locality and the vigor of law enforcement officials. The Civil Rights Act, passed by Congress in 1964, was another step forward, but we may be sure that its actualization will take many, many years.

Humanism declares ontogorically that no country is truly democratic when racial minorities of whatever stock are denied the constitutional and other rights of citizens in general. The notion of inherent white superiority in a world of peoples predominantly black, brown, or yellow in color has no standing from a democratic, ethical, or scientific viewpoint. It is utterly contrary to the Humanist outlook.

Fourth, there is *economic democracy*, the right of every adult to a useful job at a decent wage or salary, to general economic security and opportunity, to an equitable share in the material goods of this life, and to a proportionate voice in the conduct of economic affairs. Economic democracy, as I define it, goes far beyond freedom from want, since it does not mean merely material security. Such security can be established on a rather restricted minimum basis. Full economic democracy, however, implies a higher and higher standard of living for the whole population as the over-all wealth of a nation increases. While not entailing equality of income, it does imply some surplus above minimum security, so that individuals and families can enjoy the cultural amenities and have an adequate chance for rest, recreation, and travel. Of course discrimination in employment or wage scale against any particular group, on grounds of race, religion, sex, or politics, constitutes a violation of economic democracy.

In his message to Congress of January 11, 1944, President Franklin D. Roosevelt outlined an extensive program of economic democracy. After referring to the inalienable constitutional liberties of the American Republic, he stated: "As our nation has grown in size and stature, however—as our industrial economy expanded—these political rights proved inadequate to assure us equality in the pursuit of happiness. We have come to a clear realization of the fact that true individual freedom cannot exist without economic security and independence. . . . In our day these economic truths have become accepted as self-evident. We have accepted, so to speak, a second Bill of Rights under which a new basis of security and prosperity can be established for all—regardless of station, race or creed." The President then enumerated the economic rights that he considered essential to freedom.

Fifth, there is *organizational democracy*, the carrying out of democratic principles in and by the manifold nongovernmental organizations, societies, associations, councils, and committees that operate in a nation like the United States. This covers the management and activities of churches, professional associations, fraternal bodies, clubs, trade unions, political parties, veterans' associations, and pressure groups of every complexion. Such organizations are so numerous in this country and wield such public influence that their democratic functioning, both internally and externally, is of great importance for American democracy. Since World War II there has been a serious recrudescence of private censorship and "vigilante" groups, such as the Ku Klux Klan and the recently organized John Birch Society, that are a constant menace to American liberties. On the other hand, labor unions have also been guilty of undemocratic practices, especially in that some of them still maintain a color bar to membership.

Sixth, there is *social democracy*, in which every person recognizes the inherent worth and dignity of every other person as a member of the human family, and in which social stratification, snobbery, and classes based on varying economic, intellectual, or other functions no longer exist. This form of democracy includes complete functional democracy, the realization that every productive job makes its particular contribution to the total community life and that therefore everyone who does useful work stands on a plane of ethical equality with everyone else so far as the nature of his work is concerned. Humanist democracy in this sense does not ask us to forget that differences in ability and intelligence will always prevail among men; it does insist that castes and snobberies stemming from such differences be eliminated. And it is always mindful of Kant's classic statement: "*So act as to treat humanity, whether in thine own person or in that of any other, in every case as an end withal, never as a means only.*" [136]

Very important in social democracy is a feeling of inner warmth and friendliness toward our fellowmen, a sympathetic desire to see them prosper, a determination to be fair and honest in our dealings with them. This attitude includes the ability to argue firmly and uncompromisingly in private or public, yet to disagree with others in a tolerant manner; to experience victory or defeat in political affairs, yet not give way to anger, malice, or hatred. As Walter Lippmann has so well put it, democracy "is a fraternity which holds men together against anything that could divide them. It cools their fevers, subdues their appetites and restrains them from believing and saying and doing those irreconcilable, irreparable, inexpiable things which burst asunder the bonds of affection and trust." [137]

Seventh, there is *cultural and educational democracy*, the right of all to a full and equal opportunity to share in the cultural and educational, the artistic and intellectual life of the nation. True cultural democracy demands, in the first instance, the possession of enough leisure and money on the part of the masses of the people so that they can fully participate in the enjoyment of literature, music, painting, the theatre, and the like; and so that those of really professional ability may enter the cultural field as a vocation and work upward to the summits of creative achievement.

The concept of educational democracy implies the administration of schools, colleges, and other educational institutions, whether public or private, according to democratic principles, including nondiscrimination in admissions policy toward such minority groups as Jews and Negroes. It also covers academic freedom. This means that all teachers and employees in school, college, or university are entitled to full liberty of expression and association, as guaranteed under the Bill of Rights, without any interference or penalization on the part of the educational institution which employs them. The teacher has the right to speak his mind in the classroom, as long as he maintains the recognized standards of professional competence and scholarship. Students also have the right to voice their opinions and to join organizations of their choice.

Eighth, there is *democracy in religion and philosophy*, the right of all individuals and groups to profess, practice, and publicize their chosen religion or philosophy. By the very nature of their beliefs, Humanists are very much concerned with this type of democracy, which implies the liberty to be nonreligious or antireligious, to be agnostic or atheist. In the United States this right includes, according to the First Amendment, separation of church and state, and thus rules out intervention by the government on behalf of any particular religion. Yet during recent years Congress has made repeated inroads on this principle. In 1954 it amended the Pledge of Allegiance to the Flag by inserting the words "under God"; and a year later passed an Act requiring that the motto "In God We Trust" be printed on all U.S. paper currency.

Meanwhile, ecclesiastical authorities have increased their efforts to weaken the wall between church and state. In 1963 the U.S. Supreme Court counteracted these attempts to some extent by deciding 8 to 1 in the Schempp-Murray case that the reading of Bible verses or the Lord's Prayer in public schools was unconstitutional. Admittedly, religious pressure groups remain quite powerful in curtailing or preventing public criticism of supernaturalistic doctrines, especially in the press and over the air. We cannot pretend that fair and equal treatment is accorded the discussion of Humanism at the present time.

One of the battles Humanists have been waging for decades is to win exemption from military service for conscientious objectors who oppose participation in war on ethical grounds instead of conventionally religious ones. Daniel Andrew Seeger has challenged in the courts of the United States the U.S. Selective Service Act's limitation of draft exemptions to those who have faith in a Supreme Being. In 1964 a Federal Appeals Court in New York City handed down a unanimous decision in favor of Mr. Seeger in which it asserted: "The stern and moral voice of conscience occupies that hallowed place in the hearts and minds of men which was traditionally reserved for the commandments of God." The U.S. Supreme Court consented to hear an appeal filed by the Department of Justice in this case.

Ninth, there is *democracy between the sexes*, that is, equality between men and women in all relevant ways. This covers the legal, political, economic, educational, and moral spheres. In the East, where the legal and social inequality of the sexes used to be particularly deep-seated, nations such as Communist China and the Soviet Union have recently made immense strides in releasing women from traditional restrictions and giving them new freedoms. In the more advanced democracies of the West, such as Great Britain and the United States, it was only during the first part of the twentieth century that the female sex attained the right of suffrage. This has not, however, brought full political equality; and relatively few women in these countries have been elected to public office. Furthermore, many barriers remain against the female sex in the nonpolitical sectors of life.

In America we spend on the education of women a tiny percentage of what we spend on that of men. Only a small proportion of university professional schools admit members of the female sex. In the economic sphere, even in the United States with all its mechanical gadgets and labor-saving devices, women in general are still preoccupied with the routine tasks of cooking, washing, cleaning, and taking care of the children. The important careers of motherhood and home management are not given their due under what I have called functional democracy. At the same time the male tends to remain dominant in the home, with the wife spiritually subservient and curtailed in her freedom of opinion when her views happen to run counter to her husband's. The vice of "male chauvinism" has by no means become a thing of the past.

Tenth and last, there is *international democracy*, in which all peoples organized as nations live on terms of equality, freedom, and friendship, and do not interfere with the legitimate and peaceful aspirations of one another. This variety of democracy coalesces with the Humanist aim of enduring world peace. It functions in all forms of international cooperation and more especially today in the International Court of Justice and, with definite limitations, in the United Nations. International democracy and the other types of democracy closely interlock and give moral encouragement and practical stability to one another. The peace that comes with genuine international democracy creates a world atmosphere of calm and security favorable to the growth of the other forms of democracy. Conversely, a state of hostility or war between different countries creates an atmosphere of tension, fear, and crisis unfavorable to democratic institutions and likely to weaken whatever democracy does exist.

My discussion of democracy again underlines the point that the philosophy of Humanism is far more than opposition to supernatural beliefs and a corresponding concentration upon the things of this world. The mind of man knows of no adequate substitute for the democratic concept. The Humanist holds that the idea of democracy in the broad sense has permanent validity for human living. Democracy in the narrow sense of formal political democracy is not only inadequate for the needs of men, but tends to discredit the democratic way, because when democracy is so restricted in function it cannot possibly solve the economic, social, and racial problems of mankind. There can be no adequate and complete Humanism unless it is a full-fledged *democratic* Humanism.

4. A HUMANIST CIVILIZATION

A Humanist civilization is one in which the principles of the Humanist philosophy are dominant and find practical embodiment in laws, institutions, economics, culture, and indeed all the more significant aspects of individual and social life. This requires, as the eighth proposition of Humanism phrases it, "a far-reaching social program that stands for the establishment throughout the world of democracy and peace on the foundations of a flourishing and cooperative economic order, both national and international."

Humanism's thorough democratization of education and culture will result, I am convinced, in a cultural flowering comparable in achievement to the outstanding epochs of the past and going far beyond them in breadth of impact. A Humanist society will invest in education and general cultural activity sums proportionate to what present-day governments allocate to armaments and war. Particularly will schools and colleges, universities and research institutes, with their perennial budget difficulties, benefit from vastly enlarged financial resources. At long last educational institutions will be able to construct adequate physical plants and employ full teaching staffs at generous salaries. Thus current overcrowding will be done away with and the advantages of individual attention for all types of students realized to the full. It is generally recognized that the current crisis in American education is principally due to a tidal wave of students, the result of an all-time high birth rate, inundating already inadequate schools, colleges, and universities.

Humanist education naturally accents social rather than individualistic aims. This implies both more attention to social studies, such as economics, politics (including civil liberties), and sociology, and inclusion in the curriculum of courses on ethics in order to train the youth of a nation in the broad Humanist attitudes of loyalty to the social group and to humanity. Humanism would also greatly extend the teaching of science and scientific method, putting emphasis on the student's learning to think straight, but not neglecting the inculcation of basic facts. There need be no opposition between science and the Humanities, from both of which the Humanist draws inspiration, and no concentration upon one of them to the exclusion of the other.

The Humanist educational program will be a large factor in spreading a fundamental awareness of literature and art among all of the people. This does not mean any letdown in standards; on the contrary the effects will be just the opposite, by raising to unprecedented levels the average cultural understanding and by widening to an unprecedented extent the range of true artistic accomplishment on the part of both amateurs and professionals.

The Humanist stress on complete cultural democracy and freedom of expression means that artists and writers should have the widest latitude in what they produce and say. A free art and a free literature are absolute essentials for a free culture. A Humanist civilization will contain many different and contradictory currents of thought, including non-Humanist and anti-Humanist tendencies. It certainly will not bring pressure on art and literature to conform to any official philosophy; or seek to force the novel, the theatre, and the motion picture to deal with Humanist themes. Those who so wish will criticize and satirize to their hearts' content; and will be at entire liberty to present unconventional ideas that shock and stir the Humanist orthodox.

Narrowly moralistic restraints on artists and writers have ever been a bane in the history of the West; and those restraints have frequently stemmed from the supernaturalist's suspicion of earthly pleasures. As Professor Irwin Edman explains: "The traditional quarrel between the artist and the puritan has been the quarrel between those who were frankly interested in the sensuous appearances and surfaces of things and those to whom any involvement or excitement of the senses was a corruption of the spirit or a deflection of some ordered harmony of reason. The history of censorship in the fine arts, if it could be told in full, would be found to revolve in no small measure around the assumed peril of corruption of the spirit by the incitements of the flesh through beautiful things." [138]

One of the challenges to Humanist writers and artists will be to embody in artistic and literary work the general point of view for which Humanism stands; to express that sense of the beauty and glory of life which Michelangelo, for instance, so superbly portrayed in the Sistine Chapel through the medium of a subject matter centered upon the supernatural. There is nothing in the nature of art, literature, or poetry that makes treatment of the Christian myth lead to great creative accomplishment and that prevents a similar result in the representation of the humanistic and naturalistic world-view.* Genius is not confined to the delineation of any one philosophic position concerning the universe and man.

Santayana enlarges upon our point. "The naturalistic poet,"

---

* Cf. pp. 60-80 on "The Cultural Background" of the Humanist philosophy.

he writes, "abandons fairy land, because he has discovered nature, history, the actual passions of man. His imagination has reached maturity. . . . Throw open to the young poet the infinity of nature; let him feel the precariousness of life, the variety of purposes, civilizations, and religions even upon this little planet; let him trace the triumphs and follies of art and philosophy, and their perpetual resurrections—like that of the downcast Faust. If, under the stimulus of such a scene, he does not some day compose a natural comedy as much surpassing Dante's divine comedy in sublimity and richness as it will surpass it in truth, the fault will not lie with the subject, which is inviting and magnificent, but with the halting genius that cannot render that subject worthily." [139]

Great poets in the past have given expression to some particular philosophy or religion. In a general sense we can call Homer the poet of Paganism, Lucretius the poet of Materialism, Dante the poet of Catholicism, Milton the poet of Protestantism, Goethe the poet of Romanticism and Wordsworth the poet of Pantheism. As yet, however, no poet equal in rank to these just mentioned has put into enduring verse the basic themes of Humanism as a philosophy.

An essential function for artists and writers in a Humanist society will be to work out rituals and ceremonies that are consistent with the central tenets of Humanism. Such ceremonies should appeal to the emotions as well as the minds of the people, capturing their imagination and giving an outlet to their delight in pomp and pageantry. Present-day Humanists regard a festival like Christmas, which has already become secularized to a large extent in the United States, as a folk day symbolizing the joy of existence, the feeling of human brotherhood, and the ideal of democratic sharing. However, during the year's most intensive holiday season, many Humanists prefer to put their stress on New Year's Day rather than Christmas. Easter can be humanistically utilized to celebrate the rebirth of the vital forces of Nature and the renewal of man's own energies. In fact, according to the anthropologists,

Easter probably originated in just such a way. Humanism will likewise naturally make much of the birthdays of outstanding leaders of the human race, and of other important aniversaries.

The average family in a Humanist civilization will also need wedding and funeral services based on a nonsupernatural philosophy of life. It seems reasonable to suppose that even today millions of families in America and throughout the world would like to have available definitely Humanist rituals for the occasions of marriage and death. Since such families are not usually acquainted with services of dignity and beauty that are in harmony with their ideas regarding life and destiny, they tend to fall back on the traditional supernaturalist ceremonies. One result of this has been that again and again rationalists, freethinkers, and Humanists are adjudged finally in the public eye as faithful supernaturalists because their funeral services are orthodox. A number of Humanist wedding and funeral services are already in use, such as those prepared by Ethical Culture and Humanist groups.*

In general, Humanism believes in the social origin and function of art. Categorically asserting that art is for man's sake, it repudiates the superficial slogan of art for art's sake, which represented a natural reaction against the dreariness and ugliness of nineteenth-century industrialism. At the same time Humanism eschews the artificial distinction between the fine arts and the useful arts. This is another of the old, outworn dualisms and tends in the direction of an aristocratic, spectator view of art as residing in private mansions and public museums rather than as a pervasive complement of human work and play. So far as the products of labor are concerned, the Humanist theory is that they should embody a constant fusion of utility and grace, so that the quality of beauty will enter universally into the common objects of daily use.

The mass production of industrial goods by machinery does

---

* See *Humanist Wedding Ceremonies* edited by Tolbert H. McCarroll, and my own *A Humanist Funeral Service*. Both brochures are published by the American Humanist Association.

not necessarily prevent the fulfillment of this aim. An excellent case can be made for claiming that the best designed American automobile is of as high a standard aesthetically as the ancient Greek chariot, modern china as the ancient Greek vase, and the twentieth-century skyscraper as the ancient Greek temple. The finest works of art in any case have always been socially functional in some sense. Where modern economic systems have held back and hampered the development of good art is particularly in their emphasis on the profit motive. The quality of artistic and literary creations cannot be justly assessed in terms of the money that they earn; and the general spirit prevalent in a predominantly money civilization is not conducive to the highest type of culture.

All the great periods of cultural upsurge in the past have sprung from a definite material foundation, usually coinciding with or immediately following relative economic prosperity on the part of the particular people concerned. Greece of the Periclean Age, the European Renaissance, the flowering of New England in the nineteenth century, are cases in point. The lesson of history is, then, that for a dynamic and creative cultural life, a nation must have an adequate material base in the form of a healthily functioning economic system.

It is not the purpose of this book to go into the details of economics. But it is necessary to state that Humanism, whatever the prevailing economic system may be, stands behind Abraham Lincoln's statement: "Whenever there is a conflict between human rights and property rights, human rights must prevail." [140] Here we also return once more for guidance to what the Founding Fathers said in the Declaration of Independence. Instead of listing life, liberty, and *property* as the inalienable rights of men, as had John Locke, the English philosopher who so strongly influenced Jefferson and other early American statesmen, the signers of the Declaration substituted "the pursuit of happiness" for "property." This was a most significant departure.

Humanism also brings to the fore the concept of *planning*

as a key to the establishment of a sound economic order, though individual Humanists vary as to how far they favor pushing the techniques of planning. Effective thinking is in essence a form of planning and the final solution adopted for any problem constitutes a plan of action. The first level of planning is, then, problem-solving thought. The second level is a person's general planning for himself and his future, his conscious attempt to foresee and control relevant circumstances. The wise individual who looks ahead will draw up an annual budget for himself. The preparation of a budget by individuals, families, businesses, colleges, governments, or any organization whatever is always an example of planning.

The third level of planning is that which a family does for the well-being of its members, including planned parenthood through some form of birth control. Next we come to the planning of individual private businesses, whether small or large, with the central coordination of different departments and the itemized control of finances. Then there are various types of government planning, whether Federal, State, or municipal. A further and crucial stage is that of continuous national planning for the benefit of all the people and through the means of coordinating the entire industrial and agricultural life of a country with transportation, finance, and distribution. Contrary to a widespread impression, socio-economic planning is fully compatible with democratic procedures and can be utilized as a major instrument in furthering the goals of democracy.*

World planning for the welfare of all mankind is the highest and broadest level of all. It becomes possible only with a tremendous extension of international organization. A successfully functioning United Nations, with its many specialized agencies, such as the Economic and Social Council, the Food and Agriculture Organization, the World Health Organization,

---

* For an excellent discussion of planning possibilities, see Professor Joseph Blau, "Social Planning in a Democracy," in *The Humanist*, Autumn 1949, pp. 110-16.

and UNESCO, obviously entails some degree of global planning and could lay the foundation for an integrated world economy and political federation.

Manifestly any practicable and constructive scheme of world planning depends on the elimination of international war, the most terrible and destructive malady that has ever afflicted the human race. Modern philosophers have been perennially concerned with the scourge of war. Kant's succinct essay *Perpetual Peace*, written in 1795, was among the best philosophic studies of the subject. Kant included among his prerequisites for international peace that every nation should have a republican constitution, that each people should possess national self-determination, that there should be general disarmament, and that there should be a federation of free states agreeing to abolish war forever. He also suggested an eventual "State of nations," or world-republic, embracing all peoples. The Humanist, while disagreeing with the supernaturalistic aspects of Kant's philosophy, can certainly agree with his program for peace so far as it goes.

In the twentieth century the idea of a federation of free states became embodied in the League of Nations, which collapsed with the outbreak of World War II, and in the United Nations, which was created at the war's end. Both these organizations were founded upon the principle of collective security, namely that the peace-loving countries of the earth should band together against any aggressor or potential aggressor and speedily put an end, by means of collective action and mutual assistance, to war or the threat of war. For Humanism the principle of collective security is a vital one in international affairs.

The realistic Humanist, however, believing in at least a limited economic interpretation of history, will look beyond fine-sounding peace pronouncements and formal peace organizations to those fundamental economic forces and relationships that make for war. We can find an economic interpretation of war as far back as Plato when he said, "Wars are occasioned by the love of money." [141] Without contending that economics constitutes the whole story behind war, we can state that unless and until the different peoples of the world solve their basic economic problems centering around poverty, unemployment, inflation, depression, business monopoly, and the proper control of natural resources, there will be no lasting international peace.

Clearly, too, the various nations, now some 120 in number, will not be able to work out their economic problems independently. All countries in this modern age are economically, politically, and culturally interrelated and interdependent. The time is past when any national unit can be sufficient unto itself and function prosperously and securely in isolation from the rest of mankind. A long time ago Plato stressed in his *Dialogues* the theme of the good individual in the good society, showing how difficult it is for a person to achieve virtue in a bad environment. Today it is relevant to talk about the good *nation* in the good *world*. No one country, however wealthy, populous, and powerful, can fulfill its finest potentialities until it can live in a decent international environment quite dissimilar from that of the present. A truly Humanist civilization must be a world civilization.

For the Humanist it follows that beyond all questions of national self-interest, every people has a moral obligation to humanity as a whole; a duty, which is also an opportunity, to make common cause with the other peoples of the earth in man's eternal quest for peace, plenty, and freedom. All individuals of all countries are together fellow citizens of our one world and fellow members of our one human family. The Americans, the Russians, the English, the Indians, the Chinese, the Germans, the Africans, and the rest are all part of the same perplexed, proud, and aspiring human race.

Humanism is not only a philosophy with a world ideal, but is an ideal philosophy for the world. It is quite conceivable that a majority of this planet's population could come to see the truth of its underlying principles. The Humanist viewpoint, surmounting all national and sectional provincialisms, provides a concrete opportunity for overcoming the age-long cleavage between East and West. Even those who cling to some form of supernaturalism can unite with Humanists, as they did during World War II, on a program of democracy and progress that reaches to the farthest corners of the earth. Humanism is a supranational, panhuman philosophy of universal relevance; it is the philosophic counterpart of world patriotism.

In my endeavor to present a compact, minimum prospectus of the Humanist philosophy, I have naturally had to deal very briefly with certain large topics, especially in this last chapter. Yet I have tried to make explicit Humanism's clear and uncompromising answer on the major philosophic issues. In an era in which multitudes of people have lost the faith of their forebears and waver uncertainly in a no man's land of doubt concerning the ultimate problems of existence, Humanism takes an unequivocal position and offers an integrated and affirmative way of life. It provides modern man with a stable and meaningful frame of reference. The Humanist synthesis, while of course gathering strength from other philosophies, has a unity and a viability of its own. And it represents a viewpoint, still in process of evolution, that can never be restricted to any final formulation. Naturalistic Humanism is a comprehensive idea-system, but it is an *open* system.

Despite the appalling world wars and other ordeals through which humanity has passed during the twentieth century, despite the unprecedented menace of nuclear annihilation, Humanism takes the long view and remains hopeful of the decades to come. This philosophy, with its faith in man and in his ability to solve his problems through human intelligence and scientific techniques, holds to what might be called a reasoned optimism. It rejects the dead ends of despair as well as the daydreams of Utopia. I believe firmly that man, who has shown himself to be a very tough animal, has the best part of his career still before him. And there is at least the possibility that by the close of this century "the Humanist break-through," in Sir Julian Huxley's phrase, will spread throughout the globe to create a higher civilization of world dimensions.

In the meaningful perspectives of the Humanist philosophy man, although no longer the darling of the universe or even of this earth, stands out as a far more heroic figure than in any of the supernaturalist creeds, old or new. He has become truly a Prometheus Unbound with almost infinite powers and potentialities. For his great achievements man, utilizing the resources and the laws of Nature, yet without Divine aid, can take full credit. Similarly, for his shortcomings he must take full responsibility. Humanism assigns to man nothing less than the task of being his own saviour and redeemer.

Appendix

A HUMANIST MANIFESTO *

The time has come for widespread recognition of the radical changes in religious beliefs through the modern world. The time is past for mere revision of traditional attitudes. Science and economic change have disrupted the old beliefs. Religions the world over are under the necessity of coming to terms with new conditions created by a vastly increased knowledge and experience. In every field of human activity, the vital movement is now in the direction of a candid and explicit humanism. In order that religious humanism may be better understood we, the undersigned, desire to make certain affirmations which we believe the facts of our contemporary life demonstrate.

There is great danger of a final, and we believe fatal, identification of the word *religion* with doctrines and methods which have lost their significance and which are powerless to solve the problem of human living in the Twentieth Century. Religions have always been means for realizing the highest values of life. Their end has been accomplished through the interpretation of the total environing situation (theology or world view), the sense of values resulting therefrom (goal or ideal), and the technique (cult), established for realizing the satisfactory life. A change in any of these factors results in

---

* First published in *The New Humanist*, Vol. VI, No. 3, 1933.

alteration of the outward forms of religion. This fact explains the changefulness of religions through the centuries. But through all changes religion itself remains constant in its quest for abiding values, an inseparable feature of human life.

Today man's larger understanding of the universe, his scientific achievements, and his deeper appreciation of brotherhood, have created a situation which requires a new statement of the means and purposes of religion. Such a vital, fearless, and frank religion capable of furnishing adequate social goals and personal satisfactions may appear to many people as a complete break with the past. While this age does owe a vast debt to the traditional religions, it is none the less obvious that any religion that can hope to be a synthesizing and dynamic force for today must be shaped for the needs of this age. To establish such a religion is a major necessity of the present. It is a responsibility which rests upon this generation. We therefore affirm the following:

First: Religious humanists regard the universe as self-existing and not created.

Second: Humanism believes that man is a part of nature and that he has emerged as the result of a continuous process.

Third: Holding an organic view of life, humanists find that the traditional dualism of mind and body must be rejected.

Fourth: Humanism recognizes that man's religious culture and civilization, as clearly depicted by anthropology and history, are the product of a gradual development due to his interaction with his natural environment and with his social heritage. The individual born into a particular culture is largely molded by that culture.

Fifth: Humanism asserts that the nature of the universe depicted by modern science makes unacceptable any supernatural or cosmic guarantees of human values. Obviously humanism does not deny the possibility of realities as yet undiscovered, but it does insist that the way to determine the existence and value of any and all realities is by means of intelligent inquiry and by the assessment of their relations to human needs. Religion must formulate its hopes and plans in the light of the scientific spirit and method.

Sixth: We are convinced that the time has passed for theism, deism, modernism, and the several varieties of "new thought."

Seventh: Religion consists of those actions, purposes, and experiences which are humanly significant. Nothing human is alien to the religious. It includes labor, art, science, philosophy, love, friendship, recreation—all that is in its degree expressive of intelligently satisfying human living. The distinction between the sacred and the secular can no longer be maintained.

Eighth: Religious Humanism considers the complete realization of human personality to be the end of man's life and seeks its development and fulfillment in the here and now. This is the explanation of the humanist's social passion.

Ninth: In the place of the old attitudes involved in worship and prayer the humanist finds his religious emotions expressed in a heightened sense of personal life and in a co-operative effort to promote social well-being.

Tenth: It follows that there will be no uniquely religious emotions and attitudes of the kind hitherto associated with belief in the supernatural.

Eleventh: Man will learn to face the crises of life in terms of his knowledge of their naturalness and probability. Reasonable and manly attitudes will be fostered by education and supported by custom. We assume that humanism will take the path of social and mental hygiene and discourage sentimental and unreal hopes and wishful thinking.

Twelfth: Believing that religion must work increasingly for joy in living, religious humanists aim to foster the creative in man and to encourage achievements that add to the satisfactions of life.

Thirteenth: Religious humanism maintains that all associations and institutions exist for the fulfillment of human life. The intelligent evaluation, transformation, control, and direction of such associations and institutions with a view to the enhancement of human life is the purpose and program of humanism. Certainly religious institutions, their ritualistic forms, ecclesiastical methods, and communal activities must be reconstituted as rapidly as experience allows, in order to function effectively in the modern world.

Fourteenth: The humanists are firmly convinced that existing acquisitive and profit-motivated society has shown itself to be inadequate and that a radical change in methods, controls, and motives must be instituted. A socialized and co-operative economic order must be established to the end that the equitable distribution of the means of life be possible. The goal of humanism is a free and universal society in which people voluntarily and intelligently co-operate for the common good. Humanists demand a shared life in a shared world.

Fifteenth and last: We assert that humanism will: (a) affirm life rather than deny it; (b) seek to elicit the possibilities of life, not flee from it; and (c) endeavor to establish the conditions of a satisfactory life for all, not merely for a few. By this positive *morale* and intention humanism will be guided, and from this perspective and alignment the techniques and efforts of humanism will flow.

So stand the theses of religious humanism. Though we consider the religious forms and ideas of our fathers no longer adequate, the quest for the good life is still the central task for mankind. Man is at last becoming aware that he alone is responsible for the realization of the world of his dreams, that he has within himself the power for its achievement. He must set intelligence and will to the task.

(Signed) J. A. C. Fagginger Auer, E. Burdette Backus, Harry Elmer Barnes, L. M. Birkhead, Raymond B. Bragg, Edwin Arthur Burtt, Ernest Caldecott, A. J. Carlson, John Dewey, Albert C. Dieffenbach, John H. Dietrich, Bernard Fantus, William Floyd, F. H. Hankins, A. Eustace Haydon, Llewellyn Jones, Robert Morss Lovett, Harold P. Marley, R. Lester Mondale, Charles Francis Potter, John Herman Randall, Jr., Curtis W. Reese, Oliver L. Reiser, Roy Wood Sellars, Clinton Lee Scott, Maynard Shipley, W. Frank Swift, V. T. Thayer, Eldred

C. Vanderlaan, Joseph Walker, Jacob J. Weinstein, Frank S. C. Wicks, David Rhys Williams, Edwin H. Wilson.

Note: *The Manifesto is a product of many minds. It was designed to represent a developing point of view, not a new creed. The individuals whose signatures appear, would, had they been writing individual statements, have stated the propositions in differing terms. The importance of the document is that more than thirty men have come to general agreement on matters of final concern and that these men are undoubtedly representative of a large number who are forging a new philosophy out of the materials of the modern world. It is obvious that many others might have been asked to sign the Manifesto had not the lack of time and the shortage of clerical assistance limited our ability to communicate with them.*

Reference Notes

CHAPTER I. *The Meaning of Humanism*

1. Daniel Cory (ed.), *The Letters of George Santayana* (New York: Scribners, 1955), p. 390.

2. Plato, *Apology,* trans. Benjamin Jowett, Sections 38, 39, 41.

3. *Encyclopaedia of the Social Sciences* (New York: Macmillan, 1937), Vol. IV, p. 541.

4. Quoted by Willard L. Sperry (ed.), *Religion and Our Divided Denominations* (Cambridge: Harvard University Press, 1945), p. viii.

5. Walter Lippmann, *A Preface to Morals* (New York: Macmillan, 1929), p. 322.

6. Saul K. Padover (ed.), *A Jefferson Profile* (New York: John Day, 1956), p. 344.

7. Merwin Roe (ed.), *Speeches and Letters of Abraham Lincoln* (London: Dent, 1919), p. 163.

CHAPTER II. *The Humanist Tradition*

8. Diogenes Laertius, *Lives of Eminent Philosophers* (New York: Putnam, 1925), IX, p. 51.

9. Benedict Spinoza, *Correspondence,* Letter XIX.

10. Harold A. Larrabee, "Naturalism in America," in *Naturalism and the Human Spirit,* ed. Y. H. Krikorian (New York: Columbia University Press, 1944), p. 321.

11. A. D. Winspear, *The Genesis of Plato's Thought* (New York: Dryden Press, 1940), p. 150.

12. Baron d'Holbach, *Système de la Nature* (Paris: Chez Etienne Ledoux Librarie, 1821), Vol. II, pp. 170-71.

13. Denis Diderot, *Oeuvres Complètes* (Paris: Edition Assezat-Tourneaux, Garnier Frères, 1875-77), Vol. 9, pp. 15-16.

14. Ludwig Feuerbach, *The Essence of Christianity* (New York: Calvin Blanchard, 1843), p. 54.

15. Frederick Engels, *Ludwig Feuerbach* (New York: International Publishers, 1935), p. 15.

16. John Stuart Mill, *Utilitarianism, Liberty and Representative Government* (New York: Dutton, 1922), p. 79.

17. Bertrand Russell, *Why I Am Not a Christian*, ed. Paul Edwards (New York: Simon and Schuster, 1937), p. 219.

18. George Santayana, *Interpretations of Poetry and Religion* (New York: Scribners, 1927), p. 108.

19. George Santayana, *Reason in Religion* (New York: Scribners, 1926), p. 240.

20. *Ibid.*, p. 188.

21. Lin Yutang, *My Country and My People* (New York: Reynal and Hitchcock, 1935), pp. 101, 103.

22. Quoted by Stephen H. Fritchman, *Men of Liberty*, (Boston: Beacon, 1945), pp. 1, 9.

23. Quoted by Charles Francis Potter, *Humanism: A New Religion* (New York: Simon and Schuster, 1930), p. 80.

24. Paul Leicester Ford (ed.), *The Writings of Thomas Jefferson* (New York: Putnam, 1892-99), Vol. IV, p. 430.

25. Larrabee, *op. cit.*, p. 338.

26. Bound volume of the journal *Politics for the People* (London: John W. Parker, 1848), p. 58.

27. Ford (ed.), *op. cit.*, Vol. X, pp. 67-68.

28. Julian Huxley, *UNESCO: Its Purpose and Its Philosophy* (Washington: Public Affairs Press, 1947), p. 8.

29. Trans. Alfred E. Zimmern, *The Greek Commonwealth* (Oxford: Oxford University Press, 1924), pp. 203-5.

30. *Ibid.*, p. 207.

31. William L. Westermann, "Greek Culture and Thought," in *Encyclopaedia of the Social Sciences*, Vol. I, p. 17.

32. Gilbert Murray, *The Rise of the Greek Epic* (Oxford: Oxford University Press, 1924), p. 1.

33. Terence, *Heauton Timoroumenos*, Act I, Sc. 1.

34. Santayana, *Interpretations of Poetry and Religion*, p. 152.

35. John H. Randall, Jr., *The Making of the Modern Mind* (Boston: Houghton, Mifflin, 1926), pp. 381-82.

36. Quoted from *Humanism: What Is It?* (San Francisco: Humanist Society of San Francisco, 1947), p. 3.

37. Robert G. Ingersoll, quoted in Christopher Morley (ed.), *Familiar Quotations* (Boston: Little, Brown, 1937), p. 603.

38. Warren Allen Smith, *The Humanist* (Oct. 1951), p. 197.

39. Carl Sandburg, *The People, Yes* (New York: Harcourt, Brace, 1936), pp. 241, 286.

40. Karl Marx, *The Eighteenth Brumaire of Louis Bonaparte* (New York: International Publishers, 1926), p. 23.

CHAPTER III. *This Life Is All and Enough*

41. William James, *The Principles of Psychology* (New York: Holt, 1923), Vol. I, p. 348.

42. James B. Pratt, *The Religious Consciousness* (New York: Macmillan, 1928), p. 253.

43. Lucretius, *On the Nature of Things*, trans. Cyril Bailey (Oxford: Oxford University Press, 1926), Bk. III, lines 445 ff.

44. John Donne, *An Anatomy of the World*, II, lines 244 ff.

45. *Odyssey*, xi.

46. Sir Oliver Lodge, *Why I Believe in Personal Immortality* (New York: Doubleday, Doran, 1934), pp. 139-42.

47. W. Somerset Maugham, *The Summing Up* (New York: Doubleday, Doran, 1938), p. 275.

48. Anne Parrish, *Golden Wedding* (New York: Harpers, 1936), p. 343.

49. H. G. Wells, Julian S. Huxley, and G. P. Wells, *The Science of Life* (New York: Doubleday, Doran, 1938), p. 551.

50. From Dylan Thomas, "Do Not Go Gentle into that Good Night," *Collected Poems* (New York: New Directions, 1946).

51. From Don Marquis, "Transient."

52. Santayana, *Interpretations of Poetry and Religion*, p. 250.

53. Santayana, *Reason in Religion*, p. 247.

54. Frederick Tilney, *The Brain from Ape to Man* (New York: Paul B. Hoeber, 1928), Vol. II, pp. 935-36.

55. F. Zwicky, *Morphology of Propulsive Power* (Society for Morphological Research, Pasadena, Calif., 1962), pp. 368-69.

56. H. Spencer Jones, *Life on Other Worlds* (New York: Macmillan, 1940), pp. 272-73.

57. Harlow Shapley, "We Are Not Alone," *The Christian Register* (July 1956), p. 38.

CHAPTER IV. *Humanism's Theory of the Universe*

58. James Jeans, *The Universe Around Us* (New York: Macmillan, 1929), pp. 83-84.

59. Roy Wood Sellars, *The Next Step in Religion* (New York: Macmillan, 1918), p. 171.

60. Dean E. Woolridge, *New York Times Magazine* (Oct. 4, 1964), p. 66.

61. Isaac Newton, *Principia*, Book III, Rule I.

62. Albert Einstein, "Science and Religion," in *Science, Philosophy and Religion: A Symposium*, eds. L. Bryson and L. Finkelstein (New York: Conference on Science, Philosophy and Religion in Their Relation to the Democratic Way of Life, 1941), pp. 211, 213.

63. George Santayana, *Three Philosophical Poets* (Cambridge: Harvard University Press, 1945), p. 77.

64. Wm. Pepperell Montague, *The Philosophical Review* (May 1945), pp. 231-32.

65. John H. Randall, Jr., "The Nature of Naturalism," in *Naturalism and the Human Spirit*, ed. Y. H. Krikorian, pp. 370-71.

66. David Hume, *A Treatise of Human Nature* (New York: Dutton, 1926), Vol. I, p. 254.

67. Quoted by Arthur O. Lovejoy in *Contemporary American Philosophy*, eds. George P. Adams and Wm. Pepperell Montague (New York: Macmillan, 1930), Vol. II, p. 85.

68. Quoted by Will Durant, *The Story of Philosophy* (New York: Simon and Schuster, 1926), p. 318.

69. Friedrich Nietzsche, *Thus Spake Zarathustra*, Introductory Speech.

70. Durant Drake in *Contemporary American Philosophy*, eds. Adams and Montague, Vol. I, p. 296.

71. Wieman, Macintosh and Otto, *Is There A God? A Conversation* (Chicago, New York: Willett, Clark, 1932), p. 13.

72. *Ibid.*, p. 36.

73. George Santayana, *Reason in Art* (New York: Scribners, 1926)., p. 201.

74. George Santayana, *Reason in Common Sense* (New York: Scribners, 1927), p. 37.

75. Lippmann, *op. cit.*, pp. 217-18.

76. Quoted by H. G. Wells, *The Outline of History* (New York: Macmillan, 1920), Vol. II, p. 335.

77. William James, *A Pluralistic Universe* (New York: Longmans, Green, 1925), pp. 321-22.

78. John Dewey and Others, *Creative Intelligence* (New York: Holt, 1917), pp. 15-16.

79. Horace M. Kallen, *A Study of Liberty* (Yellow Springs, Ohio: Antioch Press, 1959), p. 19.

80. Sterling P. Lamprecht, "Man's Place in Nature," *The American Scholar* (Winter 1938), pp. 68-69.

81. Sterling P. Lamprecht, *Nature and History* (New York: Columbia University Press, 1950), p. 114.

82. John Dewey in *The New Republic* (April 29, 1931), p. 307.

83. Paul Tillich, *Systematic Theology* (Chicago: University of Chicago Press, 1956), Vol. I, pp. 184-85.

84. George H. Mead, *Mind, Self and Society* (Chicago: University of Chicago Press, 1934), p. 98.

85. Charles Hartshorne, "Freedom Requires Indeterminism and Universal Causality," *The Journal of Philosophy* (Sept. 11, 1958), p. 799.

86. Gardner Williams, "Human Freedom and the Uniformity of Nature," *The Humanist* (Winter 1948-49), p. 180.

87. Wm. Pepperell Montague, "Free Will and Fate," *The Personalist* (Spring 1943), p. 175.

88. Frederick J. E. Woodbridge, *The Purpose of History* (New York: Columbia University Press, 1916), pp. 5, 47.

89. Sterling P. Lamprecht, "Metaphysical Background of the Problem of Freedom," *The Journal of Religious Thought* (Autumn-Winter 1951-52), p. 16.

90. Aristotle, *Metaphysica*, trans. W. D. Ross (Oxford: Oxford University Press, 1928), Gamma, Ch. 1, 1003a 21-26; Epsilon, Ch. 1, 1025b 7-10.

91. Theodore M. Green (ed.), *Kant Selections* (New York: Scribners, 1929), p. 439.

92. Arthur Schopenhauer, *The World as Will and Idea*, Supplements to the Third Book, Ch. XXXIII.

93. Lucretius, *Of the Nature of Things*, trans. W. E. Leonard (New York: Dutton, 1941), pp. 259-61.

94. James H. Leuba, *The Psychology of Religious Mysticism* (New York: Harcourt, Brace, 1926), p. 207.

95. Henry David Thoreau, *Walden or Life in the Woods* (Boston: Houghton, Mifflin, 1927), p. 96.

96. Ralph Waldo Emerson, *Nature* (Boston: Houghton, Mifflin, 1921), p. 17.

97. Robert Marshall in *The Living Wilderness* (Washington, D.C.: The Wilderness Society, Summer 1954), inside front cover.

98. Christopher Hussey, *The Picturesque* (London: Putnam, 1927), pp. 6-7.

99. Quoted by Marjorie H. Nicolson, *Mountain Gloom and Mountain Glory* (Ithaca, N.Y.: Cornell University Press, 1959), pp. 101-2.

100. Nicolson, *op. cit.*, in a preliminary draft.

101. A. Eustace Haydon, *The Humanist*, No. 1 (1950), p. 3.

CHAPTER V. *Reliance on Reason and Science*

102. Bertrand Russell, *A History of Western Philosophy* (New York: Simon and Schuster, 1945), p. 123.

103. T. H. Huxley in *A Treasury of Science*, ed. Harlow Shapley (New York: Harpers, 1943), p. 15.

104. John Dewey, *How We Think* (Boston: D. C. Heath, 1910). In the second edition (1933), Dewey analyzes scientific method in terms of *six* steps. I prefer, however, his earlier and simpler five-step formula.

105. Copernicus, *De Revolutionibus*, Letter to Pope Paul III.

106. Quoted by Edwin A. Burtt, *Right Thinking: A Study of Its Principles and Methods* (New York: Harpers, 1946), p. 90.

107. Quoted by Graham Wallas, *The Art of Thought* (New York: Harcourt, Brace, 1926), p. 80.

108. Ralph Waldo Emerson, *Essays*: "Self-Reliance."

109. Frederick Barry, *The Scientific Habit of Thought* (New York: Columbia University Press, 1927), p. 47.

110. Frederick Soddy, *Science and Life* (London: John Murray, 1920), pp. 2-3.

111. *The Federalist*, No. 10.

112. Brand Blanshard, "Can the Philosopher Influence Social Change?" *The Journal of Philosophy* (Nov. 25, 1954), p. 745.

113. Burtt, *op. cit.*, p. 304.

114. John Dewey, *Logic: The Theory of Inquiry* (New York: Holt, 1938), p. 147.

115. Abraham Edel, *The Theory and Practice of Philosophy* (New York: Harcourt, Brace, 1946), pp. 127-28.

116. John Dewey, *Reconstruction in Philosophy* (New York: Holt, 1920), pp. 84, 86.

117. Howard Selsam, "Frederick Engels: Philosopher," *New Masses* (Oct. 8, 1946), p. 12.

CHAPTER VI. *The Affirmation of Life*

118. Santayana, *Reason in Common Sense*, p. 21.

119. Randall, *The Making of the Modern Mind*, pp. 48-49.

120. George Santayana, *Reason in Society* (New York: Scribners, 1927), p. 32.

121. John Dewey and James H. Tufts, *Ethics* (rev. ed.; New York: Holt, 1932), p. 309. In this section on Humanist ethics I

rely heavily on this book and on Dewey's *Human Nature and Conduct*.

122. John Dewey, *Human Nature and Conduct* (New York: Holt, 1922), p. 136.

123. Charles Landesman, "Thoughts on Humanism" (unpublished paper, 1964).

124. Abraham Edel, "Two Traditions in the Refutation of Egoism," *The Journal of Philosophy* (Nov. 11, 1937), p. 625.

125. V. J. McGill, *Emotions and Reason* (Springfield, Ill.: Charles C. Thomas, 1954), pp. 44-45.

126. Dewey, *Human Nature and Conduct*, pp. 196, 198.

127. Aristotle, *The Nicomachean Ethics*, trans. J. E. C. Welldon (London: Macmillan, 1923), Bk. VII, ch. XIV.

128. George Bernard Shaw, *Man and Superman* (New York: Brentano, 1903), Preface, pp. xxxi-xxxii.

129. Matthew, X, 37-39.

130. Bernard H. Hall (ed.), *A Psychiatrist's World* (New York: Viking, 1959), p. 5.

131. McGill, *op. cit.*, p. 81.

132. Thoreau, *op. cit.*, p. 65.

133. Albert Maltz, *The Underground Stream* (Boston: Little, Brown, 1940), p. 341.

134. Ina Corinne Brown in *This I Believe*, ed. Edward P. Morgan (New York: Simon and Schuster, 1952), p. 17.

135. Reinhold Niebuhr, *The Children of Light and the Children of Darkness* (New York: Scribners, 1944), p. xi.

136. *Kant's Critique of Practical Reason and Other Works on the Theory of Ethics*, trans. T. K. Abbott (London: Longmans, Green, 1923), p. 47.

137. Walter Lippmann, "Today and Tomorrow," *New York Herald Tribune* (Feb. 1, 1944).

138. Irwin Edman in *Encyclopaedia of the Social Sciences*, Vol. I, p. 224.

139. Santayana, *Three Philosophical Poets*, pp. 36, 210.

140. *The Great Quotations*, comp. George Seldes (New York: Lyle Stuart, 1960), p. 428.

141. Plato, *Phaedo*, trans. Benjamin Jowett, Section 66.

Selected Bibliography

Aristotle. *Metaphysics*.
————. *Nicomachean Ethics*.
Auer, J. A. C. F. *Humanism States Its Case*. Boston: Beacon, 1933.
———— and Others. *A Humanist Manifesto*. *The New Humanist*, VI, 3, 1933.
Beach, Joseph Warren. *The Concept of Nature in Nineteenth Century Literature*. New York: Macmillan, 1936.
Blackham, H. J. (ed.). *Objections to Humanism*. London: Constable, 1963.
Burtt, Edwin A. *Right Thinking*. New York: Harpers, 1946.
Cohen, Morris R. *Reason and Nature: An Essay on the Meaning of Scientific Method*. New York: Harcourt, Brace, 1931.
Dewey, John. *A Common Faith*. New Haven: Yale University Press, 1934.
————. *Democracy and Education*. New York: Macmillan, 1926.
————. *Experience and Nature*. New York: Norton, 1929.
————. *Human Nature and Conduct*. New York: Holt, 1922.
————. *Reconstruction in Philosophy*. New York: Holt, 1920.
———— and Tufts, James H. *Ethics* (rev. ed.). New York: Holt, 1932.
Dunham, Barrows. *Heroes and Heretics: A Political History of Western Thought*. New York: Knopf, 1964.
————. *Man Against Myth*. Boston: Little, Brown, 1947.
Durant, Will. *The Story of Philosophy*. New York: Simon and Schuster, 1926.
Edel, Abraham. *The Theory and Practice of Philosophy*. New York: Harcourt, Brace, 1946.
Edman, Irwin, and Schneider, Herbert. *Fountainheads of Freedom*. New York: Reynal and Hitchcock, 1941.
Engels, Frederick. *Ludwig Feuerbach*. New York: International Publishers, 1935.
Ficke, Arthur Davison. *Tumultuous Shore*. New York: Knopf, 1942.

Frankel, Charles. *The Case for Modern Man*. New York: Harpers, 1956.

Fromm, Erich. *Man for Himself*. New York: Rinehart, 1947.

Hartshorne, Charles. *Beyond Humanism*. Chicago, New York: Willett, Clark, 1937.

Hawton, Hector. *The Humanist Revolution*. London: Barrie & Rockliff, 1963.

Hook, Sidney (ed.). *Determinism and Freedom in the Age of Modern Science*. New York: New York University Press, 1958.

Humanist Anthology (comp. Margaret Knight). London: Barrie & Rockliff, 1963.

Huxley, Julian. *Religion Without Revelation*. New York: Harpers, 1957.

——— (ed.). *The Humanist Frame*. New York: Harper & Row, 1962.

Kallen, Horace (ed.). *Freedom in the Modern World*. New York: Coward, McCann, 1928.

Krikorian, Y. H. (ed.). *Naturalism and the Human Spirit*. New York: Columbia University Press, 1944.

Lamont, Corliss (ed.). *Man Answers Death: An Anthology of Poetry*. New York: Philosophical Library, 1952.

———. *The Illusion of Immortality*. New York: Philosophical Library, 1959.

Lamprecht, Sterling P. *Nature and History*. New York: Columbia University Press, 1949.

Lippmann, Walter. *A Preface to Morals*. New York: Macmillan, 1929.

Lucretius. *On the Nature of Things*.

McCarroll, Tolbert H. (ed.). *Humanist Wedding Ceremonies*. Yellow Springs, O.: American Humanist Association, 1964.

Morain, Lloyd and Mary. *Humanism as the Next Step*. Boston: Beacon, 1954.

Otto, Max C. *The Human Enterprise*. New York: Crofts, 1940.

Patton, Kenneth L. *A Religion for One World: Art and Symbols for a Universal Religion*. Boston: Beacon Press and Meeting House Press, 1964.

Plato. *The Republic*.

———. *Phaedo*.

Potter, Charles Francis. *Humanism: A New Religion*. New York: Simon and Schuster, 1930.

Randall, John H., Jr. *The Making of the Modern Mind*. Boston: Houghton, Mifflin, 1940.

Reese, Curtis W. *The Meaning of Humanism*. Boston: Beacon, 1945.

Russell, Bertrand. *Marriage and Morals.* New York: Liveright, 1929.

––––––. *Why I Am Not a Christian.* New York: Simon and Schuster, 1957.

Santayana, George. *The Life of Reason* (one-vol. ed.). New York: Scribners, 1954.

––––––. *Three Philosophical Poets.* Cambridge: Harvard University Press, 1945.

Sperry, Willard L. (ed.). *Religion and Our Divided Denominations.* Cambridge: Harvard University Press, 1945.

Thoreau, Henry David. *Walden or Life in the Woods.*

Trapp, Jacob (ed.). *Songs and Readings.* Salt Lake City: Porte Publishing Co., 1937.

Wells, H. G., Huxley, Julian S., and Wells, G. P. *The Science of Life.* New York: Doubleday, Doran, 1938.

Williams, David Rhys. *World Religions and the Hope for Peace.* Boston: Beacon, 1951.

Index

303

PT267   247